Cultural Reflections

Cultural Reflections

*Critical Teaching and Learning
in the English Classroom*

John Gaughan

Lockland High School
Lockland, Ohio

Boynton/Cook Publishers
HEINEMANN
Portsmouth, NH

Boynton/Cook Publishers, Inc.
A subsidiary of Reed Elsevier Inc.
361 Hanover Street
Portsmouth, NH 03801-3912

Offices and agents throughout the world

The authors and publisher wish to thank those who have generously given permission to reprint borrowed material:

Excerpt from "the teacher" by Tom Romano was originally published in *English Journal* (volume 71, no. 3, March 1982). Reprinted by permission of the publisher, National Council of Teachers of English.

Library of Congress Cataloging-in-Publication Data

Gaughan, John.
    Cultural reflections : critical teaching and learning in the
English classroom / John Gaughan.
      p. cm.
    Includes bibliographical references (p. 225).
    ISBN 0-86709-431-1
    1. Language (Secondary)—Social aspects—United States.
    2. English language—Study and teaching (Secondary)—Social aspects—
United States.   3. Critical thinking—Study and teaching
(Secondary)—United States.   I. Title.
    LB1631.G24   1997
    428'.0071'273—dc21   97-22050
                                              CIP

Consulting Editor: Thomas R. Newkirk
Production: Melissa L. Inglis
Cover design: Joni Doherty
Manufacturing: Louise Richardson

The cover features an excerpt from "Endless Journey," an acrylic painting by the author's father, John W. Gaughan.

Printed in the United States of America on acid-free paper
01 00 99 98 97   DA   1 2 3 4 5 6 7 8 9

To my parents,
who started me on
the reading-writing road

To my wife, Kathy,
who accompanies me
on the journey

To my daughters,
Amy and Kelly,
who are just
beginning the trip

Contents

Foreword

These past five years I have watched John Gaughan draft, revise, reconceive, and rerevise *Cultural Reflections: Critical Teaching and Learning in the English Classroom*. During my reading and conversations with John, I've thought often of a line from Whitman's "Song of Myself":

> He most honors my style who learns under it to destroy the teacher.

I met John in January of 1982. He had called me before Christmas break to ask if he could do his student teaching with me. I was reluctant. I'd had a student teacher just that fall, and our relationship had failed miserably. After eight weeks—with all parties' mutual consent—the student teacher began working with one of my colleagues.

"I'm not real keen right now about working with a student teacher."

John wasn't giving up. "You know Dr. Krabbe and Dr. Sherman at Miami, don't you?"

"Know them well," I said. "Krabbe was my advisor and Sherman is a jazz and swimming friend."

"They thought we had a lot in common," John said, "thought we'd get along well."

My interest piqued, I asked John to tell me about himself. He wasn't shy. He told of his return to college to become certified to teach English after graduating from Miami University with a degree in business administration five years earlier. He told me of his interest in blues and film, of a great independent reading course he had taken in high school. He told me about working on the road with a railroad crew, when he and a coworker read *Crime and Punishment* each evening and talked about it the next morning as they earned their daily bread.

"Do you like to write?" I asked him. "Do you think you'd like to teach high school kids to write?"

He would, John said, and then he told me about a writing class he'd taken the previous semester, the pieces they had written in various genres, the peer conferencing they had done.

"I'll do it," I told him.

In 1987 John appeared with me on the program at the fall National Council of Teachers of English (NCTE) convention in Los Angeles. Our session was about the "alternate style"—effective writing that purposely breaks rules of standard written English. Another friend and I showed participants the work our students had done. John was the third presenter. His job was to get participants to actually write in the alternate style. In the front row of the audience sat Don Graves. He took right to the rule breaking, zealously writing a labyrinthine sentence on a hot topic. When John asked for volunteers to read, Don was one of the first to share. Our presentation was a success; everyone on the panel glowed.

Since then John has been part of six NCTE panel discussions and has conducted workshops there on collaboration, portfolio assessment, and social constructivist issues. For the 1996 conference in Chicago, John submitted a proposal I was sure would be accepted. The theme of the conference was "Honoring All Our Stories." The call for proposals emphasized the importance of listening to and reading the stories of our students, the capacity of stories to increase our empathy. The proposal stated that stories can remove "walls of time, culture, and distance." We believed those things. But John also understood the flip side. He knew that the stories students write and tell can sometimes be problematic. One of the students in *Cultural Reflections* illustrates just how problematic when he writes about the gang rape

and murder of a Vietnamese girl by American soldiers in the film
Casualties of War:

> In normal cases rape is never justifiable. But in war there is
> chaos, and chaos in war brings out the evil animal instincts
> in man. In war anything is justifiable. She was nothing but a
> gook anyway. Her life was worthless.

When I think of John's pedagogy, I think of another Whitman quote: "Resist much, obey little." John knew he had the perfect angle for "Honoring All Our Stories." He wrote a compelling,
provocative one-page proposal and titled it "When Students Tell
Stories We'd Rather Not Hear: Teaching in the Contact Zone."

It was rejected.

We were disappointed, but I understood. "Teaching is a political act," John writes in *Cultural Reflections.*

And political acts that oppose the norm have consequences.

In the fall of 1996 I placed student teachers from Miami University
with four high school teachers, all Ohio Writing Project alums, all
my friends, all excellent teachers who featured writing as an integral part of their curricula.

Because of my close relationship with the mentor teachers,
they agreed to keep "learning portfolios" along with the student
teachers and me to trace our paths of growth and development as
we worked together. Four times during the semester the nine of
us met at a Mexican restaurant after school to share our portfolios. We combined the professional of reading, writing, teaching,
and learning with the social of margaritas, corn chips, and salsa.

At one meeting, as part of his portfolio, John shared a sheet
of comments he'd excerpted from papers his students had written about race relations. The comments ranged from humane
and inclusive to inflammatory and racist. John showed us the
anonymous comments and described his class the day he
handed them out to launch discussion. The class had become
volatile, he told us. At one point two students were screaming at
each other. A verbal free-for-all ensued. John had to step in to
calm passions. One young man went from cockiness to chagrin

when racist language he had written was met with fierce resistance. Two periods later, a young woman was crying in another class. Discussion about the discussion was carried on throughout the day.

Two of the mentor teachers at our portfolio meeting taught at a much larger, more racially diverse school than John. "If I distributed such comments in my last period class," Katy said, "there would be bloodshed." Her student teacher agreed. John explained his position: Racism was real in America. He wanted students to think about it, to explore myths about race, and to examine their own assumptions.

"You're putting a lot of pressure on the one or two African Americans in your class," said Katy.

"The alternative is not to discuss these issues," said John. "An educational setting isn't the street corner, where the only views students hear are those that confirm their own. In my classroom we can dispute claims and ask for reasoning."

Katy and John debated a few minutes more. We felt the tension ratchet up in our usually amicable meeting. The four student teachers were silent, eyes wide. Over the weeks they had grown to like and respect both John and Katy, two progressive teachers who were witty, intelligent, and committed to social responsibility. Neither John nor Katy backed off their positions; John stood behind his constructivist agenda, Katy behind the reality of her school and classroom.

This is great, I thought. The student teachers were seeing respected professionals who genuinely cared for each other in sharp disagreement. John was troubled for weeks about the dispute. It became the seed for his next NCTE proposal. Katy, of course, was listed on the panel.

John was one of the people I dedicated my second book to. I said that he knew where the constructivist and the expressivist meet.

In *Cultural Reflections,* John shows how he was incomplete as a teacher with only an expressivist side, only a side that spurred students to tell their stories in the most effective language possible. As a constructivist, however, John believes that the language and images of a culture shape identity. He wants students to take note of that. He wants them to question their assumptions, assumptions they sometimes wear like blinders.

> Students need to be taught that language not only reflects reality but shapes it as well. While slurs such as "nigger," "slut," and "red" *reflect* racial, gender, and political discrimination, children's attitudes toward blacks, women, and Communists are *shaped* when they grow up in households where parents regularly use such language.

In Keith Gilyard's *Let's Flip the Script: An African American Discourse on Language, Literature, and Learning* (Wayne State University Press, 1996), the lead article is titled "A Heightened Sense of Language as Educational and Social Critique." That's what John is after in *Cultural Reflections*. In the pages that follow, you will find John implementing a curriculum of his own design in which his students examine their culture. John chooses contemporary literature of many genres to get his students to struggle with issues of gender, immigration, racism, class, patriotism, dissent, and more. He wants his students to develop into readers and writers who are "critical and a little suspicious" so that when they consume products and ideas afloat in our culture, they will understand that they are also consuming someone's values and philosophies—values and philosophies that can be deconstructed and opposed if a heightened sense of language is in place.

———————————

At the second international conference on language and literacy in Heidelberg, Germany, in the summer of 1996, NCTE president-elect Sheridan Blau said that the history of our profession is the tension between the spirit of inquiry and indoctrination.

In *Cultural Reflections*, we see John facing that tension as he nudges and pushes students to examine their assumptions about controversial issues. John is not naive about his position in this political act.

"Constructing ourselves," he writes, "is about taking charge, setting our own agendas."

John's pedagogical identity is a blend of individual expression and social critique. But he doesn't want to brainwash students; he isn't satisfied if they simply come around to his way of thinking. "Proselytizing isn't teaching for the kind of change I want to effect," John writes. "It teaches students to veil their views." He doesn't want that. When students remain mute, the classroom becomes passionless, every voice silenced but that of the teacher.

Cultural Reflections renders a curricular possibility, the goal of which is for students to critique their culture and express their rude truths, all the while developing a heightened sense of language and a critical reading and writing sensibility. That curricular possibility evolves in John's classroom, just as he has evolved from the teacher of fifteen years ago when he student-taught with an expressivist mentor then took a teaching job and was handed a curriculum guide composed of fifty-two discrete grammar and usage objectives.

John has created what we all long for: a curriculum you can roll your shoulders in. By that I mean a curriculum flexible and transformable, responsive both to your students' needs and your own; a curriculum in which students write passionately, composing songs, poems, videos, narratives, and persuasive essays; a curriculum that requires them to conduct classes, lead discussions, interview people, and compile portfolios; a curriculum in which they must go far beyond merely memorizing rules for using the comma.

John has given us life stories in *Cultural Reflections.* We see the isolation and paranoia of a first-year teacher relegated to the only classroom in the dank basement. We see the stories of Fonika, Misty, Mike, and Steve as they grapple with who they are and why they have become what they have, as they develop an additional lens for critiquing their culture and their own assumptions about issues that divide our country.

Cultural Reflections will absorb you, entertain you, make you think and feel. The prose is clean and uncluttered, the stories revelatory, sometimes painful, always memorable. After reading it, you might revise your teaching. You might take charge in a new way.

I am part of John's story. Just a part. I think of that quotation I opened with about the student destroying the teacher. I want to alter it, not to accept even Walt Whitman's language as truth simply because our culture acknowledges him as an authority from the past. I want to socially construct a new quotation based upon my own experience as a friend of John's for fifteen years:

> He most honors the teacher's voice who takes part of it and constructs an identity.

Tom Romano
Miami University
Oxford, Ohio

Acknowledgments

I didn't tell anyone for nine months that I was attempting to write this book . . . no one. I was afraid I'd never finish and didn't want to disappoint anyone besides myself. Before that nine-month period, I revised two papers I'd written for a class, thinking they might work as potential chapters; then, during the school year, I wrote three more chapters for a total of five. Since I'd envisioned a ten-chapter book, I was convinced at that point I was committed enough to succeed. So I told my wife, Kathy, what I'd been up to all that time in the laundry room, which doubles as my office. She was surprised I'd done as much as I had and kept my mouth shut about it, but when she sat down to read, she offered such positive feedback I was convinced I should tell others.

Tom Romano was next. We were sitting in the convention hall at NCTE taking a quick break between sessions, when Tom uttered another "Ya oughta." Tom is better than anyone I know at persuading others to write, nudging them just when they need it, supporting them in the midst of projects. I can't remember what he said "I oughta" write that time, but I finally blurted out, "Tom, I am writing . . . a book."

"It's about time," he smiled.

Had I known then that I wasn't actually halfway done, that I'd end up cutting one of those early chapters, that I'd revise as much as I have, write a prologue and epilogue, and spend so much time seeking permission to include students' writing, I might never have gotten this far. Luckily for me Tom provided the follow-up support I've needed all through this process. He read a first draft of the entire manuscript, then numerous revisions as I completed them. His encouragement and response kept me writing. Thanks, Tom!

Tom Newkirk read a first draft of the manuscript too and, besides responding so positively, helped me rethink the organization of the entire book. I thank him for helping me see the big picture. I also appreciate his suggestion to include sample assignments and an annotated bibliography.

My friends at the Ohio Writing Project have made a significant impact on my professional life. Max Morenberg, Janet Ziegler, Mary Fuller, and Don Daiker changed the course of my teaching, first as my teachers, then as my colleagues. I've taught and presented with each of them, learned about myself and my writing and teaching through our friendship and professional dialogue.

The summer after breaking my silence about this book, I was fortunate to have Jeff Sommers, Karen Powers-Stubbs, and Renee Dickson as my peer group at the Writing Project. Besides reading and responding to my prospectus and several drafts of early chapters, they encouraged me to write on. They pushed my thinking and helped me shape my theoretical stance. I thank them for being a supportive peer group.

Two colleagues at Lockland High School, Linda Tatman and Sandy Burrell, supported me, too. Linda, the other half of Lockland's English department, read my work and discussed it with me, helping me understand my theory and practice; Sandy, our high school counselor, helped me obtain students' permission to publish their work.

I spent a year on leave teaching at Miami as part of its graduate program and met Jim Meyer, whose class I observed and who helped me broaden my understanding of what English teachers can do in the classroom. Jim challenged his students in ways that I hadn't seen in traditional English classes. His "quantum logic test" appealed to my mathematical side, and his knowledge of anthropology and film made me rethink my own teaching. I've lost track of Jim, so wherever you are, thanks!

This past semester I've been fortunate to work with Tom Gaffigan as his cooperating teacher. Talking and teaching with Tom, and sharing each other's writing, helped me write my prologue and epilogue.

Acknowledgments

Finally, I want to thank my wife, Kathy, who listened to me when I needed a sympathetic ear, read emerging drafts offering insightful response (in one case helping me avoid a gaffe everyone else, including me, had overlooked), and agreed to a new computer so I could type my final revisions.

Thanks to her and to everyone who helped me! I never could have done this alone.

Prologue

Our board of education instituted a new rule this year: miss five or more days in one grading period and fail the quarter. That on the heels of last year's rule: fail the final quarter of a class and fail the class.

I met Terry three years ago in Reading-Writing Workshop. She's tall, small-boned, almost frail. Her skin is smooth and white, her brown hair thick and long. Halfway through ninth grade, Terry got pre-engaged to a seventeen-year-old guy. She was thirteen.

Two years elapsed. No marriage.

Junior year Terry got pregnant. I'd see her in the hallways, body heavy, eyes sunken, long hair still thick and beautiful. Despite a difficult pregnancy, she maintained her grades and completed her junior year.

Now Terry's a senior. Her grandmother helps out with the baby. Last Thursday when Terry walked into class, I was struck by her crescent face. Then I understood the crescent: she'd gotten her hair cut. For more than three years it had hung down her back; now it barely flowed past her shoulders. Instead of parting it in the middle and wearing it back, she'd pulled the right side behind her ear; the rest covered half of her face.

Terry had been absent the day fourth-quarter portfolios were due, so I walked up to her desk, crouched beside her, and asked if she managed to finish it. "Yes," she whispered, and that's when I saw it. As she bent toward her book bag to retrieve her folder, her hair fell away to reveal the black eye she'd been trying to hide. Her boyfriend had been abusing her for some time.

That day in the fourth quarter when Terry's portfolio was due—the day she missed—was her sixth absence.

Last week in Dayton, Ohio, north of Lockland where I teach, a thirteen-year-old honor student was suspended for taking Midol from a friend. The Midol "pusher" was sentenced to four months. The school has an antidrug policy.

Kari was one of my favorite ninth-grade students. She was punctual, bright, and conscientious. I admired her honest writing and facility with words.

Three years later she could barely stay awake in class. Her face was always pale, her eyes veined with red. She missed assignments and skipped school, but I still liked having her in class the days she attended. Her writing continued to reveal insight, but darker clouds shadowed the content of each new piece. I invited Kari to enter a writing contest, which she did. One of her pieces—about date rape—was published. I think she'd make a good high school English teacher someday. Because she got into trouble senior year, though, Kari almost didn't graduate. The trouble wasn't with Midol.

The same week as the honor student's suspension in Dayton, a first-grader was suspended in North Carolina. He'd kissed a classmate on the cheek. The school has a sexual harassment policy.

Kim was reluctant to share her narrative with classmates but said I could read it. She'd titled it "Laughing in the Park." I wondered what story lay beneath that title. Apparently, Kim had fallen for a senior boy, who took her to a local park and tried to force himself upon her. When Kim said "no," he persisted until she jumped out of the car. Finally realizing he was getting nowhere, he yelled out he'd drive her home. With her purse and keys still resting on the passenger seat, she pushed her luck. He did drive her home but mocked her all the way. The last thing she remembered after scrubbing herself over and over with soap was the laughter that wouldn't rub off.

"Would Jim Link please report to the elementary office?" the intercom blared. The *elementary* office, I thought, as Jim left my seventh-period class. Turns out he had to take his third-grade sister

xxii

home; she had a 102-degree temperature. Jim's a hard worker, a model big brother. I knew he'd call a classmate that night, make up his work, and tend to his sister, too.

Jim's family had little money. His mother worked assorted jobs at odd hours and drank most of their income away; Jim's father had been out of the picture for years. Two more roles Jim has to play.

Crissy just moved to Lockland. She's fourteen, tall, thin, and blond. I knew she'd have trouble here. Sure enough, three days later, Crissy was suspended. Stephanie, a fifteen-year-old, was talking to some friends in the restroom. She said the new girl was a "stuck-up bitch," loud enough for Crissy to hear. They bloodied each other's noses before someone broke them up.

There's always a new girl. Last year her name was Stephanie.

Teachers like to hear news of recent graduates, that they're succeeding in college or paving career paths, that they've turned their lives around—especially if adolescence troubled them more than most.

The first graduate I heard about several years ago was John. Six days after receiving his diploma he was shot and killed.

Last week Jerry named my student teacher "Fag." On his way out the door he called us both "pusses." "You know where the office is," I told him. The following day, Jerry was back in class, wrists still red from the slap he'd received.

Marie wrote a personal narrative about living in a small apartment with three brothers, two sisters, her mom and mom's boyfriend, and the daughter Marie bore in eighth grade. Roaches and ants roamed the floors, water leaked from the ceiling, the heat often failed. A local official was the landlord. After asking him to spray for bugs, repair the roof, and fix the furnace, Marie and her family were evicted.

I took students to *The Notebook of Trigorin* this week, Tennessee Williams' version of *The Seagull*. My students are usually well behaved at plays. The only thing I told them before we left the bus was to leave their ball caps and Walkmans behind.

My own high school experience was so unlike that of my students. Today physical abuse is commonplace. More children are having their own. Younger students are using drugs. Graduates die violent deaths. Slumlords cast out tenants who protest too much. Parents don't know how to parent. Not that the Cleavers went to my high school or that I lived in Mayberry. But I was a lot closer to Opie than James Dean, and Kettering, where I went to high school, was more Mayberry than Lockland, where I teach.

Yes, there were "hoods" in my school; they smoked, wore black jackets, talked behind teachers' backs. I liked most of my teachers, though, and enjoyed going to school. I finished my homework on time. So did my peers. We were polite and civil—even the hoods. But the times they are a-changin'.

Teaching is different for me, too. I break up more fights between girls than boys. I deal with verbal abuse and poor discipline. I call parents at home in my "free" time but often find support lacking.

Teachers assume added roles today—we teach not only our subject but manners and decorum. We counsel troubled students who number far too many for one high school counselor. We break up fights and intervene when we suspect abuse.

Just as my peers and I weren't the Cleavers, my students aren't the Bradys. Maybe the Bundys mirror their lives more closely. Regardless of what TV family I use as a metaphor, my teaching world and their student worlds are different. What worked for my teachers doesn't work for me. Students aren't interested in sentence diagrams or prescriptive approaches to the paragraph. We may not have been either, but still we did what we were told. My students are argumentative. They've been raised on TV talk shows.

Their needs are different, too: how to escape abusive relationships, to stay afloat in a sea of drugs, to avoid domestic violence. I can't use the same curriculum that nurtured me, and hope—as my teachers did—that students will find it relevant. They may need to escape as did Walter Mitty, but his secret life doesn't provide the route they need. On their way home, they must negotiate harassment and abuse, drugs and neglect, sometimes life and death.

The very institution—the school itself—is different. Frustrated by high absenteeism, districts impose limitations on the number of absences. Scared about drug use, they combat it with rigid policies that punish girls with menstrual cramps. Threatened by lawsuits, they suspend first-graders for sexual harassment.

The district let Terry graduate—she'd been an honor-roll student for four years—and she had more important things to worry about than a sixth absence. The Midol girl served her suspension, however, and the "pusher" was finally admitted back to school after threatening a lawsuit of her own.

Institutions have to be negotiated. Individuals must learn how to negotiate because common sense doesn't always prevail. Sometimes "institutional mind" runs amok. Teachers can help students understand how institutions shape "individuality" and how individuals can challenge institutions. Teaching Marie how to write letters to housing authorities or government agencies, for example, might better serve her interests than critiquing *The Scarlet Letter*.

To remind Stephanie of what it's like being the "new girl," she might watch Rosa in *El Norte* instead of reading "The New Land" by John Smith. Jerry could reflect on Evelyn Couch's experience in *Fried Green Tomatoes at the Whistle Stop Cafe* when a teenage boy calls her "fat cow" after she's been dieting for weeks. Not that any of these strategies will necessarily change behavior, but they might plant seeds that, given a different curriculum and pedagogy, could grow into stalks of understanding and blooms of respect.

This book explores a different pedagogy and curriculum. I call it a construction in process. As students and schools change, so must teachers. We can let others take charge of our profession or take charge ourselves. We can watch our students suffer harassment, abuse, and rigid institutional policies or teach them to take charge of their own lives. I think about Terry and Kim finding healthy relationships, and Kari becoming a teacher; about Jim being relieved of roles he shouldn't have to play, and Stephanie recognizing herself in Crissy; about Jerry realizing the power of language and Marie's baby growing up warm and dry. I may not be as idealistic as I was my first day teaching, but as I see it, I have no choice but to hope for these students and their futures. This book is my seed.

Chapter 1

Constructing a Teaching Life

Mrs. Keller has taught American literature to juniors at Clarksdale High for twenty-three years. For the past ten she has been using Scott, Foresman's *The United States in Literature* as a primary text. Mrs. Keller decides to skip the first unit, called "American Mosaic," and asks students to jump right into "The New Land: 1500–1800." She particularly enjoys Jonathan Edwards' "Sinners in the Hands of an Angry God," which is included in this unit.

From there she and her students plow their way chronologically through the American canon, usually ending the year with Tennessee Williams' *The Glass Menagerie.* Mrs. Keller supplements the anthology with three novels: *The Scarlet Letter, Adventures of Huckleberry Finn,* and *The Great Gatsby.*

At the beginning of the third quarter, Mrs. Keller introduces her students to *Huck Finn,* Mark Twain, and literary realism. She begins the unit on a Monday by giving her students a list of fifty vocabulary words from the novel, including *ingots, reticule, yawl,* and *phrenology.* The vocabulary list is part of a teacher's supplement, which also includes a fifty-question objective test and study guide questions for each chapter, which Mrs. Keller uses as she teaches the novel.

After students look up definitions for each word on Monday, they will be required to use them in sentences and turn them in for credit on Wednesday. On Tuesday Mrs. Keller stands at her podium and delivers a fifty-minute lecture on the transition from romanticism to realism in American literature, explaining the importance of *Huckleberry Finn* in the realistic tradition. Students take notes.

Then, sharing slides and personal anecdotes, Mrs. Keller conveys her own enthusiasm for Mark Twain and the novel her students are about to read. At the end of the period Mrs. Keller passes out the book and assigns the first fifty pages for Thursday's discussion.

Students are surprised with a pop quiz at the beginning of the period Thursday. One question asks students to explain the significance of two encounters: Huck's with the spider and Jim's with the witches. Mrs. Keller uses the quiz as a springboard for a lecture about tall tales. She reads aloud passages she deems important to make other points about the novel and literary realism.

Using an alternating pattern of silent reading, quizzes, and lectures, Mrs. Keller guides her students through *Huckleberry Finn.* When they've finished, students take a one hundred-point objective test—fifty vocabulary questions and fifty content questions—and choose one of the following essay prompts for the final part of the exam: (1) Name three uses of the tall tale and give an example from the book to exemplify each one; or (2) In what ways does the novel reflect frontier life?

The entire unit of study takes five weeks.

Mr. Rosewald has been teaching high school English for eight years. Each year he feels his teaching improves. He attributes this improvement to becoming better acquainted with the students of Westchester High. One thing he's learned is that his students become more engaged in his class when he gives them the freedom to express themselves orally and in writing.

This year Mr. Rosewald decides to begin the course by using literature as a springboard to help his students introduce themselves to him and each other. On the second day of class he gives them a handout with introductory paragraphs from three novels:

> Whether I shall turn out to be the hero of my own life, or whether that station will be held by anybody else, these pages must show . . .

> You don't know about me, without you have read a book by the name of *The Adventures of Tom Sawyer,* but that ain't no matter. . . .

> If you really want to hear about it, the first thing you'll probably want to know is where I was born, and what my lousy

2

childhood was like, and how my parents were occupied and all before they had me, and all that David Copperfield kind of crap, but I don't feel like going into it, if you want to know the truth . . .

Mr. Rosewald asks students to circle their desks in groups of four. He instructs them to discuss these three characters and what they can discern about each based on the characters' voices. Where are they from? When is the novel set? Have the characters been formally educated? After the group discussion, Mr. Rosewald and his students write their own introductions to share in class the following day.

Once students have introduced themselves through their writing, they choose one of the three novels and spend the next few weeks (1) reading silently in class, (2) meeting in groups to discuss their respective novels, and (3) using writing to explore the novels and their own lives. Since all three books deal with young boys coming of age, their final paper will be a personal response to literature in which students show how their own adolescent discoveries connect with David's, Huck's, or Holden's.

Students in Mr. Rosewald's class write almost daily. Sometimes they freewrite in response to prompts; other times they brainstorm topics about which they might write. Often they write after reading to discover what they think a particular passage means. Every two to three weeks they write longer papers that evolve through their own writing processes until their revised paper reaches a "publishable" state. Publishing in Mr. Rosewald's class includes submitting pieces for classroom anthologies, sharing papers aloud, hanging pieces on the bulletin board for others to read, and turning favorite pieces in to the school literary magazine.

Students sometimes read novels as a class or in small groups; other times they choose novels independently from Mr. Rosewald's classroom collection. If they can't find a book that interests them there, they can check out a book from the library and get Mr. Rosewald's approval to read it. To keep track of their reactions to their reading, students keep response journals in which they write letters about their books to their peers and their teacher. In the course of these interactions, Mr. Rosewald's students learn to express their own thoughts and feelings.

At the end of the course, students peruse their writings and choose three or four favorite pieces to submit in their final portfolio. Students enjoy the freedom Mr. Rosewald allows them in choosing writing topics, pieces to publish, and books to read. Mr. Rosewald wants his students to value their independence and individuality.

Ms. Bennington is a second-year teacher in PS 891 in a large city school system. Unhappy with the eleventh-grade curriculum she taught her first year, she decides to revise it. Instead of teaching American lit chronologically, she renames her course "The American Dream" and teaches the class thematically. Students explore the following questions:

1. What is the American dream?
2. What dreams bring people to America?
3. Does attaining the American dream require a particular work ethic?
4. Do race, class, and gender affect a person's vision of the dream?
5. Is education the key that unlocks the dream?
6. Do media influence Americans' perception of the dream?

For the race, class, and gender unit, Ms. Bennington's students read poems by Mary Brosmer, a teacher and poet in Cincinnati; an essay by feminist critic Carol Gilligan; and a short story by Charles Johnson, a contemporary African American author. These are followed by two novels: *Adventures of Huckleberry Finn* and *The Color Purple*. Ms. Bennington gives students the following guidelines to focus their reading of the novels:

1. Note examples of racism and oppression of blacks.
2. Note examples of sexism and oppression of women.
3. Consider how Huck "names" Jim and how Mister "names" Celie; how does this naming shape Jim's and Celie's identities?
4. How conscious are these characters of their own oppression?
5. Does consciousness lead to self-determination? Do these

4

characters rename themselves when they escape their oppressors? If so, how?

6. How does Mark Twain's depiction of African American experience differ from Alice Walker's?

Small groups of students periodically lead class discussion using these guidelines to explore the novels. Ms. Bennington joins her students in the class discussion circle and participates by sharing her own reading, observations, and experiences. Students use writing during this particular unit to examine the effects of race, class, and gender on their own lives.

For a final project, Ms. Bennington's students interview people from the community about their own American dreams. These oral histories are published and become the last artifact students examine in their study of race, class, and gender.

For their unit portfolio, students select journal entries they've written and significant passages from the reading and oral histories that made the biggest impact on their thinking. Their reflective letters explain how the oppression they've discussed, observed, and experienced affects their own perceptions of the American dream.

Though these teachers share several things in common—using *Huck Finn* for example— the assumptions that underlie their pedagogical practices differ. An impartial visitor might observe students in each of these classrooms silently reading Twain's novel and conclude they are all doing the same thing. But context is everything.

Teachers and administrators must be aware of contexts. They should be able to articulate their agendas to themselves and each other. Every teacher and administrator has an agenda, whether it be to keep students working quietly, to prepare them for college, to raise test scores, or to help them pass proficiency tests. Sometimes they may be unaware that their agenda perpetuates the status quo. So although these three slices of English instruction might sometimes appear the same, they don't leave the same taste in students' mouths. For both the teacher and students, the means of instruction—in this case, reading *Huck Finn*—will be similar, but it will lead to very different ends.

5

Just like painting or any other art form, teaching is an evolution-
ary process. We usually begin our careers emulating our men-
tors—for many of us, the teachers and professors we most
respected. Picasso's early paintings reflect his interest in Impres-
sionism and the "straightforward approach of Velazquez and
Goya" (Murray and Murray 1965, p. 154). By 1907 his "Les Demoi-
selles d'Avignon" revealed his new style: cubism.

I've been Mrs. Keller, Mr. Rosewald, and Ms. Bennington in
the course of my teaching career and would probably still be a
much more traditional teacher had I not student-taught with Tom
Romano, author of *Clearing the Way* (1987) and *Writing with Passion* (1995). When I student-taught with him in 1982, Tom's students were using Ken Macrorie's *Writing To Be Read* (1976),
discovering what they had to say, working through their own
processes. They were using writing to learn and they were learning to write—certainly better than I ever had in high school. I
knew that what Tom was doing with his students made sense,
and I was determined to use what I learned in his classroom in
my own. Still, I wasn't able to completely relinquish the traditional pedagogy I had experienced in my own education.

When I was hired for my first teaching job, I was handed a
thick, ninth-grade curriculum guide with fifty-two discrete objectives—too many to teach in thirty-six weeks. I tried anyway. I
thought my job depended on it. The guide contained a list of over
three hundred vocabulary words, which students needed to "master" (mastery learning was all the rage then) by the end of the year.
The words were out of context, unrelated to any other course content. On my first Monday, I wrote twenty of the words on the board,
had students look up definitions, use them in sentences, and learn
them for Friday's test. We practiced writing process in this class, but
not as often as students needed because I was afraid to stray too far
from the curriculum. I'll be honest: it took me a few years.

Since I'm being honest, I must admit I was concerned, too,
about the role I played in transmitting Western notions of cultural
literacy. I believed it was my job to "expose" students to the
"great" works in the British and American literary tradition. They'd
need this exposure, I rationalized, to preserve the tradition for future generations. "This argument . . . frequently wins support by
enfolding itself within a myth of the Fall from Grace . . . Minds and

6

characters have been weakened by television, or rock music, or the automobile, or permissiveness, or the sixties, or narcotics, or the disintegrating family" (Knoblauch and Brannon 1993, p. 20). Playing "catcher in the rye," recovering for them the past they'd "lost," was just part of the job.

After a few years of fairly traditional teaching, I spent the next seven or eight as "Mr. Rosewald." I think many of my students benefited from that teaching and those classrooms. I was trying to emulate Tom Romano and not coming close, but his theoretical grounding made so much more sense to me than the theories that underlie traditional pedagogy that my teaching was more focused, enthusiastic, and credible.

Tom turned me loose as a writer, too. I experienced the same satisfaction that beginning writers feel when they express themselves well . . . and the corresponding frustrations when they don't. Sharing my struggles with writing helped create the atmosphere of trust students need to write honestly and subsequently boosted individual students' confidence.

In "Rhetoric and Ideology in the Writing Class" (1988), James Berlin names the theory that informs Mr. Rosewald's pedagogy "expressionism." Expressivist teachers function more as facilitators or coaches than do traditional teachers. They stress the importance of "process" in individual students' development because through process students ultimately discover "the true self" (p. 484).

This focus on the individual in expressivist classrooms "borrows from long-hallowed American myths of self-determination, freedom of expression, and supposedly boundless personal opportunity" (Knoblauch and Brannon, p. 21). Borrowing from these traditions paints an optimistic, indeed ideal, picture of expressivist classrooms that critics like Berlin view as naive. Unfortunately, the school systems in which many of us work still impose constraints and repressive curricula that need to be negotiated by both teachers and students. Helping students discover "authentic" voice will not help them negotiate the rhetorical situations of a community they don't understand. Teaching students the features of a particular community's writing so they can "acquire position to speak" (Knoblauch and Brannon, p. 133) in that community—whether it be to dispute a racist comment in school or to challenge sexual harassment in the workplace—can help. Although promoting societal change through individual students' progress is appealing, that route in and of itself is unlikely to effect the kind of change that will make American institutions more democratic.

Only in the last few years have I started to branch out and explore other theories. I can't give up the theoretical underpinnings of expressionism—students won't explore their place in and influence on society if they aren't confident writers in the first place. Since I want them to begin this exploration in my class, I've shifted my focus. Now I do what I know will help students gain reading and writing confidence and competence. At the same time I urge them to consider issues such as gender, race, class, and sexuality.

I teach students to read and write with "a 'critical consciousness' of the social conditions in which people find themselves, recognizing the extent to which language practices articulate—objectify—rationalize those conditions" (Knoblauch and Brannon, p. 22). Berlin names this rhetoric "social-epistemic." Within the parameters of this theory, individuality exists as a social construct: "The self is always a creation of a particular historical and cultural moment" (Berlin, p. 489).

To help students explore the social factors that shape their individual identities, teachers must reflect upon the way society and tradition shape their teaching. How did they become the people and teachers they are? What kind of teaching did they encounter in their education? Why do they teach the way they do? What theories and values support their pedagogy?

I've undertaken that same course of reflection many times myself—most of us have. One thing I've learned is that we can let others "construct" us—label us, define us, tell us who we are—or we can participate in that construction ourselves. Instead of remaining passive objects we can become active subjects. Rather than let others define us as babysitter, instructor, or pedagogue, we can help shape our professional identities as teacher, scholar, or mentor. I'd like to share part of my reflections with you so you can see how I've attempted to construct my personal and professional identity, at least for now. I urge you to do the same.

I was born in Pittsburgh during the Korean War, spent childhood shivering from cold war winds, and came of age braving the political storms of Vietnam. I suppose that's why I'm no stranger to conflict. My stomach still knots itself with each new confrontation, but I know I can weather any turmoil I confront.

Like other children of the fifties and sixties, I remember ducking under school desks during air raid drills or running home for cover in fear of nuclear attack. In 1963 when John F. Kennedy was shot, I thought God would surely raise this first Catholic president from the casket where his body lay in state. A few years later I was convinced Vietnam couldn't invade my world until Sister Felicita called Kelly Byrd to the office because his older brother had been killed. My innocence was crushed by experience.

Despite my early disillusionment, Woodstock mesmerized me in 1969 and rekindled my idealism. Even though RFK and MLK had been assassinated the year before, I wanted to believe in the possibility of a more inclusive and harmonious society. As a new teacher, I hoped to achieve that harmony, but I was pragmatic enough to know I'd need to start small. I'd work on my classroom first. It didn't take long to discover how difficult achieving harmony can be.

Lockland High School, just north of downtown Cincinnati, is a maze of a building where first-year teachers often lose their way. I know because I got lost: not just physically when I took wrong turns, but in my mission to teach.

The body proper of our building consists of three floors of classrooms, offices, computer labs, lounges, and restrooms. My classroom wasn't part of that proper body, though. I ended up in a basement classroom that was dark and dank. Sometimes when I reached school before dawn, I'd hear roaches scattering on tile like fingernails tapping Formica.

The main stairway to this dungeon hallway was fairly well lit, but two smaller stairwells were not. Because of their proximity to my class, I often followed them to daylight, surfacing to use the restroom or to escape at the end of a long day. It wasn't unusual to find gum wrappers, wadded-up English assignments, or discarded papers littering these stairs. The smell of urine, though, surprised me; I was reminded of New York City subways and wondered what kind of teaching world I'd entered. This school wasn't the comfortable suburban one I'd graduated from myself.

In some ways, being isolated that first year was comforting. I rarely worried about administrators popping in to witness my rookie-year incompetence. On the other hand, isolation from colleagues was discomforting. A mentor that first year would have helped. A colleague next door would have been welcomed. Though three other classrooms lined that basement hallway, none but mine was used.

Fortunately, most of my students were friendly and offered little resistance—except, that is, for my ninth-period boys. This class comprised "regular" ninth-graders who had been tracked for years. Some had failed earlier grades; most had attendance problems or had gotten themselves into trouble with teachers and administrators—sometimes with the law. In fact, a middle-school teacher said he wouldn't take another field trip because some of the boys in this class had been caught shoplifting the last time he'd taken them to work on research projects. That and their sneaking a small flask into the Cincinnati Public Library convinced him that field trips weren't worth it.

The year before was of little consequence to me, though, because here they were, last period of the day, in my classroom. I didn't know how to teach them. I didn't know how to control them. How would we ever achieve harmony?

Sammy bragged about driving a long-term middle-school sub to a nervous breakdown the year before. Apparently, the paper airplane he constructed and set ablaze was the last straw for her. She fled the classroom sobbing, never to return. Sammy and his peers saw this feat as the last victory in the war they'd waged for classroom turf. His defiant eyes implied the battlefield in my class could be conquered, too. I silently pledged to stay the course and sought out strategies I could use to win this classroom war.

After attending an assertive-discipline workshop, I thought I'd discovered a battle plan that would allow me to maintain some trace of the authority I thought accompanied my position as teacher. I explained to my students how assertive discipline worked and then began asking questions about that day's reading: Jack London's "To Build a Fire." These boys, however, wanted to throw flames, not discuss them. So Tim purposely interrupted me. I wrote his name on the board. He protested. I placed a checkmark next to it. Fred laughed. I wrote his name below Tim's. Within minutes most of the students had three checks next to their names meaning after-school detention for each of them. Sammy became incensed; he wouldn't give up without a fight. Rising from his desk, he stomped out of the room. "I'm going to see Mr. Vitale," he challenged. One by one his classmates followed. Only three hadn't the guts to leave.

I'd lost battles before, but that period, that day, I lost my teaching identity. Cowering before the few remaining students, I stood beaten and dejected.

A few minutes later Mr. Vitale, the principal, returned with Sammy and his army of peers. Mr. Vitale closed the door, and all of us began to scream, accusing one another of not understanding, of not being fair, of not granting each other the respect we thought we were due.

Strangely enough, things improved after our war of words. I junked assertive discipline, even though the school district had paid for that workshop. I became better acquainted with my student audience. Teaching, I discovered, is about more than content and curriculum, especially when the traditional curriculum handcuffs you and your students. These weren't the kids I'd gone to school with in Kettering, Ohio.

Fourteen years later the chasm between my high school education and my current student audience widens. In her introductory portfolio this past year, Carlsie includes a letter she wrote to an uncle who committed suicide; Cindy, a memo from her attorney regarding "care and protection" and an accompanying article about depression; Diane, two letters from her brother in prison. I can't deal with these students the same way my high school teachers dealt with me and my peers. I'm sure dealing with me is different for them, too.

As I reflect on the incidents that transpired in my first classroom, I realize that they didn't have to happen the way they did. Why place a new teacher in a basement classroom with little contact or guidance? Why dump one of the worst groups of students on that teacher last period of the day? Why track those students at all?

I wish I could say the principal's intervention ended the difficulties I confronted that year, that I escaped unscathed—but I can't. The following week I was marching to the teachers' lounge between bells. Students crowded the main stairway rushing to their next class. Most of these students' faces were still foreign to me, and suddenly I felt trapped—out of breath, out of my element. I patted my right rear pocket to check for my wallet as is my habit in crowds. It wasn't there. I turned abruptly and grabbed the wrist of the person just behind me: an African American student, who I later learned was named Krista.

"Where's my wallet?" I yelled.

"What are you talking about?" she asked, taken aback by my accusation.

"My wallet?" I repeated. Then I patted my left rear pocket and felt the familiar bulge. I felt stupid and desperate. Other students had gathered, glaring at me now. With Krista's wrist still in my hand, they asked me what I was doing. I quickly released her, mumbled something even I didn't understand, and hurried to the lounge, where I closed the bathroom door, heart pulsing, head pounding, wondering what to do next.

"This-is-it, time-to-get-out, I'm-not-cut-out-for-teaching."

I knew I had to tell the principal, so I did. He calmed me down, said everything would be all right, then suggested we find the student so I could apologize. Krista was in typing class, and I apologized, but the apology felt empty to both of us. She didn't understand what had happened, and I couldn't explain it to her.

When I got home that afternoon, the thoughts flooding my mind spilled out on my wife's ears. She couldn't believe what she was hearing.

"You want to quit teaching?" she asked incredulously. She'd just worked two years supporting us so I could earn a teaching certificate. "You have to tough this out," she said. "Things will get better next year. They always do."

Unconvinced, I somehow managed to muddle through the rest of the year. I don't remember anything traumatic happening after the incident with Krista on the stairway. (Two years later I had Krista in class. She was a model student, an excellent athlete, her class's homecoming queen—the student least likely to steal anything from anyone. We talked about how I'd behaved two years before and were able to laugh off the guilt I still felt.) But I can't deny that what happened in my early days at Lockland scarred me in ways I've never really thought about until now.

Here I was, a teacher who believed it was important to establish a harmonious community where students would trust their teacher enough to take risks, to write honestly, to share their lives on paper with me and their classmates. At the same time, though,

I didn't trust them. I overreacted when I thought my wallet had been stolen. The ugly side of my own socialization reared its head on the stairs that day when I stereotyped all Lockland students because of a few rebels in my ninth-period class.

It took me a long time to trust students again. It took them a long time to trust me. I think most of the classroom communities I've worked in since have been healthy places, but I had to battle my own prejudices and experiences to construct those environments.

I realize now how important that first year was in shaping my professional identity. I couldn't simply reconstruct a teaching self based on a teacher I sought to emulate. I had to recognize how the social contexts of Lockland High School were unique, as are all social contexts. I had to construct a teaching identity that made sense in this school with these students. Somehow I'm managing to do that.

This book is the result of one teacher's attempt to create a curricular context that makes sense to him and to his students. I write it with hope. Hope that other teachers in similar contexts will benefit from my and my students' experiences. Hope that teachers in different contexts reflect upon their own teaching identity. Hope that all of us can help students construct meaningful lives as critical citizens.

I agree with Paulo Freire, author of *Pedagogy of the Oppressed* (1971), that teachers should work to empower students. I teach to that end and in this book will explain the means I use in that attempt. But I'm also a realist. Not all students want to be empowered, at least not in the way I envision them to be as critical citizens. Many of my students claim they want to be truly independent when they leave school, able to think for and support themselves, but they sometimes don't appreciate the responsibility that entails. They want to be free, yes, but sometimes from school itself: partying with friends, cruising the malls, playing sports, listening to music. I empathize with them and understand their normal teenage urges.

They set short-term goals—winning the game, getting a date Friday night—and don't imagine their distant futures. While they admit people in power manipulate them, exclude them, or alter their lives, they often aren't willing to engage in the sort of thinking that might prevent or confront such manipulation. I still believe, though, that we need to create an environment in which critical reflection is not only possible, but encouraged, in the hope that students will leave our classes and schools more empowered than when they entered them.

That's why I try to set a reflective tone from the beginning of the year when I ask students to think about how they're named. "Take me, for example," I tell them. "John, after my father and his father, back to the apostle who sat beside Christ at the Last Supper; brother to six siblings; golfer and friend; teacher—the first person in my family to attend college and enter a profession; Irish Catholic—which explains my temper, my taste for beer and potatoes, why I attended St. Bernard's Elementary School in Pittsburgh and root for Notre Dame to win national championships."

My students explore their names, too, not only ones that welcomed them as friends, peers, or teammates but ones they'd just as soon forget, like bully, nerd, or airhead. By examining their own naming practices and those of others, they begin to see how names define them and shape their futures. Just because Mrs. Crum deflated my fifth-grade ego, naming me "troublemaker," I didn't name myself "troublemaker" in sixth grade—but I needed my parents' reassurance to overcome the label she'd imposed. In the same way, the negative connotations attached to racial slurs need not lower students' self-esteem if they realize the names say more about the speaker than the object. "Racism speaks volumes about those who hide behind it, says exactly nothing of those at whom it is directed" (Crutcher 1991, p. 107).

This exploration of how we are named and how we name ourselves can be painful. Paulette, for example, couldn't bring herself to reveal that she'd been called a "nigger lover" for dating an African American student; she told the class "black lover" instead, and even that was difficult for her to voice. But in the process of examining her feelings, she found herself taking a stand in relation to her peers and her mother, who said, "I'm not prejudiced but I don't want you dating a black guy." It wasn't easy for Paulette to call her mother wrong. "I guess I'm being defiant," she told her peers, "but I have to do what I think is right." By naming herself "defiant" but at the same time "right," Paulette began to take charge of her own identity.

Teachers, too, need to exercise more control over their professional identity. If we let administrators, state departments, and disgruntled parents define who we are—counselors, monitors, clerks—we may easily burn out. Constructing ourselves is about taking charge, setting our own agendas, agendas that make more sense for us and our students.

Knoblauch and Brannon assert that educators must actively support social change, especially in the face of oppression and prejudice. They insist that such support is not political correctness, a label conservative critics use to demean and trivialize what we do, but the "substance of a democratic country" (1993, p. 47).

This book is about setting an agenda that helps students read and write for democracy. Chapter Two is an overview of one course I teach called "The American Dream." In it I share stories of a recent journey with students as all of us contemplated our own American dreams: their evolution, the role of work and education, the advantages some people have in their pursuit of the dream. Chapters Three through Nine detail specific strategies, theories, and assumptions that underlie my own teaching. These chapters address ways teachers can help students become more critical readers and writers so they can assume more control of their own identities and be more sensitive about the role they play in shaping others'. At the same time readers will see how one teacher constructs curriculum, chooses texts, writes assignments, integrates reading and writing, and uses portfolios, in an attempt to help students think about their culture and identity. Chapter Ten suggests a concrete way teachers might begin reflecting upon their own teaching and learning as they construct a curriculum.

As I indicated earlier, my own teaching has evolved. I firmly believe in helping students work through their own reading and writing processes so they can become more confident about expressing themselves. At the same time I realize the importance of getting students to think about the social dimensions of reading and writing—how others affect the way they make meaning. I see my own teaching as a blend of individual expression and social critique. I offer this book to readers then, not as a prescription, but as a possibility.

Chapter 2

Teaching Thematically:
The American Dream

Her friends called her Mookie; I knew her as Melanie. Her skin was like ebony, her cheeks plum round, her eyes angry. She rarely spoke in class, but when she did her tone was confrontational. I wondered what had happened to Melanie that made her so hostile toward school. She usually attended class, though, and fulfilled most of the course requirements. Her writing voice was not as angry as her speaking voice; it was more friendly and conversational, expressing insight, sometimes even humor. Getting to know Melanie through her writing helped me see what lay beneath her icy exterior. As I became better acquainted with her, I occasionally cracked that frozen surface in class—sometimes even coaxed forth a smile.

One day I showed the film *Hairpiece: A Film for Nappy-Headed People* (Chenzira 1985), which I discovered while browsing through a catalogue from Women Make Movies. *Hairpiece* is a ten-minute animated film about African American women's attempt to match their hair to the media image of what was—and often still is—considered beautiful hair: the long flowing blond manes of supermodels.

Using an assortment of creams, relaxers, and conditioners didn't end black women's frustrations in this attempt; neither did uncomfortable wigs. Not until they were willing to accept the hair they were born with, letting it grow into the "beauty of its own rebelliousness," did they liberate themselves from the shackles imposed by mainstream media.

When the film ended, Melanie smiled. "That's the first time," she declared, "I ever saw anything in school that was just for me."

Her declaration caught me off guard. I wanted students to consider how media shapes their identities, how women are objectified, how society compels them to achieve a certain look, a compulsion not felt as strongly by men. Melanie recognized all of this. But the first thing she voiced when *Hairpiece* ended taught me a lesson I hope I never forget: students' presence in school must constantly be affirmed. This short film was the first thing Melanie identified with in twelve years of schooling. How incredibly sad that she had to wait until her senior year to see her reflection in the mirror of our school system.

The presence of young male students, especially white males, is constantly affirmed. They become Huck or Holden, Horatio or Hamlet. Though white females see their reflections less often in school, Jane Eyre, Scout, and Juliet do represent them. African American boys and girls are lucky to catch a glimpse of themselves.

Maybe the anger on Melanie's face wasn't directed at what school *was* for her, but at what it was *not*.

Principal Frank Vitale interviewed me for my first teaching job, explaining that he was looking for someone who could teach not only English but drama as well.

"We'd like to revitalize our drama program," he said. "Can you direct plays?"

It was late July. I didn't have any other job prospects. "Sure," I shot back. "I love plays." Then I quickly added that my wife and I had seen five plays in London on our honeymoon, and that I'd always enjoyed reading plays. I hoped that if I rambled long enough he wouldn't ask me if I had any actual theater experience—if I'd ever directed a play or acted myself.

My rambling worked: I got the job.

On the first day of school I was surprised that the mailbox bearing my name was already stuffed with mail. Among the many catalogues from publishers and advertisements from office supply stores was an invitation to usher for plays at Cincinnati's Playhouse in the Park. What better way to interest my drama students in theater, I thought; so I signed us up.

Four of my students and I ushered for each play—about one every two months. Students alternated so everyone got a chance. One of those students was Julie, a senior from a conservative

Christian background who had a flair for dramatics. Besides being a member of the drama club, Julie was also enrolled in one of my English classes, so she and I became well acquainted. The more I got to know Julie, the more I appreciated her as an actor and student. Her blue eyes danced attentively in class, her right hand always in the air to respond, question, or comment.

At drama practice outside of class, Julie and I often found ourselves immersed in lengthy discussions about all sorts of topics, among them religion. During one particular discussion, the subject of evolution arose. Julie's background "prevented" her from finding Darwin's theories plausible; she placed all her faith in creationism. As it happened, Julie's turn to usher coincided with the Playhouse production of Lawrence and Lee's *Inherit the Wind* (1955).

Ushering demanded little work of us and was more than a fair trade for the benefits my students and I received. We arrived an hour early, stuffed programs, and led patrons to their places. Once the lights dimmed, ushers were free to assume any unoccupied seats. This night fate found us. Our front-row seats just to the right of center stage made us part of Hillsboro, particularly when the jury sat a few feet before us.

As the trial of Bertram Cates unfolded, we became jurors ourselves, weighing arguments, considering rebuttals, holding Bertram's fate in our hands. Late in the play, prosecutor Matthew Harrison Brady takes the witness stand and explains he knows "exactly what's right and what's wrong" because God speaks directly to him. Defense attorney Henry Drummond counters, "What if a lesser human being—a Cates, or a Darwin—has the audacity to think God might whisper to *him?*" Out of the corner of my eye, I noticed Julie nodding her head.

When the play ended and we'd picked up the scattered programs, Julie remarked, "I never thought of it like that before."

When I first started teaching in this working-class community, I had trouble getting students to read or write anything. I had a lot to learn, which I should have realized when I reviewed the English curriculum. It looked too familiar. Nothing much had changed in the ten years since I'd graduated from high school. American lit, junior year; British lit, senior year—both to be taught chronologically, of course. My comfort zone quickly eroded, though. Student resistance rose every time we cracked the anthologies. Hawthorne and Hardy didn't stir them the way they had my college professors; nor, for that matter, did Shakespeare or Twain. Students like Melanie didn't see or hear themselves in these classical characters; nor could they relate to the characters' backgrounds. My students are, after all, city kids from the late twentieth century.

I had to search my soul. Much of the literature I'd read in high school hadn't affected me the way my teachers hoped it would. I didn't realize Shakespeare's genius until I was twenty-seven; I didn't appreciate *The Scarlet Letter* until I reread it for my master's exam.

If my students couldn't connect with the literature in the anthology, if they wouldn't even read it, I had to try something different. A thematic approach offered hope. In one class we explore American dreams: of working-class Americans in our own community; of women in history fighting for the right to vote; of Hispanic Americans in Sandra Cisneros' *The House on Mango Street* (1984). My students connect with Cisneros' Esperanza better than with Fitzgerald's Gatsby. Though none of them are Hispanic, they see their own lives mirrored in her Mango Street characters.

Chronological approaches to teaching literature construct a narrow view of what constitutes a text, especially since teachers find it difficult to get past the 1920s or 1930s when they start with Beowulf or Bradford. Thematic approaches, on the other hand, allow teachers to juxtapose classic and contemporary texts, including audio and video texts, for students' consideration. I don't want to discount the importance of classics like *The Great Gatsby*, but teachers must learn what will work with their own students. By breaking away from the rigidity of the canon, my students are finding their own voices in contemporary American literature.

In addition to hearing their voices echoed in those of contemporary characters, I want students to examine the factors from their own backgrounds that shape their American dreams. The flicker of light Julie glimpsed when she experienced *Inherit the Wind* was a beacon for me. As I was beginning to better understand my students, I knew they needed to better understand themselves. Only then would they realize that not everyone dreams the same dream, that others' visions are shaped by backgrounds quite different from their own. This chapter is about one course and how I help my students find their voices and explore the forces that shape their lives.

The first day of class I ask students to explain their conception of the American dream in a ten-minute freewriting. Here's what Chris says:

> When most people think about the American dream, they think of an immigrant coming to America flat broke, illiterate, sick, hungry, tired, etc., then he opens up his own little applecart on a small New York street corner at age ten and then gets a job in a small mom and pop grocery market at age twelve, working there for eighteen years and when the mom and pop die, he takes over the store and expands it to a mini-mart, then a supermarket, then into a department store, then a chain of them up and down the Eastern seaboard, then he starts expanding them out West across the country, and before he knows it he becomes a millionaire, then a billionaire, and then he goes into distribution and starts buying other businesses and expands into Canada and becomes the first American supermarket chain in Russia, then he moves into Britain and Australia. Then he finally gets married with news crew cameras running.
>
> *Chris Edrington, grade 11*

Chris had taken a class from me two years before, so was used to writing freely. He was a free spirit before he took that class. I'll never forget a drama picnic at a local state park, losing Chris, our scattering up and down the beach, frantic he'd disappeared, only to discover him thirty minutes later, strolling toward me from the direction of the marina. "Where were you?" I blurted out the minute I saw him.

"Oh, I just rented a canoe," he said matter-of-factly, never giving a thought to our concern for him.

Though Chris didn't always complete his work in my class—only those assignments he felt like doing—he did develop a strong writing voice. Chris' conception of the American dream obviously originated somewhere, evolving as he experienced more of America, as a citizen, consumer, TV viewer, and patriot. If you know the movies *Avalon* and *Ragtime*, you recognize the pattern Chris describes: ambition, opportunity, expansion, materialism, greed. His final cynical sentence reveals his own attitude about media and celebrity in the nineties.

To help students explore the origins and evolution of the American dream, I ask them to consider passages from familiar texts (e.g., the Declaration of Independence, the Pledge of Allegiance, and "The Star-Spangled Banner") and others providing different lenses (e.g., Kurt Vonnegut's *Breakfast of Champions* and James Clavell's *The Children's Story*) through which they can view the familiar.

Even though many of my students criticize the United States in class discussions, most defend the concept of Thomas Jefferson's Declaration and believe deep down America is the greatest country on earth. This is similar to the way they criticize their own high school among themselves but staunchly defend it when challenged by students from neighboring schools.

Being children of the nineties does color their criticism. When we examine the passage about all men being created equal, at least one person points out that Jefferson owned slaves. Occasionally, someone else will ask whether women were created equal as well as men. They wonder, too, about whether the "pursuit of happiness" is enough anymore. Nicole writes,

> I think the American dream has definitely and drastically changed. What happened to the old-fashioned, just-be-happy American dream? The entire family, and don't forget Lassie, gathered around the new black-and-white television on a Saturday night. Mom knitting, Dad smoking a pipe and reading the newspaper, John and Sally playfully bickering about which channel to watch, and the shiny Ford sitting in the add-on garage. This was my grandparents' American dream. To have a happy and peaceful home . . . the pursuit of happiness.
>
> *Nicole DeKraker Hayden, first-year college*

John and Sally traded the pursuit of happiness for the pursuit of a career and blue-collar for white-collar jobs. My high school students equate money with success and would just as soon win the lottery as work. Americans claim they're still interested in coming together as families, but more and more of us sacrifice that time for other pursuits. Why? Because we want more things: entertainment systems with surround sound, cellular phones, newer computers with CD-ROM and access to the Internet. Never mind that as some Americans acquire more and more, others survive with less and less.

Yet every morning at school, students stand and recite a pledge to their country that ends "with liberty and justice for all." When Troy sat at his desk the first time the Pledge aired on the intercom, I knew I needed to talk to him. I imagined an administrator walking down the hall, gazing through my door, spotting Troy slumped over his desk while the rest of us stood, the administrator censuring me for permitting such disrespect. (Only in the last year has the administration acknowledged that students have the right to sit quietly at their desks during the Pledge of Allegiance.)

When I talked to Troy about not rising to recite the Pledge with his classmates, he told me he didn't believe the words were true. Troy was new to Lockland and tight-lipped. He wore a flat-top black vinyl cap, with a short bill in front, and always took a seat at the back of the class away from his peers. It took months of writing before I began to understand how past experiences had made him so reticent and angry. His stance on the Pledge, though, was firm: he wouldn't stand for it.

Troy's stance made me contemplate my other students' willingness to pledge to their country's flag. I asked them if they knew what *pledge* meant. Many didn't. What about *allegiance*, I wondered. Again, many were stumped. "Who stands for 'The Star-Spangled Banner' at ball games?" I asked. Most raised their hands. "Do you know what *perilous* and *ramparts* mean?" Few did.

I decided to read James Clavell's *The Children's Story* (1963) to this class, a novel that can be read aloud in less than thirty minutes. In it a new elementary school teacher asks her students what *pledge* and *allegiance* mean, just as I had. The students are dumbstruck. Their old teacher had never interrupted them as they blindly recited a pledge that meant little to them. In twenty-five minutes, the new teacher brainwashes these children, channeling their allegiance toward a new government. Clavell says the germ for his story was a discussion with his daughter just home from school. He writes in his epilogue: "I really realized how vulnerable my child's mind was—any mind, for that matter—under controlled circumstances."

22

School is a controlled environment. We condition children to behave in certain ways, to assume certain attitudes, to become certain kinds of Americans. I don't want to create revolutionaries in my classroom, but I do want them to question their beliefs and think about how they became the Americans they are. This short lesson, which I stumbled upon because of Troy's revolt, is now incorporated at the beginning of class.

Another thing I stumbled upon that reinforces Nicole's and Chris' perspectives is a full-page ad for the St. Louis Symphony Orchestra's performance of Copland's *Lincoln Portrait.* A huge American flag flies in the background with a black-and-white portrait of Lincoln superimposed on it. Standing in front of the flag, to either side of Lincoln, are conductor Leonard Slatkin and General Norman Schwartzkopf. Students quickly point out the celebrity status Schwartzkopf achieved through Operation Desert Storm, and the advertisement's implication: both he and Lincoln are American heroes. In the bottom right corner rest five tiny words: AVAILABLE AT YOUR LOCAL K-MART. No wonder Chris is cynical. Advertisements are texts worth reading; they, too, shape our perceptions. (See Chapter Five.)

We usually read one more literary excerpt in the introductory unit to this class: Chapter One of Kurt Vonnegut's *Breakfast of Champions* (1973). Vonnegut's book is so satirical it provokes many of my students to anger; anger leads them to rethink lessons they learned in elementary school. After taking shots at the anthem and motto, and noting that a U.S. law states, "The flag shall not be dipped to any person or thing," though other countries consider flag-dipping "a form of friendly and respectful salute" (p. 9), Vonnegut writes,

> The undippable flag was a beauty, and the anthem and the vacant motto might not have mattered much, if it weren't for this: a lot of citizens were so ignored and cheated and insulted that they thought they might be in the wrong country . . . It might have comforted them some if their anthem and their motto had mentioned fairness or brotherhood or hope or happiness, had somehow welcomed them to the society and its real estate. (p. 9)

23

Vonnegut continues in this same vein, then helps us understand why we believe what we do about America and Americans:

> Teachers . . . wrote this date on blackboards . . . and asked children to memorize it with pride and joy:
> 1492
> The teachers told the children that this was when their continent was discovered by human beings. Actually, millions of human beings were already living full and imaginative lives on this continent in 1492. That was simply the year in which sea pirates began to cheat and rob and kill them. (p. 10)

Vonnegut's first chapter helps students understand how their attitudes about Americans have been shaped. They remember choral recitations of "In fourteen hundred and ninety-two Columbus sailed the ocean blue." In fact, much of their education has involved memorizing "facts," facts they translate into Truth. Rarely are they challenged to question Truth. Truth is unassailable.

Vonnegut's words are harsh. Teachers had named Columbus and his men "discoverers"; Vonnegut names them "sea pirates." Students of European descent don't want to imagine their ancestors as pirates who cheat and rob and kill. My African American students like Troy, though, find Vonnegut's depiction comforting and correct.

On this note we begin our exploration of the American dream. Most recently we focused our efforts by investigating four questions:

1. What dreams bring people to this country?
2. How hard do we have to work for it?
3. Is education the key that unlocks the door?
4. Whose dream is it anyway?

What Dreams Bring People to This Country?

My own ancestors were actually Irish, English, and German, but as far as I knew growing up, I was a hundred percent Irish. Though my father had never visited Ireland (my mom and he did go for their thirty-fifth anniversary), he always talked about the potato famine, St. Patrick driving out the snakes, and the fervent faith of Irish peasants. My father was so interested in his own background, he visited libraries, wrote hospitals, and made pilgrimages to the birthplaces of ancestors in Pennsylvania and West Virginia, in the hope he could trace his roots back to the early tribes of Irish warriors. (He does claim an Irish chieftain as one of our earliest ancestors.)

My wife's family is Swiss and Italian. Her father has relatives living in Basel, Switzerland. Her grandmother grew up in northern Italy. When we met, I quickly became acquainted with the Italian side of her heritage. My family is fairly reserved so I was unaccustomed to the hugging and cheek-kissing I encountered the first few times I visited. Kathy's grandmother lived in Highwood, Illinois, a small enclave of Italian immigrants just north of Chicago. The town is such a magnet it once attracted Pavarotti to a neighborhood dinner when he was performing in the city.

When my wife and I married in 1979, we honeymooned in Europe. I'd been working on the railroad for three years and had saved enough money for two months abroad; Kathy had completed her first year teaching and was off for the summer. As part of our trip, we visited the birthplace of each of our ancestors.

I hadn't told my father we'd be visiting Ireland, but I remembered he'd said our family had come from County Mayo, so that's where we headed. After riding the train to Castlebar and the bus to Ballina, I asked a ticket agent if anyone in town bore my last name. He pointed down the street. We had walked a few blocks when I spotted GAUGHAN emblazoned in large letters above the entrance to a small pub. I rummaged through my backpack for my camera, excited that the picture I was about to take would be the perfect gift for my father when we returned. Just as I snapped the first shot, the broad-shouldered man washing the picture window in front turned in surprise. I yelled an explanation across the street: "That's my name!"

"Mine too," he responded. So we crossed over, introduced ourselves to Edward Gaughan, walked into his pub, and agreed to drink the beers he offered us (even though it was ten in the morning). We talked of family, what had happened to the Gaughans (some had gone to England, many to the United States), and how the Gaughan name evolved.

"It used to have an 'O' in front of it," Edward explained. "And it's pronounced 'Gauhan,'" he told us. Then he suggested we visit a small coastal village where a Gaughan wedding celebration was winding down. (The party lasted a week.) We hitched a ride with Edward's help, found a room at Bridie O'Toole's guesthouse, and followed her directions down the narrow country road to the local tavern. I asked the first patron I met if any Gaughans were present, and though he'd had a few mugs of Guinness before we arrived, he turned, eyes a bit glazed, waved his hand toward the right side of the room, and exclaimed, "Why, all o' them are Gaughans!"

At that moment we could have been at Aunt Vi's Fourth of July picnic, we became so familiar with our Irish relatives. (I say "we" because they claimed Kathy looked Irish, too, though I don't see it.) We took pictures, drank beer, sang songs, told stories, and celebrated our "reunion."

The following morning Kathy and I strolled down the same road to the coast, the point, my relatives had informed me the night before, from which my ancestors sailed for America. I imagined them leaving, hungry but full of hope. I felt connected to the past at that moment, but to the present, too, knowing my name lives on in Ireland, England, and the United States.

In Basel, Switzerland, we stayed with Kathy's cousin Marianne. In the mountains of northern Italy, we visited Emilia Romagna, the province where Kathy's grandmother Mary spent part of her childhood. We established roots, understood connections, realized our own immigrant status.

Sometimes when I ask students to explain why their own ancestors came here, they look perplexed. "From Kentucky?" they ask. When they understand I'm speaking of immigrating to the United States, they recite standard clichés about religious freedom and equal opportunity, but the connections Kathy and I experienced are absent. When I survey their attitudes about current immigration policies, they usually remark that immigrants are ruining the country. They've heard parents complain about losing jobs; they know some of them might lose scholarships.

I've only taught two first-generation immigrant students in my fourteen years at Lockland. One, Kiem Hoang, immigrated from Vietnam. I nudged Kiem to write about the experiences that led him here; fortunately, he agreed. "Escape from the 'Red Heaven'" is a five-page, single-spaced narrative and the lead story in *Horizons*, the literary magazine the school funds when the money's available.

26

Kiem explained that, though "leaving" home is usually sad, escaping the "lovelessness which is communism helps overcome the emotional attachment." Initially Kiem's family left their city dwellings for the countryside to, as his father put it, "escape the look of the spy." After a few months in the country, though, Kiem decided it was time to part from his parents:

> I can remember the sunset one evening, lightly shadowing a manioc tree under the valley, the cool wind scattering the leaves. The valley was not so deep, but down there the dark evening would soon be coming. I was faced with the most important decision of my life, one of life or death. The moon was over the top of the mountains. I lied to my parents and told them that I planned to go back to Saigon. They didn't speak to me—not one word. Little did they know that my plan was to escape Vietnam altogether. I felt so sorry for my mom and dad. They're getting old, but I had to take charge of my own life. It was hard to leave my family and my country, because I felt that I hadn't done anything for my country, and I was leaving it.

Kiem hooked up with a group of refugees with similar aspirations. The rest of his story details the travails they faced as they attempted to leave Vietnam. Kiem remembers bugs so bad he had to "cover his face with dirty rags to prevent them from biting me"; swimming across a cold river in the dead of night; ignoring the pains of dysentery to keep up with the group.

> It was about two a.m. when we came to the promised point. The moon was bright, making me worried; everyone was silent. We huddled together closer, so we wouldn't lose anyone. In front of us was a big group of coconut trees, the wind flowing through the palms. The egrets started coming back to their nests. As the tide began rolling in, the fishermen began to go home. A storm was growing nearer. The sky was dark except for the lightning. Soon the rain began to drop on our innocent heads. I had to find the thicket to hide from the rain, which was so heavy. The tide got higher, so I had to stand up to avoid drowning; the salty water was pounding against my skin, stinging.

27

For nearly two hours Kiem and the others waited for the boat, which promised new life. When it finally arrived and everyone loaded their packs on board, "the boat turned its nose to the sea door."

> It was still raining. As the boat headed out to the sea, I looked back at my village. I could see the smoke rising from the house and I knew the people were preparing food for the next day. I felt so sad because that was the last time I looked back at my mother land. That feeling made my cheeks wet.

Kiem's journey to the United States was not without peril: their boat was lost at sea; the women and children were forced to board a Thai fishing vessel where "shameless things" were done to the women; they were robbed of their jewelry; some were shot and killed; others drowned. Kiem remembered a Vietnamese saying: "If you don't yet see the coffin, you're not crying." But Kiem admits he "began to see the coffin in my mind."

Only 90 of the 115 refugees remained after the pirates and storms, when they finally were able to continue their journey:

> On the evening of the sixth day, we saw the land very far from us. We continued to travel until eight p.m., and then finally knew that we had reached the Malaysia Sea Zone.
> And our freedom station was opened wide . . .

Kiem ended his story there, but he eventually made it to Lockland, Ohio, where he had relatives who had also escaped. His English was quite good, though he often asked his peers or me to clarify points made in class. Kiem loved to read, to play guitar, to laugh. My class was a richer place the year Kiem Hoang was part of it. I thanked him for telling his story and reminding us of the very real fear that drove many of our own ancestors to seek opportunity in the United States.

Not everyone's immigrant past was driven by fear. Hunger, poverty, even a thirst for adventure motivated millions to leave their old homes for new ones across the oceans. I want students to consider different immigrant experiences and the effects of those experiences on an evolving United States. Early in the semester we read Joseph Bruchac's "Ellis Island" (Columbo et al., 1989, pp. 218–219).

When many of us hear the words "Ellis Island," we immediately imagine excited immigrants spotting the Statue of Liberty, relieved they have finally made it across the Atlantic. Bruchac, too, echoes that image in the first part of his poem. His last verse, however, expresses quite a different sentiment because of his mixed Slovakian and American Indian ancestry. Bruchac reminds students that immigrants seeking opportunity displaced Americans already here. Many of them identify personally with Native American displacement because they, too, have been displaced. I use Sandra Cisneros' *The House on Mango Street* (1989) as a catalyst for their own "immigrant" or "migration" stories. Although none of them are first-generation immigrants like Kiem Hoang, many have been uprooted from their homes. (See Figure 2–1.)

Cisneros' main character, Esperanza, dreams of living in a "real house" someday, one with "at least three washrooms so when we took a bath we wouldn't have to tell everybody." The house would be "white with trees around it," and have a "great big yard." Instead, after moving from Paulina Street to Keeler and Loomis, her family ended up on Mango Street, in a small red house with "tight steps in front and windows so small you'd think they were holding their breath." "Bricks are crumbling," the front door is "swollen," there is no front yard. "Everybody has to share a bedroom."

"You live *there?*" a nun from Esperanza's school once asked her, spewing forth "there" as one would an epithet, making Esperanza "feel like nothing" (pp. 3–5).

Still, Esperanza dreams, makes friends, lives her life on Mango Street. "Like it or not you are Mango Street," a friend tells her (p. 107).

None of my students are Hispanic, but most identify with Esperanza. They are not Mango Street, but Cooper Avenue, Shepherd Lane, or Williams Street. Janette's journal response echoes Cisneros' first chapter:

> First we lived in Deer Park in a trailer; next was Reading in a great big blue house with white stars around the sides; then we moved to Kenwood in a little brick house with a back yard for our dog to run around in; we moved back to Reading to a brown house that was always real cold; then there

29

The American Dream: *The House on Mango Street*

The House on Mango Street by Sandra Cisneros is a different kind of novel. Instead of a typical plot unraveling chapter by chapter, Cisneros shows us a number of scenes or vignettes unified by place: Mango Street, where all of these characters live. Taken together, we get a sense of what it might be like growing up Hispanic in the United States.

Cisneros' novel is about more, though, than growing up Hispanic; all of us can relate to Esperanza and the characters who live on Mango Street. We share similar dreams, know how it feels to be displaced, learn through experience that the world isn't always kind. After reading the novel, show in writing how you connect with these characters' lives.

Write one- to two-page responses to at least two of the following:

1. After reading Chapter One, write about the importance people place on owning a home.

2. What was Louie's cousin's motivation in the chapter called "Louie, His Cousin and His Other Cousin"? Do you blame him for what he did? Can you empathize with his cousin?

3. What does the chapter "Those Who Don't" say about the American Dream? Relate this chapter to Vonnegut's quote from *Breakfast of Champions*: "Color is everything."

4. How does pursuing the dream in "The Family of Little Feet" turn into a nightmare?

5. After reading "A Rice Sandwich," explain how each of the following affects people's self-esteem: (1) where they live; (2) what they own; (3) what they can afford.

6. Show how other people's perceptions of Sally affect her dreams in the chapter called "Sally."

7. Esperanza says in "Bums in the Attic" that she won't forget who she is or where she came from. How important is social responsibility in relation to individual pursuits of the American Dream?

Figure 2–1

8. How do "pride" and "shame" relate to "A Smart Cookie"?

9. How do things that appeared pleasant or appealing when we were younger grow unpleasant or unappealing as we get older (in the same way they do for Esperanza in "The Monkey Garden")?

10. How does marriage affect Sally's dream in "Linoleum Roses"?

11. Explain what Esperanza means at the end of the book when she says, "I have gone away to come back. For the ones I left behind. For the ones who could not get out."

Write one- to two-page responses to at least two of the following:

1. Write a "chapter" of your own life modeled after Chapter One, "The House on Mango Street"; think about where you've lived, where you'd like to live, etc.

2. Write the story of your name as Esperanza does in "My Name."

3. Have you or has anyone you've known ever done something similar to what Louie's cousin did? If so, tell the story showing what happened.

4. Can you tell a story similar to "The Family of Little Feet"? Tell it!

5. Tell your own story patterned after "A Rice Sandwich."

6. Show that you won't forget your roots by writing a chapter similar to "Bums in the Attic."

7. Have you ever experienced anything like what Esperanza relates in "A Smart Cookie"? Show what you mean.

8. Did you have a "Monkey Garden" of your own when you were younger? What happened to it? How has your attitude toward it changed?

Figure 2–1 Continued

was Lockland, the yellow two-family, the white two-family, the apartments.

We have everything now, but it's not ours. From the outside of the house and the pink color, you'd think the perfect family lived there, but I can't wait to move out.

Janette Wurtzler, grade 11

Although most of my students hadn't moved as many times as Janette, they understood her displacement. Rebecca talks about being shifted from room to room each time a new sibling was born:

As my baby sister Rachel grew older and Patti matured, I had to move in with Rachel. It seemed as if every time I became comfortable in my surroundings and grew attached to my room, I had to leave. I know it's strange to feel bonded to a room, but I was young and I felt unwanted because it seemed as if I was the only one in my family having to do all the room hopping.

Rebecca Alcorn, grade 12

Fonika spent most of her life in the same room in the same apartment. In her journal she talks candidly about never living in a home of her own:

Since I don't own a home and I have never lived in a house, I have no idea of what it may be like. I can only imagine how good it feels to know that you no longer have to pay rent, you no longer have to ask your neighbor to turn down his/her music so that you can sleep, and you no longer have to ask someone to move their car from your parking space.

Fonika can identify with how Esperanza felt when the nun inquired about where she lived:

One of the things that really bugged me was when my friend wasn't allowed to play in the park in my neighborhood because her parents thought that it was infested with drug dealers. That's one of the reasons why I am trying to get an education so my children won't have to grow up ashamed of their home.

Fonika wrote these journal entries her senior year. I valued her presence in class, because of her E. F. Hutton influence: when Fonika spoke, people listened. Besides her oral contributions, she was one of the best writers I taught. She worked hard and meant what she said about valuing education. Fonika graduated first in her class.

Just as Esperanza dreamed, so did Fonika. After reading the chapter from *Mango Street* called "Bums in the Attic," Fonika wrote a similar piece in her journal. Here's the beginning:

> I want a house surrounded by trees with a big yard like the ones in Madeira and Wyoming. I used to love to go driving through these neighborhoods, but I don't anymore. I used to imagine how beautiful my own house would be when I got older. Now I hate it because I always have to come out of Dreamland to face reality—my small apartment in a town that hardly anybody knows.

Fonika plans to leave Lockland one day, just as Esperanza did, but like Esperanza, she pledges to remember her roots. The ending of the same journal entry mirrors Cisneros' ending, except her "bums" aren't "rats":

> Some days I'll have really wild parties and my new neighbors and I will sit in the living room sipping champagne. They'll hear people talking loud and having a good time. They'll become annoyed and wonder who invited hoodlums to the party.
> "Bums?" they'll ask.
> "Boys from the hood," I'll say, and I'll be happy.
>
> *Fonika Thomas, grade 12*

How Hard Do We Have to Work for It?

After spending this first major unit dwelling on the dreams that drive immigration, or migration, and the importance of roots, we shift our emphasis to work: a work ethic, different kinds of work, people's attitude toward jobs or careers.

Since one stereotypical image of the American Dream derives from the "rags-to-riches" stories of Horatio Alger, we read

Ragged Dick (1868/1985) first. The novel's alternate title is *Street Life in New York*, and Dick literally grows up in the streets. In fact, when asked where he lives, Dick replies, "The Box Hotel . . . I slept in a box on Spruce Street" (p. 16).

Dick's nickname reflects his appearance: his oversized pants are torn, buttons are missing on his vest, his coat is too long, and his shirt "looks as if it had been worn a month . . . But in spite of his dirt and rags there was something about Dick that was attractive" (p. 4).

Dick shines shoes to survive in the streets and swears he would never steal. He does have minor character flaws—smoking, playing pranks, cussing—but his "frank, straight-forward manner . . . made him a favorite" (p. 4). Alger wants his readers to admire Dick: "I hope my young readers will like him as I do, without being blind to his faults. Perhaps, although he was only a boot-black, they may find something in him to imitate" (p. 7).

Alger implies that those who perform honest work will find good fortune as Dick does. Of course, when opportunity knocks, Dick answers. Though he admits to being "awful ignorant" (p. 40) and not "much on readin'" because it makes his head ache (p. 28), he does agree to get an education. By the end of the novel, Ragged Dick is "Richard Hunter, Esq.," not yet rich, but on his way.

Alger's stories reinforce romantic notions of individualism. People willing to work hard enough can achieve anything in America. They make their own luck. They're patient. They seize opportunities. When I show students comparative average incomes earned by high school dropouts, high school graduates, college graduates, and so on, I can bet at least one student will point out an exception from her own family or neighborhood. "My uncle didn't graduate from high school and he makes more than you teachers driving a truck." We all want to believe we can control our destinies, and many times, to a great extent, we can. But students need to examine other perspectives about work and success.

Patrick Fenton's "Confessions of a Working Stiff" (Eschholz and Rosa, 1991, pp. 251–57) provides another angle from which to view the world of work. Fenton works as an airport cargo handler at John F. Kennedy Airport in New York. His day begins at 5:45 A.M.:

> I make my living humping cargo for Seaboard World Airlines . . . I don't get paid to think. The big thing is to beat that

race with the time clock every morning of your life so the airline will be happy.

So what keeps Fenton happy on the job? A silly note in his lunch bag that reads, "'I Love You—Guess Who?' It is all that keeps me going to a job that I hate" (p. 252). After reading "Confessions of a Working Stiff," I ask students to respond in their journals. Brian writes,

> This short story describes most middle-class workers in America. They work because they have to, not because they love their jobs or the pay is good . . . They realize they are nobody to society except a number on a time card, but still they bust their ass everyday working harder than any professional for far less pay. I thought hard work in America got you where you wanted to go. All it does is get you what you need to survive. Most middle-class workers have very important jobs, jobs that have to be done for America to function, but still they weigh less on the scale of life because they can be easily replaced by many job-hungry Americans. Since I was young I was told you want to be a doctor or a lawyer, not some poor, petty middle-class worker. Why can't you be what you want to be? Because it's not socially acceptable, because you don't want to be looked down upon. Middle-class workers are prisoners. They have to work, there are bills to pay, food to buy, nothing extra, no bonus, just pride.
>
> *Brian Nelson, grade 12*

Brian addresses the story then quickly moves to a very personal observation of the world of work. Middle-class workers, most of the people in his community, are seen as inferior, even though Brian believes they perform important jobs and work harder than most professionals. The Horatio Alger myth is a lie as far as he's observed. Working-class people merely subsist. Despite the condescension blue-collar workers sometimes experience and the fact they feel their jobs imprison them, many perform their work with pride.

Not Mike LeFevre, though, a steel worker from Studs Terkel's *Working* (Columbo et al., 1989): "You can't take pride anymore . . . It's hard to take pride in a bridge you're never gonna cross, in a door you're never gonna open. You're mass-producing things and you never see the end result of it" (pp. 520–521). LeFevre has different dreams for his own child: "I want my kid to tell me he's not gonna be like me" (p. 527).

I know that many of my students work, so I'm interested in how they feel about their own jobs. I wonder if they find it difficult to take pride in their work. If Hank, a roofer I hired to repair a leak near the chimney in my house, exhibits an attitude typical of contemporary workers, then I would have to answer yes. This journal response I wrote with students explains what led me to this conclusion:

> I hear Hank on the roof again, so I leave my computer in the laundry room and head toward the ladder in front of the house. I'd been typing a "letter-to-the-editor" assignment for students in my American Dream class. The sky is high-pressure blue, just right for fixing a leaky roof. I climb the ladder and join Hank.
>
> "Found your problem," he says as the sole of his right work boot sinks into a spongy spot on the newly shingled roof. "My boys must've forgot to nail the boards under here."
>
> Ten months, two roofing companies, $3,500 later, and my brand new roof still leaks in the same place. The American Dream isn't dead, but fewer Americans want to work to achieve it.
>
> "I don't have any plywood with me today, but first thing Tuesday I'll take care of it," Hank continues, and that's the last I ever see of him. I am reminded of Wimpy and his promise to pay Tuesday for a hamburger today.
>
> Speaking of hamburgers, how often do you find yourself checking the bag before you leave your local fast-food pick-up window? I've learned myself, but it took a few missing burgers to teach me. It's just a job to these teenagers, and one that doesn't pay that well; if I want to keep my family happy, I'd better check the bag before I drive.
>
> When the Japanese criticized the American work ethic a year or two ago, they struck a raw nerve many of us feared would be exposed. Now we can't look away, and the truth

hurts. Sure there are plenty of hard-working people in this country, but if there were no truth to this criticism, why did Americans react so defensively?

"We've had everything given to us," Kim explains. "Why should we work for it?" She doesn't even say this cynically.

I don't think pride motivates people the way it used to. It's too easy today. I don't roof the house myself; I pay someone who advertises their expertise and five-year guarantee. Fast-food employees don't check to see if they've included your burgers and fries; most people will be home before they complain. And students today don't need to read or study; they'll usually be promoted anyway.

When SAT tests come along, parents pay for preparatory courses to make up for their child's lack of reading. Instead of modeling real literacy at home, parents complain when test scores decline, and criticize the schools. Appoint a commission, push for greater accountability, jump on the back-to-basics bandwagon.

There's always a simpler, more expedient way to reach the American Dream. Even we teachers buy lottery tickets. Unless we are prepared as a society to once again value work for its own sake, we will continue to seek short-term solutions to long-term problems.

In the meantime, a few politicians may get themselves elected with superficial promises, and test scores might even improve a point or two, but the American work ethic will continue to deteriorate. For now, learn to live with leaky roofs and see your fast food gone before you eat it.

After sharing my reflections, I ask students to write about their own observations or experiences of work. Vicky calls her paper, "Take This Job and Shove It," but her title is misleading:

"I hate my job," a friend of mine complains as she picks at the few bits of pink color which still remains on her nails. (It's a rule where she works that all girls have to have their fingernails polished.)

"I guess," I sigh and dry my hair.

"I mean, you wouldn't believe some of the crap I have

to put up with," she whines. "They made me close last night. I mean, I'm not even old enough to close but they made me do it anyways. They could have let Terry do it, she's twenty-four. I'm only *seventeen* and they make me stay at that store until midnight . . . just to close!"

A few days later Vicky hears the customers of a "neighborhood watering hole" wailing out the chorus of Johnny Paycheck's "Take This Job and Shove It": "He was accompanied by the shouts and hollers of several drunk patrons whose lack of musical talents was made up for by their volume. The many verses of the song were jumbled and hazy, but the chorus was sung with such pride and enthusiasm that a foreigner could have easily mistaken it for the national anthem."

But then the surprise:

Call me crazy but I love my job! That's because I have a . . . SUPER JOB! Many people have asked, "How can I find a 'Super Job'?" Well, you can't look in the paper for one because it won't be there. I mean, do you actually expect to see this in the classifieds:

> Super Job Opening: Wanted, someone who doesn't mind "working" for four hours, two of which will be spent sitting on your butt, eating, and checking out members of the opposite sex in bathing suits. Must be willing to walk the grueling twenty feet to pick up your uniform which has already been washed out and ironed. Must be experienced in standing for a half-hour and banging on a steel drum. Only one drawback: you must be willing to listen to a grown man yell at you for his mistakes! Apply in person. (Must look good in loud, tacky, K-Mart outfits.) Pay: $44.00 a day. (By the way, you'll only work two days a week if employed . . . unless it's raining, snowing, or too cold.)

Who in their right mind could hate a job like mine? Yes, I spend the summers working at Kings Island in the water park, playing the steel drums. Talk about a dream. This is the best job in the entire world.

Vicky admits her job isn't "changing the world or saving the rainforests, but it does help brighten other people's days." Vicky says she likes her job because "it's self-fulfilling." Then at the end of her paper she writes a response she may not have the nerve to voice to her friend:

> You think that your job is hard? Look on the streets. There are people out there who can't get a job, don't have a home, and can't afford to eat! So you think you have it bad and you think your job is hard? Living without a job is ten times harder. Now take that information and shove it.
>
> *Vicky Edrington, grade 12*

Vicky is proud of the job she performs because she finds it "self-fulfilling." Finding self-fulfilling jobs leads students toward discussing means and ends. Why work? What do they expect from a job? If they define success as possessing as many things as they can, will any job that pays them enough to acquire those things be fulfilling? Or must they like their jobs to feel as fulfilled as Vicky does playing steel drums?

Besides describing their own work experience, students need to consider the different contexts in which people work. One context we explore is the capitalistic society in which students already work, or will work. We begin this exploration by watching John Sayles' *Matewan* (1987), a film set during the Depression in a small West Virginia mining town. The plot revolves around Joe Kenehan's attempt to unionize the coal miners so they aren't exploited by the Stone Mountain Coal Company. Tension exists among the workers, because the company has been "importing" Italian immigrants and African American miners willing to cross picket lines. Joe's job is to unite *all* the miners:

> You ain't men to that coal company—you're equipment. They'll use you 'til you wear out or break down or you're buried under a slate fall, and then they'll get a new one. And they don't care what color it is or where it comes from . . . If you stand alone, you're just so much shit to those people. You think this man [Few Clothes, a black miner] is your enemy?

This is a worker. And any union keeps this man out isn't a union—it's a goddam country club. They got you fighting white against colored, native against foreign, holler against holler, when you know there ain't but two sides to this world: them that work, and them that don't. You work; they don't. That's all you need to know about the enemy.

Matewan works well in conjunction with Steinbeck's *The Grapes of Wrath* (1976). Both are about labor-management disputes. Both are set in the same era. Workers are treated similarly by management: they're paid with company scrip redeemable exclusively at the company store; they live on company property; they're required to buy their equipment from the company.

Still, there are two sides to every story. It might be said that both owners and workers pursue their own version of the American Dream: the owners risk money, provide coal to consumers, and turn a profit; the workers risk their lives to provide for their families' security.

When we finish the movie, we conduct a mock trial in which students argue the worth of labor and management: that a capital theory of value (with entrepreneurs risking their money) is necessary for a capitalistic economy to thrive, or that a labor theory of value (with workers providing their muscles and time) is more essential than all the money in the world. (In *Matewan* the coal remains buried in the ground until someone mines it.) Each side must also justify the violence that occurs in the course of the dispute. (See Figure 2–2.)

Students use their notes from the movie but conduct library research, too. One group explores the history of capitalism and company "bosses" such as Carnegie and Rockefeller. The second group examines labor history and organizations such as the IWW (International Workers of the World or "Wobblies").

John, Steve, Andy, and Michelle use facts from the Pullman Strike to support their case and argue that companies initiate violence. David, Joey, Kim, and Johnny argue that capitalism encourages inventiveness and results in higher quality products and services than other economic experiments such as communism.

Watching the movie, conducting research, and role playing combine to produce thoughtful student papers that are often bet-

---

Work and the American Dream:
Matewan Research and Mock Trial

At the end of this unit we will conduct a mock trial based upon the movie *Matewan*. We will divide into two teams (the Stone Mountain Coal Company and the Union). The Union will be on trial for disrupting the daily business of the Stone Mountain Coal Company. Each group should help prepare and defend their team's case.

To help prepare your case for the Company, you might consider the place of real company bosses (such as Carnegie and Rockefeller) in American business, the benefits of a capitalist economy, and the weaknesses of a socialist economy.

To help prepare your case for the Union, you might examine the labor movement in this country (and why it was necessary), the International Workers of the World (IWW or "Wobblies"), the weaknesses of a capitalist economy, and the benefits of a socialist economy.

Of course, both teams will have to review the movie and gather evidence in the library to support their cases.

A judge, jury, lawyers, and representatives of the Union and the Company will be assigned. Be ready to make your case.

Figure 2–2

ter supported than typical research papers. Students make connections, too, to other units already completed, showing me they haven't forgotten what they've learned.

A movie we sometimes watch during the immigration unit is *El Norte*. Two Guatemalan peasants escape their tiny village, which has been overrun by guerrillas, and head to "the North," in search of their American Dream. Kelly recalls a scene from the film before Enrique and Rosita left their village:

> In this movie a father told his son that to rich people, poor people are just "a pair of arms." I think this relates well to

41

Matewan, because it fits right along with how the miners were treated like equipment . . . People who are better off than you or are in a higher position will use you for their benefit and never once think of you as a normal human being like themselves.

Kelly Smith, grade 11

Examining the capitalistic world in which Americans work from a variety of perspectives (a novel, film, oral histories, personal narratives, and library research) helps students place their own jobs and future careers in meaningful contexts. They think about what work means to them and what work is for. They see, too, that the workforce is a political place, where different parties have different interests and stakes. Exploring the power struggles that occur in *Matewan* allows them to vicariously experience what they surely will experience firsthand later in life as they work for American Dreams of their own.

Is Education the Key That Unlocks the Door?

Students are lumps of clay; teachers are sculptors.
Students are empty vessels; teachers are founts of knowledge.

All through middle and high school, math came easily to me. I liked it so much that I worked the even problems when only the odds ones were assigned. I did extra proofs in geometry class, especially the toughest ones in the enrichment section at the end of each chapter. I enjoyed finding solutions after lengthy struggles (call me weird).

English, on the other hand, was not enjoyable. Not that I didn't like to read, but listening to teachers analyze symbols and "lecture the classics to death" wasn't my idea of fun.

Senior year, though, I signed up for an elective class called Guided Independent Reading. Eldon Miller taught it. This was 1970. Mr. Miller explained that we were expected to choose books we wanted to read and then write about our reading. Mr. Miller had a varied assortment of paperbacks to choose from in class, but agreed we could bring in books from outside class, too. He let us work at our own pace and periodically conferred with us about our reading and writing.

Mr. Miller was the only teacher I ever remember who held conferences with students. He got to know us and our reading tastes, and made helpful suggestions for future reading—when I was on my antiwar kick, for example. After I finished Leon Uris's *Exodus*, Mr. Miller suggested Dalton Trumbo's *Johnny Got His Gun*. When it finally dawned on me how little remained of Joe's body in that novel, I was astounded. Mr. Miller's suggestion was perfect.

Of course, I didn't think any book could follow Trumbo's, but when I turned in *Johnny*, Mr. Miller handed me *Slaughterhouse-Five*. Vonnegut's book was unlike any I'd ever read. The novel puzzled me, intrigued me, spurred me to read on and figure out what Vonnegut was trying to say. The style and voice were so distinct. Reading it inspired me to write a paper analyzing the repetend "So it goes," which seems to pop up every time someone dies. So here I was in Mr. Miller's Guided Independent Reading class, doing independently what I despised having English teachers do to me: analyzing literature.

When Mr. Miller and I discussed my paper, I asked him if my analysis was correct. His answer shocked me. "I don't know," he replied. "I'm not Kurt Vonnegut so I'm not sure what he intended, but what you've written makes sense to me."

Never in my recollection had an English teacher not known a writer's intention. They knew what the green light symbolized in *Gatsby*, what Hester's scarlet *A* represented. My question to Mr. Miller revealed my own assumptions about the teaching of literature—about teaching and learning, period: Correct answers exist. Teachers know those answers. Students learn by listening to teachers tell them what writers mean. Symbolism, imagery, and figurative language are codes teachers have cracked. In their classes they reveal how the codes work. But Mr. Miller didn't know the code. "Your guess," he told me, "is as good as mine."

I want my students to examine their own assumptions about education. I doubt much has changed since I went to school. Teacher-talk still dominates classrooms. I am often guilty of talking too much myself.

At the beginning of this unit, I ask students to choose one of the following metaphors that best describes them as learners: a piece of clay, a rosebush, a vessel, or a voyager. Once they've chosen a metaphor, they write about why that one best reflects

43

their own learning. Their responses convey not only how they feel about themselves but also how they've come to view our educational system. Amanda's response implies a sense of help-lessness:

> As far as learning goes, I feel that I am most like a vessel. Everything that I learn from others is dropped into this con-tainer. Most of the time it gets so filled up that it's hard to sift through the contents to find the answer to the question.
>
> *Amanda Patton, grade 12*

Andy realizes he needs individual attention:

> I think I am like a rosebush . . . I just have to be watered more than others.
>
> *Andy King, grade 12*

Bobby admits he's a passive learner who resists pressure:

> My mind can be formed like clay, but with too much pres-sure I will go splat.
>
> *Bobby French, grade 12*

Misty's response doesn't surprise me. She's clearly an indi-vidual who carves her own path. Her responses aren't always popular, but she voices them anyway:

> As a learner, I feel the metaphor of the voyager best suits me. I feel as though I go out searching for the things I *want* to learn . . . I am a searcher, a wanderer, a nomad, going from place to place, from book to book, till I find what I'm looking for. Learning is my mission and I will never complete the voyage.
>
> *Misty Tackett, grade 12*

As students explore their own education, I want them to consider what methodologies best suit their learning style. Are lis-tening to lectures and taking notes, for example, the best way to learn, I ask them? What about memorizing facts?

We start with this quote by Mr. Gradgrind from Charles Dickens' *Hard Times* (1961):

Now what I want is Facts. Teach these boys and girls nothing but Facts. Facts alone are wanted in life. Plant nothing else, and root out everything else. You can only form the minds of reasoning animals upon Facts: nothing else will ever be of service to them. This is the principle on which I bring up my own children, and this is the principle on which I bring up these children. Stick to the Facts, sir! (p. 11)

While a few students claim they agree with Gradgrind (memorizing facts is easy for them), most vehemently disagree. Debating controversial issues in this class, for example, drives home the point the world isn't as simple as this quote implies. Mr. Miller couldn't tell me my analysis of *Slaughterhouse-Five* was "correct." I had written a convincing argument, though.

We read Tom Romano's "the teacher" next (Daiker et al., 1985, p. 714), in which a teacher addresses his students: "I don't teach you anyway, I think, / just lead you like a scout master / and hope you'll dip your hand / into the brook—cold like no / tap water you've ever felt." Students appreciate Tom's metaphor. They enjoy "doing"—hiking through the woods, hearing a brook around the bend in the trail, stooping to scoop cool water in their hands.

To engage them in a reflection on their own education, I ask students to compose a portfolio of artifacts representing the work they do in each of their classes—e.g., an assignment and their response; a paper; a quiz or test; a project. In this way they "do" the analysis of their own education instead of me lecturing them about different ways to learn. They collect artifacts from each class; select one that best represents typical work; and reflect on each item and what it implies about their education. (See Figure 2–3.)

The following are excerpts from Vicky's portfolio:

The Scopes trial packet is from my American History class. Ms. Zickuhr lets the class re-enact trials from history. I feel that this is a very effective way of teaching. Students seem to learn better if they can find a way to relate to the material and find a way to get involved.

I especially enjoyed the Scopes trial because I was H. L. Mencken, the Baltimore journalist who covered the trial. Therefore, I wrote articles covering and summarizing the

Education and the American Dream: An Education Portfolio

1. Assemble a portfolio of items representative of the work you do in each of your classes (an assignment and your completion of that assignment; a paper you wrote; a quiz or test; a project; a poem you had published; a drawing or illustration; etc.). You might also include two to three items from past years that have made a significant impact upon you as a learner (a positive or negative impact). You may include the work itself or written reflections upon that work.

2. Collect others' views (those of parents, administrators, classmates, friends, siblings) of what makes a good education. Please include at least two teachers' views. Write down four to five questions to ask each of these people. Consider some of the following:

   —Describe a memorable learning experience, a time when you learned something well.

   —Describe an ideal education.

   —Is it better to specialize or be well rounded?

   —Why is your subject important for students to learn?

   —If you could change anything about education here at Lockland, what would you change?

3. Read and respond to one of the following pieces:

   —"Angels on a Pin" by Alexander Calandra

   —"Learning to See" by Samuel Scudder

   —"The Lesson" by Toni Cade Bambara

   —"Theme for English B" by Langston Hughes

   —"Shame" by Dick Gregory

4. Explain in writing the contents of the portfolio and why you included what you did. How has each item contributed to (or detracted from) your own education? Based on your observations and reflections, what makes for a good education? Consider the list of educational myths we generated; has any of your reading or research led you to challenge some of these myths?

5. Be ready to share your conclusions orally with the rest of the class.

Figure 2–3

46

events of each of the court days. I felt really comfortable with this role and feel that it has helped me to better define my future career.

School is an institution for the training and conforming of young minds. Think about it . . . you are told only the facts the teachers think you should be told. You are forced to take many of the classes on your schedule. You sit in even rows or columns of desks which are all the same shape.

You are being trained! (Trained to learn, trained to think, trained to conform . . .)

If you refuse to conform or go along with this training, measures may be taken. At Lockland that may be days spent in In-School-Suspension. In the case of Pat Conroy's character in *The Water Is Wide*, it was a thick, leather strap.

Why must punishment be issued to those who do not wish to be treated like robots or like machines?

School limits the imagination . . .

I must say that there are a few teachers brave enough to break the mold, strong enough to reach out and personally connect with the students they teach. Those are the ones who feel that the students in their classes should not be confined. Those are also the ones who take the action suggested by Elizabeth Segal in *Gender and Reading*.

I agree with Elizabeth that males should be given the chances from childhood to read stories which deal with female characters and their emotions. Why not? Females read about male feelings and male characters all the time.

For instance, in my Contemporary Culture class we were given the book *The Secret Diary of Adrian Mole*. The main character was a male, and the feelings felt by him were depicted on the pages of his diary. So why not a book about a female and her diary? It certainly would be a change and change is something good for education . . . good for you!

Let's put the "you" back in Ed "u" cation.

Vicky isn't afraid to challenge traditional practices she believes confine her and her peers. Education should be personal, it should be relevant, and it should reflect different voices (Bobby's and Andy's, but Melanie's and Vicky's as well).

Students are also required to interview others (including at least one teacher) about their views on education. Vicky's interview with a fourth-grade teacher is interesting in light of her comments about change and putting the "you" back in education. This teacher's recollection of a memorable learning experience centered on an eighth-grade assignment about Russia. "It was memorable because it was the first time we were given a real hands-on assignment. We had to do all of the work ourselves," the teacher told Vicky. But when asked to describe an ideal education, the teacher insisted that schools return to the basics. Students should study the classics, there should be no vocational education, students need a "solid core." It's ironic that this traditional teacher who "delivers" a basic education to students recalls a nontraditional learning experience as most memorable in her own education.

Besides these artifacts Vicky includes journal entries describing gym (which she hates) and band (which she loves); a group project from her mass media class; a business plan from entrepreneurship; the chapter six pretest from trigonometry; and a *Don Quixote* quiz from Spanish. Her final artifact is a paper from the American Dream class entitled "A Lesson You Never Forget."

> There are many things that have not been approved by the school board, have not been accepted into the curriculum, that you learn while in school.
>
> Shame is one of those lessons. In Dick Gregory's "Shame," (Madden-Simpson and Blake, 1990) the lesson is bluntly stated in the first two sentences of his story. "I never learned hate at home, or shame. I had to go to school for that" (p. 285). This story was Gregory's childhood experience of being taught to be ashamed of himself and his background.

Vicky compares the lesson Gregory learned in school to one she learned about guilt when she denied her own mother's presence at a basketball game so she'd be accepted by her peers.

Vicky ends her paper like this:

> There are many other lessons which are taught in school besides 2+2=4 and "*i* before *e* except after *c*." But I truly be-

lieve that we'd never get through them all in our lifetime. Because even though we are good in school, we are even better in life, and these lessons are the easiest to learn and the hardest to forget.

Vicky Edrington, grade 12

Vicky reminds us of the often permanent effects of "life lessons," the kind she learned watching a basketball game with a boy she wanted to impress, the kind Dick Gregory learned when his teacher humiliated him by pointing out he was a fatherless "relief" boy.

Can education unlock the door to the American Dream? Maybe not—if students are simply lumps of clay or empty vessels. Not if attaining the American Dream means learning to think actively in a system that teaches students to sit passively.

Vicky rails against this kind of teaching in her portfolio but admits that not all her teachers confine her thinking or train her to conform. The best kind of education engages students. School lessons need to be as poignant as "life lessons." If they're not, students may assume smart teachers, smart people, possess the correct answers. They may never learn to think for themselves. They may never realize their dreams. They may accept the names others impose upon them as the seven-year-old Dick Gregory does. They may never risk dipping their own hands into the brook of life.

Whose Dream Is It Anyway?

Rayford Butler raised his hand one day in Miss Gordon's primary classroom and asked if he could sing one of his own songs. When Miss Gordon relents but insists Rayford keep it short, he sings in his high voice:

Suh-whing a-looow
suh-wheeeet ah charr-ee-oohh . . . (Inada 1993, p. 9)

The whole school and neighborhood glow in the "radiance" of Rayford's song, until Miss Gordon corrects his pronunciation of "chariot" and effectively stifles his and his classmates' voices.

Lawson Inada, a Japanese American poet, grew up in a multicultured classroom in Fresno, California. "Our classroom was filled with shades of brown . . . The only white person in our classroom was our teacher. Our textbooks had pictures and stories about white kids named Dick and Jane and their dog, Spot. And the songs in our songbooks were about Old Susannah coming 'round the mountain and English gardens—songs we never heard in our neighborhood" (Christensen 1993, p. 9).

Who is the American Dream for—migrants working in the San Joaquin Valley or professionals living along Chicago's Gold Coast? Rayford or Miss Gordon? Melanie or me? Should all Americans have access to the dream? As teachers, should we let students sing their own songs? Should the books we use in our classrooms reflects "shades of brown"?

"Rayford's Song" proves an appropriate transition between our unit on education and this unit on race and culture. Though many of my students are white, they can identify with Rayford because most of them have been silenced, often in school. This poem makes them think about power and privilege—the songs that get sung, the stories that get read, the voices that get heard.

One way students give voice to their own songs is through the poetry they write. After they read "Rayford's Song," I ask them to write their own poems. T'Keesha sets her poem in the antebellum South, but its essence could just as easily be contemporary:

You call me
"Nigger"
But this is not the
name my
mother
gave to me.

God made us both,
but you claim that there
is something different between
you and me besides
color.
So you treat me like a beast.
You took me away from
My family,
My man
My children . . .

Then my life is placed into the hands
of a stranger:
The white man.
All for a small sum of money.
"Yes suh, mastuh, No suh, mastuh."
Who are you to be called
"Master"?
You see that I'm
Hot, tired, and sweaty
but you tell me,
"Keep workin', Nigger."
"What?"
"Don't you 'what' me you dirty—"
I have to bite my lip
to keep words from coming because I know
Another word said and the
whip will be mine.
As I wipe the sweat from my brow, I begin
to wonder
if you have mistaken me
for a
dog.
Take a closer look.
You'll prove yourself
wrong.
Soon you will come to
the realization that I'm
Human
Just like
You.
That won't be enough.
The truth you will
deny.
I'm not an animal.
Not a beast.
You give your dogs a bowl to lap their
water—
My cupped hands
serve as

my bowl from which I suck the water to my mouth
to drink.
I'm just a hard-working
"Nigger"
to you.
Only in your eyes
Not the One that made me.
Why is it so hard for you to
believe that
I'm human?
Over the years you have not found it
too easy to accept.
I am your plow,
Your servant,
Your cook.
You expect me to break my
back just to see you smile.
But I'm not as
dumb as you think.
One day God will open
your blinded eyes. Then
you will
see that I am
nothing more than a person.
Just like you.
Flesh and blood.

T'Keesha Chapman, grade 11

T'Keesha's poem could be tightened and polished, but she effectively captures the themes of this unit. "I have to bite my lip to keep words from coming," thinks her protagonist, silencing herself just as Rayford and his peers do after Miss Gordon's criticism. "You call me 'Nigger,'" but "Who are you to be called 'Master'?" she wonders. The white man names her "beast" and "dog," "plow" and "servant," but she names herself "human." A day will come she insists when her master's "blinded eyes" will open, and she can realize dreams of her own.

Melissa's "The Two Worlds of New York" contrasts the lives of two New Yorkers and their access to the American Dream:

The Two Worlds of New York

She steps out of her chauffeured car,
As he walks along the street.
She enters an expensive bar,
As he prays outside for something to eat.
When she exits she covers herself in mink,
As the wind whips through his flimsy shirt.
Her manicured hands hold a fancy drink,
His head to toe is covered with dirt.
She spends her day in Cartier and Saks,
He wanders aimlessly through the snow.
Tavern on the Green is where she snacks,
As he looks for *anywhere* to go.
The snow and wind come harder and stronger,
"What a nuisance," the lady mutters.
He knows he cannot take it much longer,
As he slips and falls into one of the gutters.
She waves her hand towards the passing cabs,
As he looks for a bench on which to nap.
"Ten Park Avenue, please," as she hands him her bags,
All *his* worldly possessions can fit on his lap.
The sunset for both is exactly the same,
The Empire State Building has the same height.
The glitter of Broadway for each has its fame,
While the Brooklyn Bridge gives to both the same light.
But when viewing the city through two separate faces,
One which does poorly, the other well,
New York can seem to be two different places.
To one it's heaven, the other a hell.

Melissa Luckman, first-year college

Near the beginning of this unit, I ask students to brainstorm myths of race. This is a no-holds-barred group brainstorming session: they spit out the myths, I write them on the board. I tell them we want to explore the assumptions that underlie these myths and how they were constructed. Here's a partial list from a recent class:

Lebanese people are terrorists.
Blacks are lazy.

53

Asians are more intelligent.

Native Americans are alcoholics.

Hispanics deal drugs.

Italians are in the Mafia.

Black youths are in gangs.

White people can't dance.

Indians run convenience stores.

Each of these myths is a potential research topic. Students could read, conduct interviews, review films, listen to songs, for two purposes:

1. to explore the "truth" of the myth
2. to explore how the myth evolved

One artifact we read as a class to dispel myths about African Americans is called "The 10 Biggest Myths About the Black Family" by Lerone Bennett, Jr. (1986). One myth he addresses is naming loose morals the root cause of the "black family problem." Bennett writes that although some blacks do have children out of wedlock, so do millions of whites. In fact, in 1983 there were "more births to single white than to single black teenagers" (p. 124).

An excellent film for examining the construction of myths about African Americans is *Ethnic Notions* (1967). Tracing the evolution of black stereotypes from the antebellum South to the present, the film explains how African Americans were perceived by the dominant culture. For example, the "Sambo" caricature was a childlike figure who preferred food, dance, and song to work. In a scene from an early film, a black man tells his wife, "Can I help it if I gotta desire for music," to which the wife responds, "You better get a desire for work." The myth of the Sambo was a rationale for slavery. How could Sambos run plantations, many white Americans asked. The image of a Little Black Sambo impressed upon young whites that this stereotype was not only acceptable, but funny as well.

In the film *Birth of a Nation* (1915) a more damaging stereotype is depicted. According to the film the Reconstruction era "unleashed a savage black upon the American landscape." Whites in black face chased white virgins, legitimizing, in many people's minds, the killing of free blacks after the Civil War. A call arose to go back to the times of the "happy darky." Jim Crow segregation was thought an appropriate means of "social control."

In a journal freewriting, Mike, a white eleventh-grader, explores constructed images of African Americans:

> Ghetto dwellers, gang bangers, gun a-blazing, drug dealers, Niggers.
>
> "Land of the Free," Statue of Liberty, the Thirteenth Amendment, thirteen stripes and fifty stars, FREEDOM.
>
> Slavery, KKK, cross burnings, hangings, the swastika, Poverty.
>
> Quotas, Financial Aid, athletic scholarships, people who care, a CHANCE.
>
> Why hasn't opportunity knocked for America's black society? Does America even really understand the black society? Many people of a different race would answer that they do . . .
>
> In actuality, though, what they probably understand is the distorted, mythological, racist views adopted by America from the days of slavery.
>
> The racist's view:
>
> Those poor black alley rats. Niggers. They're not fit for anything. They want, want, want, though they never work.
>
> Those lazy welfare recipients. They're ruining AMERICA, "the land of the free."
>
> *Mike Erwin, grade 11*

Mike's entry captures stereotypical images of African Americans and shows an understanding of how racists view blacks and how those images evolved.

Besides poetry and journal responses, I ask my students to explore race and the American Dream through alternate style papers. (See Tom Romano's *Writing with Passion*.) Molly examines the way language constructs images of white and black people in her paper, "Gray Matter." She begins with two crots (an obsolete word meaning "bit" or "fragment"; see Weathers 1984, p. 136):

WHITE: HAVING THE COLOR OF PURE SNOW OR MILK
    OPPOSITE TO BLACK; MORALLY OR
    SPIRITUALLY PURE; SPOTLESS; FREE FROM
    EVIL INTENT; HARMLESS; HAVING A LIGHT-
    COLORED SKIN; HAPPY, FORTUNATE.
    "white is good   good   good
    milk is good for you: builds bones
                                                makes strong
                                                healthy
    don't lie: to lie is bad   bad   bad
    pure
    white lies are ok   why?
    harmless
    light skin   happy   light skin
                            fortunate"

BLACK: OPPOSITE TO WHITE; THE COLOR OF COAL;
    WITHOUT LIGHT; SOILED; DIRTY; HAVING
    DARK-COLORED SKIN AND HAIR; EVIL;
    WICKED; HARMFUL; DISGRACEFUL; FULL OF
    SORROW OR SUFFERING; NEGRO; SAD;
    DISMAL; GLOOMY; DISASTROUS; ANGRY;
    WITHOUT HOPE
    "not white, next to white, second to white
                    don't mix
    miners' work is hard gloomy   dismal
            breathing black air
                    causes black lung
                    death
    mourning? wear black . . . witches do
                                        evil
                                        mean
                                        scary
    black black black black black black black
    scary?
                            stay away"
                    Molly Shafer, first-year college

56

Diane uses two lists as part of her alternate style paper to reflect upon the epithet "Oreos" as it is used to ridicule interracial couples:

The Cookie	The Cream
black	white
too bitter	too sweet
branded	smooth
some only	some only
eat the	eat the
cookie	cream
scraping off	twisting off
the white cream.	the black covering.
the cream is too sweet.	throwing it away.
It's a matter of	It's a matter of
impressions.	impressions.

Oreos
were made to be eaten
together.

Diane Marsh, first-year college

"It's a matter of impressions," Diane writes. Those impressions don't originate in a vacuum. People construct them, media reinforce them, adults perpetuate them. As educators, we can help students explore their own impressions of others so they understand how those impressions evolved. Our job may not be to change students' impressions, but I believe it is to help students use language to explore their assumptions. It's one thing to understand why you think what you think. It's quite another not to think. Espousing unexamined views won't help students write more effective papers or discuss controversial topics intelligently.

To help students examine their own views, especially their own prejudices, I assign them collaborative research papers. With a partner, students investigate the meaning of the American Dream firsthand by observing and interviewing persons whose perspective differs from their own. (See Figure 2–4.)

The students' research base is typically their own community or adjacent communities, but some of them venture further:

57

Difference and the American Dream: Collaborative Research Paper

Assignment: Along with your partner, investigate the meaning of the American Dream firsthand by observing and interviewing persons whose perspective is different from your own. Then write an interesting paper that reveals your findings to the other members of our class.

Topics: You should choose a perspective about which you know little but would like to know more. Your research base will probably be Lockland, Wyoming, or Reading, but some of you may want to venture further, perhaps to Clifton, Cincinnati, or Oxford. Differences to consider might include gender, race, class, or sexual orientation. Perhaps you've seen individuals on Fountain Square who wear alternative dress and hairstyles. You might interview members of this counterculture and find out their views on America and the American Dream.

Or maybe you heard about the incident at a local high school involving two boys who wore KKK robes to school on Halloween. You might get their story.

Maybe you could get in touch with an engineer from General Electric or a feminist teacher from the University of Cincinnati or a recent immigrant to this country. Whomever you decide upon, your interview source should be from outside the school.

Once you've selected a topic, begin to explore. Decide if you'll go out together, where you'll start, and whom you'll interview. Take notes recording what you hear and see. Look for related articles in the library and decide whether or not that information might enrich your understanding and your paper. Consider what we've said about good writing up to this point in the course. Above all, your paper should be interesting and informative.

Memo: When you finish your paper, please complete the following memo individually. Your partner need not see this.

1. How did you go about choosing your topic?
2. Explain the process by which the two of you wrote this paper. What were your individual contributions? Be specific.
3. What did you think of working with this particular partner?
4. What did you think of the project itself?

Figure 2–4

perhaps to Clifton, where the University of Cincinnati is located; downtown Cincinnati twelve miles south; or even Oxford, Ohio, thirty miles north and home of Miami University.

Stephanie and Chris decide to interview individuals in Clifton who wear alternative dress and hairstyles. Randy and Kevyn arrange a visit to one of the most exclusive private schools in Cincinnati. Mark and Steve take their lead from an editorial cartoon series drawn by *Cincinnati Enquirer* and Pulitzer Prize–winning cartoonist Jim Borgman. Each night for a week, Borgman had depicted cultural differences between the east and west sides of Cincinnati. While Westsiders grill burgers in the backyard for outdoor fun, Eastsiders sip cappuccino at sidewalk cafés. (My students live on the Westside.) Mark and Jeff call Borgman and ask him which side of Cincinnati he prefers, and, as you might expect, his response is noncommital. So they decide to explore for themselves, interviewing people from both sides of "the wall," or Vine Street, a lengthy divider running north and south.

One of the most provocative searches belongs to Misty and Jeremy, who travel to Oxford to interview a member of the Gay Lesbian Bisexual Alliance (GLBA). Jeremy admits his prejudices up front but, at Misty's urging, decides to confront his fears. I include excerpts from their paper below:

> Michael Burkhart is a sophomore at Miami University. We asked what he was majoring in to break the ice and to see if we would be comfortable with him and vice-versa. His reply was mathematics and statistics.
>
> He leads a rough life like many other college students who are away from their homes and their families. Except, his life is full of discrimination and personal hatred. He is a minority in today's society. He's a homosexual. He is the co-chairman of the GLBA.
>
> Michael was quick to add that they (the GLBA) prefer to be called "gay" instead of "homosexual." Homosexual makes it sound like "it's a bedroom issue," which it is not. Just like a heterosexual, gays just want someone to love and someone to love them. Affection in general. Part of Michael's American Dream is to have "a lover, a good social life, and be involved

in the arts while living in Manhattan." Just like a heterosexual except he does not want to have kids.

When first asked what his American Dream is, he changed the question, saying, "The American Dream for most straight [males] is to have a loving wife and live in a suburban community; you know with the little house, small yard, the white picket fence, and of course kids." All of this is the same for him except for the kids. He joked and said, "We all know why."

Misty and Jeremy's research explores "coming out," AIDS, and specific examples of discrimination. They end their paper like this:

Homophobia basically means fear of homosexuals to people that are straight. We wonder if this changes the pursuit of happiness and the American Dream for most gay people. With all the discrimination who would let them be free to be themselves in a prejudiced society which causes those who are straight to rebel against the homosexuals . . . with words like faggot, fairy, dike, or lesbo. The old cliché says, "Sticks and stones may break my bones but words will never hurt me." Michael commented, "Words hurt!" When the day ended, we had learned something not only about Michael but about ourselves. "It is better to be hated for what you are than loved for what you are not."

At the end of the semester, both Misty and Jeremy included this paper in their course portfolios. Below are excerpts from their reflective letters:

We learned so much from someone who was just a bit older than us. I learned a lifetime worth of education. Something that they don't teach you in school, something that you must learn for yourself. I hope I never forget the things that prejudice has taught me.

Misty Mardis, grade 11

Much to my surprise, Michael is a lot like normal men. He shares some of the same dreams and views as I did. I decided to include this in my portfolio because I feel it is the best paper I've written in my three years of high school. I thank Misty for all of her help.

Jeremy Larkins, grade 11

Besides writing a collaborative paper, Misty and Jeremy explain their research orally in class. Part of what they share is a questionnaire given them by Michael, twenty-seven questions for heterosexuals that are actually questions often asked of people who are gay:

1. What do you think caused your heterosexuality?
2. Why do you insist on being so obvious and making a public spectacle of your heterosexuality?
3. Why do heterosexuals place so much emphasis on sex?

I use the handout in subsequent classes because it helps students empathize and examine their own sexuality. The firsthand research, though, is so much more meaningful. Not every administrator I've worked for is as willing to support these efforts, but when I find one who is, I take advantage.

Students have to arrange their own interviews and transportation, and get permission from their parents and our administration if they conduct their research during the school day. Some administrators have immediately understood the value of this project; others have insisted students remain in school. I want students to have access to resources outside of our school district in the same way that I believe all Americans should have equal access to the dream. Part of this final unit helps students see that all Americans aren't equal, that achieving equality and attaining dreams is more difficult for some than others.

In this American Dream course, students read novels, short stories, poetry, essays, and advertisements. They write journal entries, poems, alternate style papers, and personal narratives. They conduct research, watch films, and examine the effects of language on identity. They explore their own assumptions and how those assumptions are constructed over time.

They consider how their own lives are reflected in the literature they read and the films they watch. They discuss the effects

61

of society on individual attitudes and behavior. Though they may not read some of the classics juniors in other high schools read, they do learn to read and write. Most of my students who go to college return after one semester, report cards in hands, showing me the A's they've earned in first-year English. I don't think teaching American literature thematically cheats my students. In fact, I think critically examining the dream makes it more accessible to them. I'm convinced it gives them a better understanding of America and Americans than would a traditional curriculum.

Who is the American Dream for? I wish I could answer, "All Americans." I hope, for now, that it's for Melanie and Julie, Fonika and Kiem, Chris and Mike . . . all my students. And yours.

CHAPTER 3

Naming Ourselves
and Our World

On May 19, 1986, Evelyn Couch, in Fannie Flagg's *Fried Green Tomatoes at the Whistle Stop Cafe* (1987), leaves her home for the grocery store on the ninth "hard" day of her diet "with a feeling of euphoria." She vows never to eat anything again unless it's "crisp and fresh," the way Evelyn feels herself. She is confident, "in control of her life." This is a "new" Evelyn Couch, one who names herself "willowy and graceful" (p. 231).

How we "name" or define ourselves reveals a great deal about our self-perception or how we believe others perceive us. Evelyn Couch had always felt "fat" and "unattractive"; the media mirror into which most of us gaze convinces her she's overweight. As Evelyn slowly sheds pounds, she feels better about herself and willingly shares her new image with others.

Fat Ass . . . echoes in my head.

"Oh, it was just childish prank. Kids can be so cruel."

But it was so much more. They weren't just being cruel. They were destroying the little girl inside me. Making me grow up way too soon. I remember it vividly. Take a look at our fifth-grade class picture. Yep, that's me, the short little fat girl. The object of recess fun. The wallflower of every school dance.

I was huge. Pleasantly plump. Chunky. But when I looked in the mirror every day, I saw a fat, ugly girl that would never get a boyfriend. A pig. I became severely depressed . . .

I decided I wanted to kill myself. Yes, I was twelve years old . . . I dreaded school. I cried a lot. In the bathroom, at school, at home. None of these cruel little brats knew what they were doing to me. I hated them.

Annie Moore, grade 12

"Girl, you are so skinny!" My friend smiles and closes her locker. "See ya later."

As I walk to first bell, I notice the other girls in the hallway and think, "Skinny? What's skinny? Who set the standard?"

So what's wrong with skipping meals, watching what you eat, not indulging in ice cream or chocolate? What's wrong is that I'm never satisfied with my outward appearance . . . Sometimes when you're told something over and over, you begin to believe it. I only wish I did, but it's "skinny" that I constantly feel pressured by.

Rebecca Singh, grade 11

How we "represent" ourselves to ourselves and each other can empower us, marginalize us, or subordinate us. At issue is representation: "the practices by which people name and rename the world, negotiate the substance of social reality, and contest prior names in favor of new or different ones" (Knoblauch and Brannon 1993, p. 3). I want my students to explore this practice of naming or representation because, while names can empower us, they can also devastate us.

Students start by considering the significance of their "given names"; more significant to many, though, are the names "given" them after birth, the names they receive from their peers and society, the labels that stick, like "Fat Ass" and "Skinny," which damage self-esteem. By reflecting on the names they bear, students begin to see just how damaging the names they "give" others can be. In this chapter I want to broaden the concept of naming to include not only names we receive at birth, but also names we acquire from peers, names we use to represent others, and names we give ourselves as we learn confidence or doubt.

Exploring Our Given Names

The first humans were poets; they named the world, giving birth to language. They had to in order to survive. Imagine the first little cave baby crawling too close to the flames, one parent too far away to do anything but yell. Or a child on the savannahs of Africa unaware of an approaching predator. The word "fire" or "lion" alerts the other parent of impending danger, and from that moment on, all three of them remember and use what might be the first four-letter word. I'm joking, of course; none of us can know how fire or lion were named, but from similar moments language was born.

Naming the world is powerful. Children delight in it. When they name their parents and siblings, they often "rename" us. My sister-in-law, Lisa, will always be "Yicken" because that's the best my daughter Amy could do when she was two. When her younger sister Kelly came along, we didn't even bother to teach her "Lisa." Amy's name stuck.

Think about naming your own children. What factors contributed to their names? Relatives, maybe? Celebrities? I was always told Catholics should name their children after saints. That's why I'm "John," my parents tell me. Heritage probably has something to do with naming children, too. My Irish ancestry helped my wife Kathy and me name our daughter Kelly, though Kelly looks more like the Italian side of Kathy's family. Amy looks more Irish, but since both of us like Pure Prairie League's song, and hadn't met an Amy we didn't like, Amy she was named (we opted not to use the song's unconventional spelling: "Aimee").

Teachers often won't name their children after troublesome students. We won't have a Robert or a Billy, my wife told me. Even though Robert is my brother's name, and my middle name is William, Kathy couldn't look our own children in the eye and name them after two "demented" third-graders she once taught.

The point of this rambling is that names are significant, they carry meaning for both the name giver and the name bearer, and names are socially constructed.

I ask my students to explore the social construction of their own names. How were they named? For whom? What is the significance of their name? What does it mean to them? The chapter "My Name" in Sandra Cisneros' *The House on Mango Street* (1989) prompted Vicky to reflect on her name:

65

Victoria . . . as in the word victory. A synonym for the words triumphant, successful, unbeaten.

The name of my great-grandmother, passed onto me. She, like the name itself, was powerful. The others who were her peers were content to lie dormant, waiting to be plucked by any man who felt in the mood for a wife. This was much like picking flowers, letting the prettiest catch the eye, not bothering to look past the pretty petals to see if there were something more to the girl's beauty.

But Victoria would not allow herself to be plucked. She was a school teacher and didn't marry until her late twenties, which was old age back then. This power, this triumphant, unbeatable power, made Victoria the person she was. She was strong-willed, wanting more from life than a family. This was quite unusual for a woman of her time.

It seems . . . as the name Victoria is passed down through the family, so are the character traits which accompany it. So here I sit, knowing the future I have planned is so much like that of my great-grandmother. (With the exception of the marriage deal, I'm still a bit uneasy about that part . . .)

You know, I have had many different names thrown at me and plastered to me over the past eighteen years—hoe, slut, nerd, bitch, spoiled, stupid, idiot, ugly, wanna-be, buck-toothed, dork, and a few I will not mention. (Funny how some people think you can't hear them talking about you.) Yet I would have to say that Victoria is my favorite. Not because it doesn't degrade me, but because it was my given name. I know some people who hate their names and wish to have them changed. I am very happy with my name, with my life, and I am quite certain that my great-grandmother felt the same way.

Vicky Edrington, grade 12

Vicky is happy with the name she was given, but Vicky has taken or assumed the qualities that she says accompany her name. "Victory" is fitting for this class salutatorian, a rank Vicky achieved the last week of her senior year as she vaulted over three of her peers who were ranked higher until then. Vicky's parents, neither of whom is named Vicky, are not teachers like her great-grandmother. But Vicky's goal as she enters college this fall is to teach, just as her great-grandmother did.

Not all my students attach as much significance to their given names as Vicky does; some aren't even aware of its origin. Many don't know their ancestry. Some claim not to care how I pronounce their names or if I address them "Randall" or "Randy." Writing about their name gives students pause and forces them to question what they never may have before. Whether or not they attach much significance to the names they've inherited, most of them do acknowledge the significance of names they've acquired *since* birth. These names are the ones that continually shape and reshape their identity.

How Society's Names Construct "Individuality"

Listing the names they've acquired since birth helps students realize the influence of others upon their identity, the "individuals" they've become. Missy lists the following names:

friend

daughter

student

sister

listener

leader

salesperson

American

vegetarian

Caucasian

Catholic

female

clutz

Missy could have written about any of the names she listed above and shown how each defines her or relates her to other people and institutions. "Daughter" shows her relationship to family; "student," to school; "American," to country; "Catholic," to church.

Expressivist teachers encourage students to express their individuality and to develop their writing voices, both of which are important to young writers' maturation and confidence. Social-epistemic or constructivist teachers want students to understand that even their individuality is socially constructed: "one's sense of 'self' is made possible through the essentially social identifications—family, home, country, culture, religion, gender, ethnicity—in terms of which selfhood defines itself" (Knoblauch and Brannon 1993, p. 162). Daughter, friend, and vegetarian are different constructions. Missy doesn't represent herself the same way to parents, peers, and carnivores. She is, in fact, a different "individual" in each of these communities.

The first time I asked Missy to reflect on the practice of naming, she immediately thought of an incident involving one of her friends and decided to relate what she observed.

While she was out getting a bite to eat with a friend, who happened to be Filipino, a group of young men at a nearby table began "making karate gestures [and] squinting their eyes" at Missy's friend. Their implication became explicit when "they told him to go back where he belongs." Missy writes she was "in a state of shock" because she'd never confronted xenophobia firsthand. For her, such blatant hatred was "a thing of the past," but this incident confirmed it "evidently is not." Missy's example shows how "naming" can marginalize people who don't belong to the dominant culture.

Reflecting later on the name "female," Missy explains how she challenged her education in eleventh grade. She realized that the majority of literature and art her junior class studied was written or created by white Protestant males. "That got me frustrated because white males are not the only talented people in this world," she said. So Missy suggested they study works from both "sexes and from a variety of cultures," which they finally did her senior year. In this case the name "female" inspired Missy and empowered her.

Another student, Michelle, says, "A name is a starting point for a domino effect of traits and meanings" that others attach to it. Michelle's brother sees her as "silly, caring, and sarcastic"; her best friend considers her "confident, giving, and fun"; others who don't know her well name her "timid" or "self-centered." A "mere acquaintance" told her brother, "Michelle never parties" and "her friends are lame." Michelle claims she's "bewildered" that people who don't know her make such judgments. This "bewilderment" contextualizes the process of naming for her, becoming the first domino, to use her metaphor, to be toppled, but this time in a chain of awareness that shows her how naming labels, derides, or excludes.

The "representation" or "naming" of a culture is usually the responsibility of a powerful elite: politicians or patriarchs, academics or generals. Ernest Hemingway's *A Farewell to Arms* (1929)—a white male's account of war-torn Europe—counts as part of the cultural canon. Zora Neale Hurston's *Their Eyes Were Watching God* (1937)—a black female's account of self-discovery in the rural South—does not (or at least hasn't until recently). In *Critical Teaching and the Idea of Literacy,* Knoblauch and Brannon state that "naming is inevitably political, entailing a struggle among opposing interests and competing possibilities, where the power to name, and also to enforce the subordination . . . of alternative voices, figures crucially in the distribution of cultural standing and social privilege" (1993, p. 4).

Missy is frustrated by the "representation" of male writers and artists to the exclusion of female writers and artists. Michelle is labeled and excluded herself by peers who name themselves "popular." As teachers interested in helping students critically examine their own participation as subjects or objects in this continual process, we need to become self-conscious about the political nature of representation, and help our students do the same. Asking them to reflect upon how they name or represent the world and how others name or represent it is a crucial first step.

Assuming Names for Ourselves

I'd been teaching high school for six years before I knew what it was like to be named "professional," and it took a year's leave of absence to find out. Fortunately for me I was dealt the perfect cards just when I needed them; I didn't weigh the pros and cons for long before I played my hand. If my school district would grant me the leave, I'd apply for the teacher-scholar position at Miami University and take my chances.

Luck was with me: my district said yes and so did the directors of the Ohio Writing Project. "Come to Miami University," they said. "Teach two courses of first-year English each semester and take classes in composition and rhetoric. We'll pay you your teaching salary and send you to the conference of your choice (the College Conference on Composition and Communication was in Seattle that year)." You can see why I didn't waste time applying.

That year away from my regular teaching position gave me time to reflect upon the work I'd done to that point but never had time to consider at length. The teaching and studying I did then informs my teaching now. It was during this time that I began to name myself "professional" because I learned what it was like to be treated professionally. I was given an office and a telephone, a key to that office, another for the English department, and a third to unlock the doors to the building that housed both. I was trusted to perform professionally. New graduate students asked if they could observe my class and I asked to observe theirs.

This year away from my school district helped me gain perspective. I got a better sense of the kind of teaching Miami students, many of whom had taken advanced placement (AP) courses, encountered in their high school's college preparatory curriculum. The status report assignment described below helped me understand their anxiety toward writing and further convinced me that I needed to address this anxiety when I returned to my own high school classroom.

I ended up teaching part-time at the college level for four years after that initial experience and came to appreciate the similarities and differences between high school and college teaching.

Though the majority of student examples I include in this book are from high school students, I do include a number of writings from students I taught in introductory college English. Most of my high school students are from working-class backgrounds. Helping them become critical learners is important because they need to understand how others might manipulate, marginalize, or disempower them.

My college students, on the other hand, were mostly from privileged backgrounds. When they graduate, most find themselves in positions to keep existing power structures in place. For years they've heard members of their communities rationalize that power structure: "There are plenty of jobs available to anyone willing to work." "People have to take advantage of the opportunities this country offers." "This country was built on hard work."

These students rationalize privilege themselves. Why should they criticize the status quo? It's worked for them, their families, their peers. From my perspective these students need to become as critical as the disprivileged students I teach in high school, probably more so. That's why their teachers need to challenge them now.

Teaching at the university level gave me a confidence I didn't possess before. I realized I could teach at another level; I learned to theorize about the teaching I'd done; I felt comfortable translating that theory into new practices that I could develop when I returned to my high school classroom.

Students need to take similar journeys so they, too, can develop confidence. They need to reflect on their learning so they can hurdle obstacles that have tripped them up in the past. To start them on the right path, I ask them to journey back along the reading-writing roads they've previously traveled. First, to writing.

When I ask my students if they consider themselves writers, most reply NO. Writers while away solitary hours in secluded Cape Cod beach houses, coffee shops, or darkly furnished dens. Muses inspire them, possess their souls, make the writer a medium through which the muse pours eloquent verse or prose.

Many of the college students I've taught haven't actually done much writing before entering my class. They've filled out grammar worksheets and written short responses to prompts or prescriptive analyses of literature, but they've never really generated enough written language of their own to regard themselves as writers.

I want them to start generating written language immediately, so I have to convince them to write honestly. I ask them to describe their attitude toward writing and how they got to be the writers they are. This initial paper is like a president's State of the Union address, except it's about the current state of the student's writing. "It's okay," I tell them, "to say you hate writing as long as you reflect upon what led to that state." I share examples of past "status reports" so they can see I'm not lying. The following example was written by Stephanie, a high school senior:

Senior Status

Writing . . . oh gee's, here's that word again. After months of sleeping in late and watching TV, I find myself facing thousand-word essays, research papers, and hours of typing. A couple of months ago I was having the time of my life, but now, ughh, writing. Just the sound of that word makes my skin crawl.

I don't know exactly why writing bothers me so much. It's just that something inside of me loathes writing with a passion. It's a never-ending internal battle every time I pick up a pen. I often wonder why I have to struggle. Is it because of the writer's cramp I get after scribbling down a few pages, or is it the typing I have to do? I'm not totally sure, but maybe with a little digging I'll be able to find out.

Even though Stephanie immediately expresses her distaste for writing, she is nonetheless writing. Yes, it may be a struggle, it may make her skin crawl, she may even loathe it with a passion, but this particular piece unleashes her passion. She's even willing to do a "little digging."

There are a few distinct memories I have left from my childhood that deal with writing. My first true memory is from Mrs. Sherwood's class in second grade. Nobody liked writing the weekly stories involving our activities from our spare time. I hated those white sheets of paper with lines that were two inches wide worse than anything that year. I always wrote the same thing. I went to the store with my mom and we'd end up being kidnapped and taken to Canada or something like that. However, what I realize now is that those were probably the best years I had for writing. Why? I wasn't forced to deal with my feelings on paper. There were no issues to deal with, just plain fun to let our imaginations take us some place.

Third- and fourth-grade English class became just what is expected. We had grammar lessons, spelling tests, vocabulary. You name it, we did it. Everything involved logical thinking and reasoning, and if I remember right, we all did pretty well. I didn't mind doing the work. In fact, it didn't affect me at all. I just thought that was what English class was about.

The result of Stephanie's "digging" reveals things she hadn't realized. Though she claims she hated writing the "same thing" week after week in second grade, she did appreciate using her imagination. She wasn't "forced to deal with my feelings on paper." Though she did less writing in third and fourth grade, she didn't "mind" the work; in fact, those classes fulfilled her expectations.

> My sixth-grade experience was very different. Two bells in a row every day of the week with Mrs. Wadsworth. I loathed that class more than any I had ever had. We started off with diagramming sentences, freewrites, letters, summarizing articles and research papers. I never figured out why teachers liked that last assignment so much. They must get some sort of sick pleasure out of seeing us sweat, looking up information on topics we could care less about, trying to stretch the information enough to make the bare minimum of the word requirements.

Recalling how much she "loathed" certain classes and assignments drives Stephanie's status report. Her writing is full of vigor, insight, and humor. The last sentence in the preceding paragraph shows how well Stephanie can build rhythmic sentences, one gerund phrase upon another.

> Writing changed in high school. Until then it was pretty much considered an extracurricular activity which few people, if any, participated in. In ninth grade we were forced to write day after day about things we could care less about. We wrote journals, poems, stories and anything else that dealt with an issue of some kind. I hate issues. I hate to be told what to write about. I don't always have an opinion or feeling on these so-called issues. Therefore, I end up writing what everyone else seems to think and passing it off as my own idea. So tell me, wouldn't you get tired of writing opinions about things you truly do not have any opinions on? It drives me crazy.
>
> I remember freshman year so well. I would wait until the night before an assignment was due and in an hour's time, I'd write the first, second, and third drafts. I could never understand why my papers came back with comments about rushing through the story before, but now I do. You see I've learned to appreciate good writing since then. The famous

To Kill a Mockingbird book, *A Separate Peace*, and Jennifer's collection of Stephen King novels have shown me a new light. I can now truly say that I love the written word.

Vigor, humor, and insight combine to create Stephanie's voice. Rather than imitating someone else, assuming others' positions as her own, Stephanie writes passionately in her own voice. She doesn't need to "borrow" ideas for *this* paper. She knows what she thinks, she knows her audience: "So tell me," she says, "wouldn't you get tired of writing opinions about things you truly do not have any opinions on?"

> I do love the written word as long as it's not my own. I already know what I feel and think, and I really don't care to share it. I'd much rather hear what someone else thinks. I really have to push myself to write a good piece and I don't like to do that. I don't think I've ever done the best I can do, because I haven't been driven that far yet. I came close a couple times, but it wasn't for my own satisfaction. Maybe if I could find something to write about that really interests me. Then maybe I would find out that I actually do like to write. I haven't gotten any pleasure out of writing thus far and I don't consider myself a writer. I feel that you have to like what you're doing to be a writer, and I haven't come to that point yet, and I don't think I ever will. If anything ever happens to change my mind, then you'll be the first to know. I wouldn't hold my breath, though, because I doubt the Russian firing squad could get me to change my mind about this.
>
> *Stephanie Cromer, grade 12*

I submit that Stephanie has found something to write about that really interests her; though she doesn't name herself "writer," she's generated more than 750 words about why she doesn't like to write—witty and insightful words to boot. Think about what Stephanie's "digging" uncovered: that she doesn't like to "deal with my feelings on paper"; that her expectations of an English class were to study grammar, spelling, and vocabulary; that she's rarely gotten an opportunity to write about things that interest her; that "passing off" other people's opinions as her own "drives me crazy"; that she now understands past teacher comments about "rushing" through emerging drafts; that she's learned to "appreciate good writing . . . as long as it's not my own"; that she's come close to realizing her potential as a writer (but to please others, not herself); and that the possibility exists she might someday discover she actually does "like to write."

This self-conscious exploration helps students understand why they do or do not name themselves "writers." It is one of the first times many of them have reflected upon their academic selves. Often this paper frees students from the various constraints imposed upon them in earlier composition classes, whether those constraints were real or imagined. They find out when they're permitted to write honestly about themselves they have something to say and can say it well. Status reports also give students opportunities to sound off. Listen to Steve:

> English teachers, and most other teachers, are funny. They test us with their assignments, searching for a fine line between the amount of work we'll complete and the amount of work we'll refuse to do. In this ongoing search, they inevitably overstep the barrier, and burnout, often mistaken for apathy, results.
>
> Burnout can be cured by lowering the amount of work in the class, allowing more freedom in writing assignments (instead of strict topics to stick to), and by ending the practice of reading our papers to the class. Each of us has a certain reputation to protect. We have a wall built around our innermost feelings to keep them from accidentally being exposed to the general public. This wall is what keeps each of us from being labeled as corny, or weird, or wimpy by our peers.
>
> *Steve Schwettman, grade 12*

Steve reminds me again of how crippling names can be. Rather than risk being named "corny," "weird," or "wimpy," Steve typically suppresses his academic identity. What interests me about this particular example, though, is that Steve agreed to read it aloud to his classmates even though he claims to fear "exposure." Maybe it's being forced to expose themselves through their writing that students dread. That's why I usually ask for volunteers

75

to read (I admit I sometimes nudge). What I see happen with status reports, though, is that students are willing to bare their feelings on paper even if, like Stephanie and Steve, they admit it scares them.

Another strategy I use to boost students' academic confidence is what I call an introductory portfolio. This portfolio serves three purposes: (1) it helps my students and me get to know each other; (2) it allows them to reflect on their reading-writing histories; and (3) it begins to convince them that naming themselves readers and writers is legitimate. One of the requirements of the portfolio is to log the reading and writing they do over a forty-eight-hour period.

Melissa's reading log includes, among other things, keyboarding instructions, Garfield comic strips, the Surgeon General's warning on a pack of Pall Malls, the *Trading Post* (a local paper for buying and selling personal property), her horoscope, and a lemon meringue pie recipe. Jason's includes supermarket tabloids, the almanac, and frozen pizza instructions. Molly lists a restaurant menu, Andy's T-shirt, and a *People* magazine in her log. Most students list assignments they read in their civics book, math problems they work, or stories I assign in English class. Others read chapters from novels they've started or poems they find in popular magazines.

Another requirement for this portfolio is to include five or six artifacts that show what the student typically reads and writes. These might include papers they saved from last year's classes (if they didn't throw everything in the trash on the way out the door in June); excerpts or the cover from a favorite novel; articles from *Sports Illustrated* or *Seventeen* magazine; letters they've written or received.

Once they've gathered their artifacts, they write a "Dear Class" letter explaining how these items represent them as readers and writers. I ask them to focus upon a few questions, too, that help them think about their attitudes toward reading and writing:

1. What were some positive and negative reading and writing experiences?
2. Who helped you learn to read and write?
3. Who hindered your reading/writing development?
4. How important are reading and writing to you?
5. What do you hope to gain as a reader and writer from this class?

Molly describes the significance of an article she read about hip dysplasia in dogs because her golden retriever suffered from it. Michael traces his reading history from *The Three Little Pigs* to Stephen King novels. Kelly reflects upon her earliest recollections of reading:

> When I was about four years old, my mom would always read to me, and while she would read, she would point to the words so I would know which "bunch of letters" spelled which word. At four I [thought] all words [were] a bunch of letters. I remember the first book I ever read by myself was *Green Eggs and Ham*. That was my all-time favorite book.
>
> Kelly Whitson, grade 9

I encourage my students to be honest in these portfolios whether or not they like to read and write. It's early in the semester, and I want them to know they can express what they feel even if they suspect I might be disappointed.

When students finish their portfolios, we sit in a large circle and take turns explaining what we included and then finish by reading a portion of our "Dear Class" letters. Most students complete this assignment and seem to enjoy sharing their artifacts. Though many of them have negative attitudes toward reading and writing, most realize they are readers and writers. Their logs confirm this. They also see that they're able to express themselves on paper. I hope this introduction will encourage them to continue reading and writing, and perhaps even change their attitudes by the end of the course.

To this end I ask students to write a second status report at the end of the semester reflecting on the work they've done since the first. Some of them report the same attitudes and abilities they did at the beginning of the course, but many report differently. Lori, a first-year college student, said she "always hated to write," "didn't care if my papers were well written," and "never even considered" revising them. An excerpt from her second status report reveals how her attitude changed:

> I have never felt comfortable reading my papers in front of others. Even people such as my boyfriend or my mother,

people who didn't care if I could write or not . . . I was too embarrassed. When we first got into peer groups, I was scared. If I wouldn't let people who loved me and cared about me read my papers, how could I let these strangers read them? I'd rush through my papers when I read them, cringing when I heard their comments. I was sure I was a *horrible writer* (my emphasis). As time passed, I became more comfortable letting them read my papers. They didn't think I was so bad after all. They still talked to me outside of class. They still like me . . .

The biggest step for me was during our presentations. I decided to read part of my paper to the class—I don't know why. It wasn't as bad as I thought. No one fell on the ground laughing. No one yelled, "What a bad writer!" No one threw rotten tomatoes at me. I realized I can write.

Lori Ott Federer, first-year college

Revealing ourselves through our writing is like standing naked in front of a mirror. Our peers' reactions reflect our evolving self-image. Lori named herself a "horrible writer" at the beginning of the course, but when her peer group listened attentively and considered her writing seriously, she liked the reflection they offered her. She even braved the waters beyond her peer group, diving head-first into her class presentation. She revealed herself and liked what she saw. She realized she could write.

This revelation was socially constructed. Lori never would have perceived herself as a capable college writer had she not been named so by her peers. Lori's earlier self-image as a "horrible writer" was wiped away and replaced with a new image as a "confident writer."

Carolyn, too, reflects upon her writing self in her second status report. Speculating early in the semester about her college peers' writing ability, she was convinced the only suitable name for herself was "unworthy":

I felt unworthy being surrounded by people who had most likely been AP students, while I had taken only college prep. I was tense, nervous and scared to death. Then John walked in. No, John isn't a student; he's my English professor. He was wearing white shorts and a blue T-shirt. He proceeded to ask us to arrange our desks to form a giant circle. This wasn't like any English class I'd ever had. The nuns always made us sit up straight, in neat, orderly rows. He began to describe the course, but I was too busy studying the tiny pictures on his T-shirt: the Golden Gate Bridge, San Francisco Bay, and streetcar trolleys.

He gave us our syllabus. I soon learned that we would be writing six papers. I couldn't believe it. I don't think I wrote six papers in the four years that I was in high school. Right then, I wanted to drop the course, but I couldn't. It was required.

Then I was hit with the first assignment. "Did I or did I not consider myself a writer?" That was simple: HELL NO! I was ready for the next assignment, but it wasn't as easy as that. I had to explain, to "show" why I felt as I did.

Carolyn finishes the paper with the following two paragraphs:

As a writer, the area in which I've grown the most is the spontaneity of writing down my innermost feelings at the spur of the moment. Last week, for instance, I was really confused about a relationship. In the middle of calculus class, I found myself writing a poem followed by a letter to this person. The poem probably isn't very well written, and I'll probably never send the letter, but it helped me to discover and express my feelings. It enabled me to think through my situation and realize how I felt and what I should do.

Now, I remember looking at my English text the first day I got it. It was entitled *Write to Learn* (Murray 1984). I had never thought of writing as something you do to learn, but now I realize it is probably the most important skill required for learning.

Carolyn McGowan, first-year college

At the beginning of the semester, Carolyn felt "unworthy." Was she a writer? "Hell no!" At the end she names herself "writer." Not necessarily because she can write publishable poetry or even letters she'll send, but because writers learn about themselves and others by writing.

79

If Carolyn is right about the usefulness of writing to reflect upon how she learns and names herself, then we, as teachers, need to move students beyond what many of them initially perceive about themselves and their writing. Had I allowed Carolyn to simply answer my question early in the semester, I would have received a two-word paper: HELL NO! Nudging students to show why they think what they think, and how they've gotten to that point shows them how useful writing can be. It can influence their very perception of themselves and their relationship to others. Carolyn proved to me she was adept as a writer and as "worthy" as her peers.

Naming Our World

We continually name and rename our world as we test new waters, as Lori did, or swim further into what we thought were familiar waters. We use naming to make sense, create order, or take charge of our lives and experiences. When new experiences validate attitudes and impressions, we continue to use the names we've created. For example, if we've already named professional athletes "greedy" because of the huge salaries they make (especially in relation to our own), and then major league baseball players go on strike to oppose a salary cap, we're convinced "greedy" was the right name. If, on the other hand, new experiences challenge the way we've named other people, if they create dissonance with existing perceptions, we may rename those people—usually after an initial bout of resistance.

When Sarah went away to college, she expected to see students with "long hair and love beads," unlike the "fluff chicks" she was used to seeing at home:

> I thought that fluff chicks were an endangered species in a collegiate environment. I was under the false notion that their migration patterns were limited strictly to shopping malls, bowling alleys, and "Guns 'N Roses" concerts. No one ever told me that they also flock to facilities of higher learning. However, to my dismay, they have appeared with their characteristic permed-heightened hair, frosty pink lips, and fluorescent apparel. Imagine that.
>
> The people that I have seen have been girls like Wendy

WorkoutWorld, Mary Make-up Maniac, and Felicia Fake-Bake Fanatic and well, people like at home. No peace rallies, no incense and Deadheads, just fluff chicks that congregate in front of the mirror and hover over the salad bar.

Sarah Heinrich, first-year college

Sarah said she expected "free spirits" in college, people who looked like the Beatles. Instead she got "fluff chicks." Sarah's writing is amusing, her perceptions insightful. Some might say her reflection isn't particularly consequential; nevertheless, the tongue of her pen is sharp, her eye observant, her reading sophisticated. She meets preconceived notions head-on and renames her new peers in college.

Steve's renaming bears more personal consequence than Sarah's. Notice that in his narrative Steve reflects on how he names others, how others name him, and how that juxtaposition sparks significant conclusions:

Those Words

"Dad, Donna Summer is a Nigger." I had spoken with pride, almost as if I was revealing something my father hadn't known. He knew—he yelled—he knew—he sent me to my room—he knew—I didn't. I sat in my room and cried about my dad and Donna. I sat in my room and cried about Niggers. My dad made me sit through three hours of *Roots*, and now I couldn't even have a snack before bed—I kicked the wall. I yelled—I kicked the wall—I said to myself "Nigger"—I said aloud "Nigger"—I said over and over louder and louder "Nigger, Nigger, Nigger!" The repetitive statement began to seem almost blasphemous. I didn't know why. For all eight years of myself, I couldn't understand the power, the intensity, and prejudice behind a word, something so semantic—I kicked the wall. When the door opened I said, "Get out." When my father walked in I said, "Get out!" He sat down and looked defeated. "You missed the point." He said it dryly—something so semantic. "What did you think of the movie?" he asked of *Roots*. "It was long." I was pouting, though I wasn't sure why anymore. "I just want you to know that our skin is

81

white and theirs is black, but that doesn't make them any different—never say 'that word' again." He looked in my eyes
for comprehension, hoping not to have to supply further explanation. I figured I'd take a stab at it. "Nig—that word, is a
bad word for black people, and just because Donna Summer
is black, or those people getting whipped are black, doesn't
mean they're bad—people just thought they were bad because they're not the same color." I saw relief in my father's
face—I understood. Beliefs are instilled. Feelings about blacks
are not innate. "That word" made me cringe.

"If I find out who did it, I'll kill him!" Shorty was pissed.
"David, what's wrong with Shorty?" David pulled me aside
and said with a grin, "Last night, I put a swastika on the
school wall with spray paint."

"Oh." I didn't know why David painted it—it didn't
seem all that important. A swastika was a symbol against
blacks—Shorty was black—a symbol—just a symbol. David
was my best friend—Shorty was pissed. At recess, I stared
at the symbol. I wondered if David could teach me how to
draw it—it looked hard. I spent the rest of the afternoon
trying to draw it—I did it. I looked at it—I drew it—I
looked at it—I looked at it—I drew it—just a symbol—
Shorty was pissed—David was grinning—he was my best
friend.

Hebrew School—World War II—the Holocaust—they
killed millions of Jews. I'm in Hebrew School learning about
the Holocaust in which millions of Jews were killed. I looked
at my book—I looked at my book—I looked at the symbol—
David was grinning—Shorty was pissed—David was my best
friend—just a symbol? He wrote on the wall, he drew a symbol, he understood the symbol. I stared at the symbol in the
picture in the book in the Holocaust in Hebrew School and I
felt a lump in my throat. "Donna was a Nigger, I was a Kike."
Beliefs are instilled. Feelings about blacks and Jews are not
innate. "Those words" make me cringe.

Steve Futterman, first-year college

Steve's paper shows his own learning about the significance
of names and naming. He initially believes a name is just a name:

82

"a rose by any other name would smell as sweet." "Nigger" and "black" are interchangeable as far as eight-year-old Steve is concerned. *Roots* doesn't do much to change his perceptions, though he does tell his dad what he wants to hear. The power to offend, though, that he begins to recognize in Shorty's reaction to the swastika, the power of that symbol to justify murder, the power of the name "Kike" to label Steve an object of hatred, finally convinces him that a name isn't just a name. Calling Donna Summer "Nigger" isn't just as sweet.

If we want students to understand the power of naming, we have to focus their attention on how they name the world and how others name it. We have to ask them to test new waters as Sarah did when she entered a new community, to swim into deeper waters as Steve did when he explores familiar names and symbols from other perspectives. We have to ask them to write specifically about how they name others and how others name them. We have to create a safe environment where they feel free enough to reveal both their vulnerability and their cruelty. We have to support them in these explorations and help them see how their perceptions of themselves and others have been constructed by their environment and experiences. As Steve says in "Those Words," "Beliefs are instilled."

Unfortunately for Evelyn Couch of *Fried Green Tomatoes,* who named herself "crisp and fresh," "willowy and graceful," experiences do construct our self-perception. As much as we try to take charge of our lives, to gain some measure of control over who we are and how we name ourselves, one negative experience can alter our self-perception.

As Evelyn Couch leaves the grocery store, a teenage boy entering through the exit door knocks Evelyn back on her way out. He calls her a "bitch," and a few moments later, when Evelyn attempts to explain his mistake, he insults her again, calling her a "stupid cow" (p. 232). Evelyn is shocked at his reaction. Running after the boy, she asks him, "Why are you being so mean to me?" At that, he pushs her to the ground, where her groceries spill everywhere and Evelyn sits, "her elbow bleeding, old and fat and worthless all over again" (p. 233).

In only a few minutes Evelyn goes from feeling good to worthless. Even though the Piggly Wiggly cashier had told Evelyn earlier how pretty she looked, it is this experience with the teenage boy that plagues her.

Teachers can relate to Evelyn's story. Think about end-of-the-year surveys we sometimes ask our students to fill out explaining their perceptions of us and the courses we teach. We read nineteen glowing evaluations, some telling us ours was a favorite class. A boy admits he read his first book; a girl thanks us for encouraging her to write. Then we read one that suggests we play favorites, that the student wasn't graded fairly, that the class was "boring." When we wake up at 3 A.M., we only remember the negative comment and wonder what we did wrong.

If one negative comment can damage our self-esteem the same way it did Evelyn Couch's, imagine how negative names can damage the self-esteem of our students—teenagers in the midst of identity crises not knowing who they are from one day to the next. We have to make students aware of how others name us and how that awareness can help us rename ourselves. But we have to offer constant support because negative feedback is so difficult to overcome.

Even though Rebecca, whose peer named her "skinny," is winning a battle with bulimia, she needs support because every day is a struggle:

> Sometimes when I cough too hard or laugh too deeply, I can still feel the pain of those dry heaves. Clothes that fit are very hard to find, especially size one jeans!
>
> Every now and then, when I look into the mirror, I face the eyes of a complete stranger.
>
> *Rebecca Singh, grade 11*

While Rebecca is getting better, Evelyn Couch of *Fried Green Tomatoes* is getting angry. Reflecting upon how men name women, she thinks: "Why always sexual names? And why, when men wanted to degrade other men, did they call them pussies? As if that was the worst thing in the world" (p. 237). The more Evelyn thinks, the more angry she becomes. She begins to imagine herself a female vigilante righting the wrongs she and her "sisters" have suffered. She names herself Towanda the Avenger. When her husband Ed calls from the den for another beer, "before Evelyn could stop her, Towanda yelled back, 'SCREW YOU, ED!'" (p. 240), and Evelyn was beginning to take charge again, to fight against the negative names women have long endured.

My student Annie, who was "Fat Ass" in fifth grade, lost weight:

> All of a sudden the popular girls liked me. The guys stared when I crossed the room. But I ignored them. So I was given a new name: BITCH.
>
> *Annie Moore, grade 12*

If we want our students to take charge of their names, to build confidence and forge new identities, we must offer constant affirmation. If we want them to think of themselves as writers who have something to say that is worth hearing, we've got to name them writers ourselves and show them their words are worthwhile. It might take a semester, it might take a year. We may never see evidence that our efforts have paid off. Though we don't want to create a society of Towanda vigilantes, at least we can plant seeds to help students name themselves "confident," so they, like Evelyn, Annie, and Rebecca, can overcome the negative names they will surely be called.

CHAPTER 4

Understanding Language: Assumptions and Bias

"Teachers' Biases Belong Outside the Classroom"

The title of this letter to the editor caught my attention so I read on to discover that the writer himself was a teacher criticizing a feminist colleague who had just left their school amid controversy. Near the end of the letter, he wrote, "A teacher must recognize *his* biases and strive to counteract them on *his* own [my emphasis]."

At the same time that this "biased" feminist was espousing her supposedly radical views, Cincinnati Reds owner Marge Schott was alleged to have made racially biased statements about former employees (e.g., calling Dave Parker a "nigger"). Although major league baseball suspended her for her insensitivity to African Americans and fans condemned her, most of the community ignored this male letter writer's insensitivity to women. Clearly this teacher did not recognize his own bias (as he claimed teachers "must"), or he wouldn't have used the masculine pronoun "his" to represent all teachers (effectively excluding most members of the profession). Although his language is less offensive than Marge Schott's racial epithets, a significant segment of the population nonetheless takes offense.

All language is laden with values and bias: the sexism of a male-dominated society; the elitism of academia; the exclusivism of gang slang. Teachers' language cannot be neutral either.

Given that, I think we should lay our language on the desk before us and our students for their scrutiny. Admit up front that it's loaded with values and go from there.

We need to show students how language can stir patriotism

as well as hatred; persuade citizens to vote for a political candidate or send money for hurricane relief; disseminate lies during the Third Reich or discriminate against African Americans for skin color. We want students to appreciate the power of language and be cognizant of its effects on them and their world.

Students need to be taught that language not only reflects reality but shapes it as well. While slurs such as "nigger," "slut," and "red" *reflect* racial, gender, and political discrimination, children's attitudes toward blacks, women, and Communists are *shaped* when they grow up in communities where parents or peers regularly use such language. Unless these children find out differently on their own, they will accept the naming of others and perpetuate their parents' prejudice.

In this chapter I suggest ways we can help students examine racist, sexist, and political language. Through reading, writing, research, and discussion, students can become more conscious of the language they take for granted and the way language shapes lives.

Racist Language

"Sticks and stones may break my bones but words will never hurt me." Whenever I hear this, I'm reminded of the ending of Hemingway's *The Sun Also Rises*: "Isn't it pretty to think so" (1986, p. 247). Anyone who has ever been called "fat" or "skinny," "stupid" or "ugly" knows this cliché is easier advice to give than receive. Our language reflects not only that we differentiate among one another (by weight, intelligence, appearance, and so on), but that we judge one another as well.

To help my students think about how language reflects judgments, we examine the bias built into color. I ask students to list words and phrases they commonly associate with "red," "yellow," "black," and "white." Here are examples of common associations:

Red: redskins, rednecks, Indians, bloodshot eyes, anger
Yellow: scared, Chinese, slant-eyes, orientals, Asians
Black: night, death, cats, hats (as in "bad guys wear")
White: wedding, innocence, angelic, spotless, good

These lists remind me of how I used to teach denotation and connotation—out of context. Helping students understand the concept was enough, I reasoned. The curriculum guide I was handed certainly demanded no more. So I explained denotation: "black" is the absence of light; "red" and "yellow" are part of the visible spectrum; "white" is maximum light.

"Seeing red," on the other hand, connotes anger; "yellow," cowardly behavior. Once I thought they grasped the difference between connotation and denotation, I'd give them multiple-choice tests to gauge their understanding. Then we'd move on to the next objective.

Now, I try to make my extension of this lesson more socially and historically relevant. I want students to understand the power language has to influence their attitudes toward people and events. For example, society's perception of Native Americans is powerfully expressed in the Grand Council Fire of American Indians' "Tell Your Children." This 1927 speech clearly shows how connotative language implies a particular view of history:

> [History books] call white victories, *battles,* and . . . Indian victories, *massacres.*
>
> White men who rise to protect their property are called *patriots*—Indians who do the same are called *murderers.* (my emphasis; in Miller et al., 1982, 4 pp. 476–477)

Indians are "treacherous"; white men, "honorable." When students consider "savagery" and "civilization" in light of this speech, they are more likely to reinterpret what they've been taught in previous history classes.

After reading "Tell Your Children," students brainstorm impressions of other Americans. Here's Fonika on Asian Americans:

> Strong work ethic. Smarter than any other race. Rice. Dragons. Costumes. Karate. Gong. Study all day. Get the jobs. Build the best cars.
>
> *Fonika Thomas, grade 12*

After Fonika shares her brainstorming with the class, we read Anne Kim's editorial in *The Los Angeles Times:* "Burdens on Asian Americans." Kim writes that "everyone assumes Americans come in only two flavors, chocolate and vanilla"; her ancestors are Korean. She's bothered that people bow when introduced to

88

her and that they ask her if she speaks English; she was born in the United States. When asked by a nurse if she were good in math, she responded no, and the nurse replied, "Really? Too bad. You're supposed to be."

Until students are made aware that Korea, China, Japan, and other Asian countries have distinct cultures of their own, that Asian Americans are just as "American" as the many German Americans in Cincinnati, they will stereotype and make assumptions supported by shaky foundations.

In an article in *The Cincinnati Enquirer*, Vicky Roland argues that news from the Middle East is as biased as historical accounts of the struggles between Native and European Americans. She quotes another *Enquirer* article that reads, in part, ". . . Arabs killed three Jews. A dozen Palestinians also died, most from Israeli army gunfire." Roland responds,

> In the first sentence, the "three Jews" who lost their lives are placed as the object of "Arabs killed," connoting the idea of Jews as victims and Arabs as aggressors. The Palestinians who lost their lives merely "died." How they died—"most from Israeli army gunfire"—is relegated to a subordinate position and thus to lesser relevance. They were not killed by Israeli soldiers, but by the more inanimate and less accusatory "gunfire."
>
> Perhaps most inhumane of all is use of the phrase "a dozen" in reference to Palestinians killed, especially since it follows the very precise "Arabs killed three Jews." A dozen eggs? A dozen doughnuts? ("The Bias in Mideast News" 1990)

By focusing on the use of language, students begin to understand that no historian's or reporter's "interpretation" is free of bias or full of fact (sometimes it is full of something else). It depends on who is telling the story. The Grand Council Fire, Anne Kim, and Vicky Roland implore listeners and readers to consider another version.

One version that works with my students is W. P. Kinsella's "Mr. Whitey." (Kinsella wrote the novel *Shoeless Joe*, known in movie land as *Field of Dreams*.) Most of his short stories about Canadian Indians are narrated by Silas Ermineskin and set in western Canada. When Silas proves his worth as a hired hand, Mr. Whitey tells him, "Most guys would have stolen twenty dollars worth of tools by now. You're a good Indian, Silas." To which Silas responds, "I ain't dead." In Mr. Whitey's language we see racist stereotyping; in Silas's self-deprecating humor, his awareness of his boss' racism.

Later in the story, when Mr. Whitey has hired Judy Powderface at Silas' urging, Mr. Whitey's racist, and sexist attitudes surface in his behavior. Silas, when awakened by noise in the middle of the night, overhears Judy say, "All you had to do was ask . . . You figure cause I'm Indian you don't have to ask" (1978, p. 13). I want students to see that language does matter. That besides reflecting their beliefs, it often can, as is the case with Mr. Whitey, manifest in their actions. Like Silas in "Mr. Whitey," I want them to be self- and culturally aware. "What is needed is not so much a change in language as an awareness of the power of words to condition attitudes" (Moore 1993, p. 158).

We can help students gain awareness by asking them to reflect upon their own and others' use of language. Just by discussing "black and white" (and I don't mean "bad" and "good" here), students begin to see that "black" has gotten a "bad" rap. Look at the evidence: the daughter who goes out and gets pregnant is the "black sheep" in the family; a pledge who doesn't cut the fraternal mustard is "blackballed" from other fraternities; a cheating spouse is "blackmailed" for adultery, which leads to *The Scarlet Letter* and Roger Chillingworth's "black sin." On the other hand, a "white lie" is just a fib, hardly an ethical breech; a "white man" is an upstanding member of the community.

While attempting to sensitize students to racist language, I try to exercise caution because I don't want to censor their language or thoughts. Colleen helps us see in her response to "Racism in the English Language" that we need to maintain an objective perspective:

The entire notion of political correctness proves that the power of language can be overestimated. Take for example "black eye" which the author describes as a "mark of shame." This is not a racist word in any way. A black eye is a bruise. Bruises are usually dark, black. If bruises were generally orange, it would be called an orange eye. No one ever argues that the "pink-eye" infection is offensive to communists.

I also submit that there are many words and phrases with "black" in them that have favorable connotations: "In the black" (operating at a profit) and "black belt" (a sign of great skill) are just two examples. Black is also associated with elegance, such as in "black tie." In the same way, there are negative connotations of the word "white": "white feather" (a symbol of cowardice); "white slave" (a woman forced into prostitution for others' profit); and "whitewash" (concealing of faults).

Colleen Joyce, first-year college

I didn't expect such a response to this essay, but Colleen shows how effectively she can use language herself. While I believe it's important that we all be sensitive to others' feelings, I don't want students to become so sensitive (or politically correct) that they're afraid to speak their minds.

One danger in social-epistemic or constructivist classrooms is silencing students whose views differ from the teacher's. Most of us like to think our worldview makes the most sense, but we shouldn't cross the line between teaching and preaching. Sure, I want to change the world, to persuade students to appreciate difference—so I'd better appreciate it myself. I don't want to cow students into compliance—to write what they think I want to hear just to earn a grade. We all know students can play this game; unfortunately, I've seen it happen all too often in the best-intentioned constructivist teacher's classroom.

Proselytizing isn't teaching for the kind of change I want to effect; instead, it teaches students to veil their views. Rather than empowering them to change the world, we teach them to play by its rules. Teachers must be careful of the messages they send students through their own use of language and practice the tolerance they expect of students.

In addition to exploring how language can discriminate against others, students must also recognize that language can reflect race, class, and cultural differences. Defining ourselves through language is crucial. Vicky realizes this in her journal response to Gloria Naylor's "Mommy, What Does 'Nigger' Mean?":

Nerd, Pimp, Slut, Wop, Jap, Dago, Nigger, Honkey, words . . . created by our culture . . . to describe certain types of people.

We all know . . . these words are meant . . . to discriminate against others. But in Gloria Naylor's "Mommy, What Does 'Nigger' Mean?" you learn that the word "nigger" itself can change meanings depending upon the speaker, the context, the tone.

Gloria, for many years, had heard her family use the word "nigger" to describe one another as a term of endearment. But it wasn't until a white boy in her third-grade class used the word against her that she questioned its meaning.

The word "nigger" and others like it are not always an "internalization of racism. [Gloria's family] transformed 'nigger' to signify the varied and complex human beings they knew themselves to be."

Gloria goes on to say, "[I heard the word 'nigger' before] . . . but I didn't hear it until it was said by a small pair of lips that had already learned it could be a way to humiliate me" (Naylor, 1990, p. 200).

Vicky Edrington, grade 12

The argument some of my white students use to rationalize their own use of the word "nigger" often involves someone saying they hear blacks calling each other that all the time. Naylor points out the importance of "contexts and inflections." She recognizes, as Vicky points out, that the third-grade boy who spoke it wasn't using it as a "term of endearment" or a mark of distinction—two of the ways her relatives used the word when addressing each other. "Words themselves," Naylor says, "are innocuous; it is the consensus that gives them true power" (p. 198).

In Chris Crutcher's short story "Telephone Man," the main character, Jack, uses "nigger" matter-of-factly, as does his bigoted father. Just as he wears his telephone belt around his waist, he wears the prejudicial attitudes his father taught him. Near the end of the story, after a fearsome-looking black student rescues Jack from a gang of boys who try to steal his telephone belt, Jack considers asking his school's African American principal for advice instead of his father. I ask students if they notice a change in Jack's language, and someone always points out the last para-

92

graph: "What if my dad found out I went to a 'you-know-what' instead of him? . . . if he made a mistake about *them*, I wonder if he could of made a mistake about the other colors, too?" (Crutcher, 1991, p. 123). Though the change may appear slight on the surface, the reader realizes that "you-know-what" marks a pivotal point in Jack's appreciation of difference.

By examining language in context, students begin to appreciate just how important context is. A word one person uses to define herself or her culture could be construed a slur if directed toward her from someone outside her culture. I'd much rather my students and I address language head-on instead of misconstruing what we read or hear. By reading Naylor and Crutcher before August Wilson's *Fences* (1986), students understand the protagonist Troy's use of "nigger" and aren't nearly as likely to take offense as they would if we hadn't discussed the importance of context.

Naylor admits that even if "nigger" disappeared from white society, she isn't naive enough to think it would disappear from white minds. Helping students explore language through brainstorming, reading, and discussion can lead them to greater understanding, awareness, and better communication. The context we create for language study is everything.

I want my students to appreciate the power of language, to understand its effects on their attitudes and behavior, to be more aware of how they use language themselves, so that as they write the drafts of their own lives, they, like Jack in "Telephone Man," won't be afraid to revise.

Sexist Language

"Write a short paragraph," I tell students in my Women and Men class, "describing your observations of a professor teaching students one of the following lessons: (1) how to improve their writing; (2) why the United States entered World War II; or (3) how to find the area of a triangle."

I admit it. These are simply diversions to convince students that the writing has another purpose. I want to find out if sexist language is embedded in their own writing, and a one-paragraph diversion doesn't seem too unfair on my part. I tell them not to assume the persona of the professor (because then they'd most likely use "I" and "you" instead of "he" and "she"). Here are typical excerpts from their paragraphs:

> I am sitting here in Geometry 101 watching the *professor* carefully draw a rectangle on the board. *He* explains to the students that to find the area of such a figure, you must multiply the length times the height.

> "I believe this method will indeed improve your writing skills," said *Mr. Johnson.*

Not surprisingly, 76 percent of the students named the professor "male." On the other hand, 14 percent visualized a female professor:

> *Professor Smith* pulled out the green math book and opened it to page 451. "We are learning about the area of a rectangle today." *She* spoke softly. "*Paul*, would you please come up to the board and draw us a rectangle?"
> Paul was a little hesitant but *he* did what *he* was asked.

> *Jammie Kirby, grade 12*

Jammie had anticipated this lesson. She not only placed a female in the position of power, but also named the student "male" and "hesitant," to emphasize who was in control.

Like Jammie, Jack "psyched me out":

> I see a professor explaining how to improve writing. The professor discusses the use of pronouns in writing and how politically correct writing does not use gender pronouns such as "he" when referring to vague or unknown persons.

> *Jack Singh, grade 12*

Even though a few students saw through my assignment, most of them were genuinely surprised when they realized that they did use "he" when referring to vague or unknown persons. Kellie, the valedictorian, literally turned red. Others grew defensive. Andrea voiced a typical argument: "We've always used 'man' to refer to both men and women. It's tradition. There's nothing wrong with it." In fact, Andrea made some of the strongest arguments for maintaining the status quo. She claimed that feminists were focusing on trivial issues and destroying the sanctity of the family. "I don't see why we should waste time talking about sexist language in this class anyhow," she reasoned. Like Rayford, Andrea needs to sing her song. I listened to her arguments hoping she'd listen to mine.

To help Andrea and her peers think about the power of language, I asked them to design a survey to find out more about sexism. I offered a few suggestions but told them not to be limited by my imagination. They might think about adults' reactions to a woman taking her husband's name in marriage; teenagers' response to being called "boys" or "girls"; the use of female names to ridicule males.

After they administered their survey, they were to draw conclusions based upon the responses they received and present their data to the class.

I also asked them to write memos explaining (1) their contributions to the survey; (2) what they learned; and (3) what they would do differently next time to improve the survey or any other part of the project.

In the past I have attempted to give students information in the name of teaching them what I want them to know. I was the "depositor" in what Paulo Freire calls the "banking" concept of education, and students were the "depositories."

"Instead of communicating," Freire says, "the teacher issues communiques and makes deposits which the students patiently receive, memorize, and repeat . . . the scope of action allowed to the students extends only as far as receiving, filing, and storing the deposits" (1970, p. 58).

I knew from their initial reactions, though, that lecturing them about something they considered trivial would not be as effective as letting them discover for themselves the pervasiveness of sexism in our society.

Kellie, Jammie, and Lea surveyed the ways males and females "name" colors. The results did not meet their expectations (or mine). We thought males would use names such as green or blue instead of aqua or turquoise, but they surprised us. In her memo Kellie writes,

> I've learned that we just expect males to use the common
> names for colors, when actually they use the same names as

females. We incorrectly prejudged the males. I guess that in a sense *we* were being sexist!

Kellie Taylor, grade 12

Even though these three students didn't learn what I thought they would—that males name the world differently than females—they did learn about their own sexist bias.

Amy, Vicky, and Cindy's research replicated Stanley's (1977) about labeling sexually active women and men. They asked seventy-five students to list labels for men and women who are involved with more than one sexual partner. For the most part, male labels bore what the students considered positive connotations: "player," "stud," "lucky," "the Man!," "master," and "stud muffin." Labels for women were mostly negative: "slut," "scuzz," "fluzie," "skank," "sleeze," and "sure thing." There were also more labels for women than there were for males. Stanley's research turned up 220 names for sexually promiscuous women and only 22 for sexually promiscuous men.

The language clearly reflects society's double standard. Cindy said that "all the female students surveyed spoke out strongly against the double standard," but men said, "The double standards weren't as bad as everyone thought."

Besides uncovering terms that were new to many of us (e.g., "ginch" and "lot lizard" for promiscuous females), we discovered what many male students think about females. The survey reinforced an all-too-common media stereotype. This positive and negative reflection of men and women respectively can't help but shape children's attitudes. If most of the names they hear directed at women are derogatory, they are bound to think less of women than if they were differently named. Amy said,

Men obviously think that they are cool if they have many women when women think men are more or less jerks if they aren't monogamous. Men also see women as "hoes" if they see many men. That's so sexist! How can they see themselves as "studs" but women as "sluts"? That's not fair!

Amy Davis, grade 10

Of course, we as teachers have long recognized what Amy is just now coming to know. But telling her and allowing her to reach these conclusions herself do not have the same effect on her as a learner. Letting students generate the means by which they will learn and then asking them to reflect upon the results they've generated empowers them instead of controlling them. They are at the center of their learning, as they should be.

Misty, Lana, and Andrea wrote a two-part survey. The first part asked respondents to check each statement they thought was sexist:

1. _____ A wise man changes his mind, a fool never.
2. _____ "Hey babe, what's shakin'?" he said.
3. _____ The mailman's name is Sally.
4. _____ Pink is for girls, blue is for boys.
5. _____ Mrs. Henry Smith is the baker's wife.
6. _____ She is a sportsman.
7. _____ "Women are inferior," said Jack.
8. _____ "I'm getting a piece of ass tonight," said Johnny.

These three students graphed their results to show the percentage of respondents finding each sentence sexist. Only sentences numbered four, seven, and eight were listed as sexist by a majority of the students. Andrea, who had initially been so resistant, said,

> The point of our survey was to use some everyday language and see if people recognized it as sexist or not. So why did I feel so guilty about saying some of these things? I think it's because ever since I began taking this class, I've been learning what kind of language is sexist. The sad thing is, it's the kind of language we use everyday. I've learned that sexist language is very easily disguised.
>
> *Andrea Davis Wheeler, grade 12*

The second part of their survey listed words often associated with a particular gender such as "divine," "shit!," or "lovely." Respondents were asked to label each as more likely to be spoken by a male or a female. Students explained some of their responses to the entire survey in the following ways:

97

I don't find traditional words to be overtly sexist (e.g., "chairman"); I do find some of the "new" words to be silly (e.g., "personhole cover").

—male

Wah, wah, wah, wah, wah.

—male

I think a "wise man" is "universal" man.

—female

"Mailman" would not offend me because it is a pretty traditional term.

—female

Once they compiled their survey results, Andrea said, "Next time I think we should use less obvious words and sentences. We should make it tougher to identify the sexist language. That would make people look closer at what they say." Lana added that she would interview respondents after they took the survey to help clarify reasons why people had answered as they had.

Because students had so much control over this project—they chose the topic to study, brainstormed ways to conduct their research, wrote the survey, administered it, compiled the results, analyzed them, drew conclusions, and presented their conclusions to the class—they were truly engaged in their study. They "owned" their learning and the responsibility for it. The project empowered them as independent learners.

As a follow-up to students' research, we discussed how sexist language can exclude, define, and belittle both women and men. For example, the generic masculine pronoun insidiously excludes females. MacKay's conclusions suggest that the masculine generic "has all the advantages of the best propaganda in its potential for influencing people: frequency of occurrence, covertness, and association with high-prestige sources (in Henley et al., 1990, p. 396).

Sexist language also defines through words or phrases that (1) group, (2) ridicule, (3) reflect status, or (4) trivialize. Grouping "men and women," "his and hers," and "women and children" (as in evacuating the women and children first) effectively subordinates women to men. Labeling a man a "wimp" or "wuss" challenges his (hetero)sexuality, and at the same time implies that "acting like a female" is unworthy. Even when men and women do the same work, the terminology used to define each trivializes or confers status: women are "cooks"; men are "chefs." When a judge recently labeled a female lawyer "girl," he trivialized her education and experience; imagine calling a male lawyer "boy."

The research Amy, Vicky, and Cindy did clearly shows how language can belittle females. The "chicken metaphor" reinforces this. A young female is a "chick"; when she marries, she feels "cooped up"; so she goes to "hen parties" and "cackles" with her friends; then she has her "brood" and begins to "henpeck" her husband; finally she turns into an "old biddy." The first time I shared this with students, I thought to myself how outdated the language seemed. I hadn't heard anyone recently labeled "chick." Then listening to the radio on my way to work the next morning, a disc jockey related a story about a peacock rebellion in a wealthy L.A. suburb. A bold peacock claimed a portion of one resident's lawn for nesting. Neighbors complained about the nightly squawking, pledging to do something about the noisy peacock. The male disc jockey said there was a bright side: the peacock's squawking was drowning out the "old biddies." I realized then that a chicken-metaphor mentality still exists. Until students are aware of this frame of mind, their own language will likely reflect sexist attitudes and beliefs.

Political Language

I think there's a new feeling of patriotism in our land, a recognition that by any standard America is a decent and generous place, a force for good in the world . . .

We've come through some rough times but we've come through them together, all of us from every race, every religion and every ethnic background. And we're going forward with values that have never failed us when we lived up to them: dignity of work, love for family and neighborhood, faith in God, belief in peace through strength, and a commitment to protect the freedom which is our legacy as Americans . . .

America's future rests in a thousand dreams inside your hearts. And helping those dreams come true is what this job of mine is all about . . .

May I suggest that those who gave us double-digit inflation, record interest rates, tax increases . . . and told us that it was our fault that we suffered from a malaise, they're not exactly experts on the future of growth and fairness in America . . .

But I didn't come to dwell on their failures. I came to talk about how, together, we're going to make this nation even greater.

"The Ronald Reagan Basic 1984 Campaign Speech,"
The New York Times, 1991

"Comrades, I trust that every animal here appreciates the sacrifice that Comrade Napoleon has made in taking this extra labour upon himself. Do not imagine, comrades, that leadership is a pleasure! On the contrary, it is a deep and heavy responsibility. No one believes more firmly than Comrade Napoleon that all animals are equal. He would be only too happy to let you make your decisions for yourselves. But sometimes you might make the wrong decisions, comrades, and then where should we be? Suppose you had decided to follow Snowball, with his moonshine of windmills—Snowball, who, as we know, was no better than a criminal?"

"He fought bravely at the Battle of the Cowshed," said somebody.

"Bravery is not enough," said Squealer. "Loyalty and obedience are more important. And as to the Battle of the Cowshed, I believe the time will come when we shall find that Snowball's part in it was much exaggerated. Discipline, comrades, iron discipline! That is the watchword for today. One false step, and our enemies would be upon us. Surely, comrades, you do not want Jones back?"

George Orwell, *Animal Farm,* 1946, pp. 59–60

George Orwell wrote in 1946 that the "great enemy of clear language is insincerity." His "Newspeak" from *1984* was designed to make only "correct thought" possible. Hence citizens in that future society found slogans such as "War as Peace" plausible. In the same way Ronald Reagan expected Americans to find "Peace Through Strength" just as plausible. This classic example of "doublethink," holding two contrary ideas in one's mind at the same time and believing them both, is a good place to begin a study of insincere and manipulative language. From there we move to the Orwellian world of *Animal Farm*.

The first time I taught this novel, ten years ago, I emphasized its symbolism. My students and I discussed the relationship of the fable to the Russian Revolution and how Old Major, Napoleon, and Snowball represented Marx, Stalin, and Trotsky. Although I still believe that making students aware of this representation is worthwhile, I've shifted my emphasis from symbolism to language. We don't live with Marx, Stalin, and Trotsky today, especially since the cold war has ended, but we do live with political language. "All animals [people] are equal, but some animals [people] are more equal than others."

Juxtaposing political speeches ("The Ronald Reagan Basic 1984 Campaign Speech" and Squealer's) shows students how politicians use language to manipulate constituents. Both Reagan and Squealer use positive connotations to enlist support ("legacy as Americans" and "comrades"); both stack the cards against their foes (the Democrats and Snowball); both appeal to a sense of patriotism ("a force for good" and "loyalty and obedience"); both resort to name-calling ("failures" and "criminal"). Both claim to be empathetic: Reagan, with every race, religion, and background; Squealer (for Napoleon), with every animal, whom he regards "firmly" as equal.

Once students understand that we will focus on language as we read the book, they begin to notice what they otherwise might overlook. It's like buying a new Chevy Lumina and realizing how many other Luminas already fill the roads. As with same-model cars, political language, "designed to make lies sound truthful and murder respectable" (Orwell 1991, "Politics," p. 494) surrounds us—in *Animal Farm* and in our government. It isn't difficult to find contemporary examples of political language, but presidential election years are especially ripe with opportunities. So when we finished the novel, we plucked the fruit of the Clinton-Bush presidential campaign.

Students were to analyze in writing the language used in a variety of media in conjunction with one political event or issue. For example, I told them to listen to a political speech and examine how the content of that speech is reported on TV, in the newspaper, or in weekly periodicals. Another possibility was focusing on one political issue such as the environment and examining one politician's views as aired in different media. Students were to consider how the medium shapes the message.

In addition to analyzing political views and the representation of those views, students were to write a speech or commercial of their own on the same issue or a school-related issue and publicize their position in two different media. I asked them to reflect upon their own use of language in relation to their intended audience and purpose and explain in a written memo the choices they made. Everything was to be submitted in a project portfolio.

Jenny included political cartoons and articles, which she analyzed; a speech and collage she "published" in her presentation to support Bill Clinton's candidacy; and a position paper on politicians demeaning the political process by "digging up dirt" instead of discussing substantive issues.

A magazine article she analyzed shows the emotional appeal of language in conjunction with patriotism:

> President Bush is standing in front of a large American flag. Decorating his neck is a navy blue tie. But not just any navy blue tie. This tie is special. It has little pictures of the Capitol Building and American flags decorating it. Oh, how American. Now what kind of picture did my verbal explanation paint for you? One of patriotism, right? One of loyalty to country, right? This is the man we want running our country, right? He's wearing an American flag tie, he must care, right? WRONG! Nine times out of ten we are not hearing or seeing the real candidate, we are seeing a robot, a prototype of someone who is what we imagine the perfect president to be. These people are appealing to our basic instincts—our need to be patriotic and feel American. He wants our votes and his image directors are helping him get there.
>
> Words like "warrior" and "regular Joe" appear a lot in the text . . . These words at once contradict and support each other. Many people don't utter the words "warrior" and "regular Joe" in the same sentence. My image of a warrior is a long-haired man, muscular and tan, with a spear in his hand chasing after a buffalo . . . and when I hear "regular Joe," I imagine a lanky man in suspenders standing on his

front porch, out in the middle of nowhere, spitting chewing tobacco. But these two images can be used together for the benefit of the candidate. If he is portrayed as a "warrior," then he's going to fight to the death for our country. And if he's a "regular Joe," then that means after he's fought the wars of this country, he still has time to go home and kick his feet up and catch the ball game. These words are important in forming a concrete opinion.

Jenny explains the dilemma a first-time voter might experience when reading about Bush as "warrior" and Clinton as "draft dodger." Jenny realizes her responsibility to question what she reads, to take into consideration the power of language to paint images—images carefully constructed to elicit particular responses: to get votes.

To extend students' awareness of the power of language to manipulate, I ask them not only to analyze what politicians or journalists speak or write, but to speak and write themselves. Jenny designed a collage with Bush on one side and Clinton on the other. She juxtaposed words and photos, again to paint a picture. Though her design was simple, it was nonetheless effective. Bush was labeled "schizophrenic" while Clinton offered "A New Vision for America"; Bush favored the "status quo," but Clinton offered "change"; Bush said, "Read my lips" and Clinton said, "Put America back to work." Just a quick glance at either side conveys the negative or positive connotations. In her speech of support for Clinton, Jenny said,

> [Clinton] wants what we want: CHANGE! Rome wasn't built in a day, and the U.S. can't jump back into the mainstream right after the elections, but with Bill Clinton's help, we will be headed in the right direction. That's why this country needs Bill Clinton. His fresh face and liberal ideas will help to lift the heavy burden that George Bush has dropped on our country.

As a class, we had discussed how "liberal" had become a dirty word during the 1988 Bush-Dukakis campaign; Jenny isn't afraid to use it in her speech several years later. For her, "fresh," "change," and "liberal" aren't dirty words, but four more years of "status quo" are.

The last thing I asked students to do for this project was write a memo reflecting upon what they had learned. Jenny said,

> The last thing I wanted to do when I started in this class was study the presidential campaigns of these men. But now I'm glad I did. At first I was willing to let Bush back in the White House without a fight. I just didn't care. But now I do. Even though I can't vote, at least I can say I nudged someone toward my side. Even though my mother was going to vote for Clinton before I talked with her, she's not just a voter anymore. She's a supporter.
>
> *Jenny Price, grade 12*

I should say that there were nearly as many Bush supporters in Jenny's class as there were Clinton supporters, and a few Perot holdouts, too. While students knew my own leanings in the election, that didn't intimidate or silence them. Jon, an ardent Bush supporter, kept leaving Republican pamphlets and leaflets on my desk. One pictured a grinning Jimmy Carter accompanied by the caption, "It's easy to forget how bad it was." Another portrayed Clinton as a pickpocket. In his analysis of this flyer, distributed by Ohio Republicans, Jon writes,

> I automatically assume this is a pro-Bush ad. The cover is black, and in big red letters . . . it says, "One Promise Bill Clinton will keep . . . "
>
> When you open up to the first page, there's a picture of someone getting their pocket picked, and next to it in bold letters it reads, "Raise Your Taxes!" Although my first instinct says that this ad is pro-Bush, his name isn't even mentioned. This ad is all the way against Clinton. This is an appeal to the American people's sense of fright. We are scared of crime and people who would pick our pockets. This is an example of transfer, thinking of the bad associated with crime and pickpockets [and] the tax increase that Bill Clinton is proposing.
>
> The next page of this ad says, "Politicians will say anything to get elected!" Following this is a list of facts about Clinton's terrible credibility. This is an example of card

104

stacking, stacking the negative facts against Clinton in order to convince people not to vote for him.

The last page is a graph showing the number of Ohio jobs that will be lost under "Clintonomics." This is an appeal to the homeland, convincing Ohioans that he obviously isn't the best choice for our state.

Jon King, grade 12

All of the students became more critical about the message they were reading and the media vehicle used to transport that message. Jenny admitted that calling Bush "schizophrenic" was unfair and untrue. Jon recognized that the pamphlet he analyzed stacked the cards unfairly against Clinton. After sorting out the different messages they heard, many students became supporters of particular candidates—and in some cases, if they were old enough, voters.

Examining the assumptions that underlie the language we use is one of the primary goals of my classroom. I agree with Robert Yagelski, who writes, "Literature should be removed from the center of the secondary English curriculum and become part of the study of language that should be at the center" (1994, p. 35). Instead of studying *Animal Farm* as a fable, for example, the novel serves as a means of teaching students about language in context, how it reflects and shapes attitudes, whether that context be Native American or African American history, student or teacher sexism in the school or classroom, an Orwell novel or a presidential campaign.

Unlike the teacher who argues that "biases belong outside the classroom," I want my students to recognize how impossible that is. Instead of pretending that teachers, like Switzerland, can remain neutral, that we don't teach values, let's study language to uncover our biases, to reveal our motivations, to understand ourselves and each other.

CHAPTER 5

Reading Cultural Texts

Culture.

Reading Melville's *Moby Dick*. Gazing at Monet's "Garden at Giverny."

Listening to Beethoven's *Ninth*. Studying Michelangelo's "David."

Right?

E. D. Hirsch, in his book *Cultural Literacy: What Every American Needs to Know*, lists 6,000 things with which every culturally literate American should be familiar. Among them are 1066 and 1492, Acropolis and aficionado, Botticelli and Byron, Clemens and cubism.

But that's not all. Included, too, are desalinization and divestiture, Engels and estuary, fission and fusion, Ganges and Garibaldi.

Are you culturally literate?

Try this "'Real-World Cultural Literacy" test (Barber 1993):

1. According to television, having fun in America means

   a. going blond
   b. drinking Pepsi
   c. playing Nintendo
   d. wearing Air Jordans
   e. reading Mark Twain

2. Familiarity with *Henry IV, Part II* is likely to be of vital importance in

a. planning a corporate takeover
b. evaluating budget cuts in the Department of Education
c. initiating a medical-malpractice lawsuit
d. writing an impressive job resume
e. taking a test on what our seventeen-year-olds know

Culture is defined differently by different people. Cultural "conservatives" subscribe to a notion of "high" culture: the "great books," classical music, art collections housed in famous museums—works often written, composed, or painted by white men. Cultural "populists" include artifacts from contemporary culture as part of their definition. The Coca-Cola logo, Murphy Brown and Dan Quayle, gangsta rap and new country all fit under this contemporary umbrella of cultural studies.

As teachers we often find ourselves bound by tradition when it comes to sharing culture with students. I know because I was shaped by traditional teaching, as were, I suspect, my teachers. I listened to lectures about Emerson, took copious notes on Whitman, and regurgitated "teacher-thoughts" about transcendentalism on quizzes and tests. I read assigned novels (or sometimes "Cliff's Notes"—especially when we "read" *Crime and Punishment*), but never ventured beyond safe readings toward the wooded paths of my own imagination. Instead, I believed in the "definitive" interpretations of teachers who surely knew the terrain better than I. Besides telling me what to think—about literature or religion, math or science, music or art—my teachers implicitly told me what to think about education, culture, and power. For example, that educators "possess" knowledge that students "consume," that the only culture worth knowing is western European, that one obtains power by earning the cultural capital that counts.

I don't subscribe to similar notions. I'm not out to clone myself 130 times each semester. Rather, I want students to think for themselves. I don't profess to have access to literary truth. The way I conduct my classes allows room for critical reflection. Instead of defining culture narrowly, I include popular cultural texts that most of my own teachers would have deemed illegitimate. In addition to studying print texts (not just works from the canon, but contemporary essays and young adult novels, too), my students analyze audio texts (songs and radio ads, for example) and video texts (commercials and music videos). In fact, if we teachers don't help our students read cultural texts critically, I think we're doing them a disservice.

So what counts as a cultural text? What texts are worth reading?

I split this broader notion of "texts" into three categories: (1) print texts, (2) institutions, and (3) artifacts. TV shows, commercials, and popular magazines count as print texts. Though these texts are not as traditional as short stories or novels, poems or plays, they bear more resemblance to traditional texts than do cultural institutions or artifacts. Each has its roots in print even if no print text actually appears before the viewer.

Marriage and malls, churches and Churchill Downs are cultural institutions. Each has established itself in our society as a practice or custom, meeting place or organization. Each reflects relationships important in a given community. Each attracts certain segments of our population and has its own rules—explicit or implicit—governing everything from dress to behavior.

Mountain bikes and Mountain Dew are cultural artifacts. Like Levi's and Lincoln Logs their popularity is ephemeral. While they are popular, though, contemporary artifacts often explode through our senses, permeating our subconscious like steam from a vaporizer. Producers of cultural artifacts squeeze every dollar they can out of cultural consumers, as fast as they can, because rollerblades and Mello Yellow may be just around the corner.

Students are all too familiar with cultural texts. I use two different invention strategies to help students make their familiarity with these texts more explicit. Sometimes I ask them to form groups and generate lists of texts, institutions, and artifacts collaboratively. I give them overhead transparencies so spokespeople from each group can share the texts their group generates:

Jeremy, Nikki, and Amy came up with these:

Texts
Bible
billboards
Pulp Fiction
The National Enquirer

Oprah

the Shopping Channel

Institutions

political conventions

universities

the Superbowl

NCAA Final Four

McDonalds

Artifacts

Sega

Nikes

microwaves

Guess jeans

tanning salons

VCRs

A second invention strategy that works well is the introductory portfolio my students in Contemporary Culture produce the first week of the semester. To help us all become better acquainted as individuals (and, in this class, as cultural consumers), I ask them to compose a portfolio of five to six artifacts that reflect personal connections to our culture. The items they choose, which might include pictures, lists of favorite TV shows, postcards, clothing, product advertisements, toys, children's books, pins, buttons, or jewelry, should have personal as well as social meaning. In other words, they should say something about the individual but also something about the society in which we live.

Below are a few of the artifacts included in the most recent portfolios:

condom

Seventeen Magazine

recycling magnet

Jimmy Buffett T-shirt

gold chain

car keys

calculator

Cincinnati Cyclones jersey

"Not-so-great-moments-in-sports" video

Seven Mary Three CD

Michael Jordan basketball card

Walkman

Larosa's Pizza Police badge

Each of these cultural texts can be read and is worth reading. We only need to let students know how. First, I ask them to reflect upon what they value and what they believe their society values. I suggest they look for emerging patterns of meaning as they review the items they've chosen. Then they write a letter to the other members of our class explaining the personal and cultural significance of each artifact.

In her portfolio Amy focuses on our society's obsession with physical appearance and the effects of that obsession on self-esteem and interpersonal relationships. Her letter begins like this:

> I'm sorry to say that our values have gone consistently down hill in the past few decades. We seem to believe that the best things in life aren't peace and world love, but how much the world loves *us* and the peace of mind that brings. Our bodies have become the center of attention. Women's bodies, essentially made to reproduce, have become mere objects.

The artifacts Amy includes in her portfolio are a *Muscle & Fitness* magazine, an article from *Essence* called "Dying to Be Thin," a picture of a woman's midsection, three pictures of adolescents in "love," and the lyrics of a song called "I Ain't Too Proud to Beg." In the following excerpts from her letter she explains how these artifacts relate to each other and the significance of each one:

> We all walk around like we're on a runway and passersby are the audience . . . We've become a vain society and I'll admit that I've fallen under its spell many times.

Looking through the *Muscle and Fitness* magazine, I see nothing but ads for weight-lifting mechanisms and tiny (though sometimes not so tiny if you know what I mean) women posing in skin-tight "work-out suits." Yeah, I always go running in a bikini, don't you? Flip through the magazine. Do you feel yourself being pulled into the "world of fitness"? That's exactly what the people who make this magazine want to happen . . . They're feeding off of your misery.

My next artifact talks about just that. Misery. The people in this article from *Essence* are in pain, and people are taking advantage of this pain and using it to make money. Are we really that sick? They don't need all these ads to bring their self-esteem down even more. These are women who suffer from bulimia. Bulimia and its counterpart anorexia are, and have been, gripping our nation in a headlock ever since this obsession with our bodies came into focus.

The following artifact is a picture of a woman's midsection to upper thigh. Believe it or not this is a jeans ad, not a 1-900 number. I don't know about you, but I think I would like to see more of the jeans and less of the body before I purchase a pair.

It used to be fashionable for women to be overweight. It showed they were well fed and, therefore, wealthy. Just look at the statue of Venus, the Goddess of Love. Do you think even three percent of the population of men in the U.S. today would want her to be *their* "love goddess"? This just strengthens my theory that we've become a nation ruled by hormones.

Amy Price, grade 11

Amy's reading of these contemporary cultural texts shows her ability to analyze individual artifacts and to recognize cultural patterns. Examined independently, the muscle magazine suggests nothing about interpersonal relationships. When juxtaposed with the other texts and artifacts in her portfolio, though, Amy "reads" how damaging the obsession with physical appearance can be on a person's health, self-esteem, and relationships with others.

In the introductory letter to her portfolio, Marisa recognizes the way make-up affects a woman's self-esteem and relationship with other women:

I don't wear make-up often. Not a lot anyway. I wear the powder stuff, that's about it. We women care so much about how we look, we turn to make-up to cover up what we don't like about ourselves. And it's not because of men, it's because of other women. That's who we're in competition with. Men have something to do with it. Not much. Men are who we're competing for, not with. I wear it for the same reason. Some women go too far with it, though, then they look fake (too slutty, in other words).

Marisa Moore, grade 11

Students dealt with more than physical appearance in their portfolios. T'Keesha asked an interesting question at the beginning of her introductory letter, which made me wonder what possible cultural significance she could attach to Kool-Aid:

Does anyone drink Kool-Aid besides me?

Seems like everyone is into drugs and alcohol these days. Every time I go to the store there's always someone buying a six-pack, requesting cigs, or lighting up a "Black 'N Mild."

I've watched people on crack pace the streets continuously asking every person they approach for money. The next day they'll try to sell you the shoes off their feet or someone's bike that they have stolen. Life like this has got be miserable. I wonder if they can see that they're killing themselves. For every problem there's a drug to take, a bottle to drink, and a joint to drag on.

I've talked to some friends who have described some of their experiences being high and to me it's scary. So if it ain't Kool-Aid, I don't want it. I've seen enough people on drugs to know what they can do. I'm too scared to try drugs let alone take a chance on getting hooked.

T'Keesha Chapman, grade 12

Though T'Keesha's discussion doesn't relate to Amy's or Marisa's concern with physical appearance, she does mention misery, as Amy does and as Marisa implies. One of my responsibilities as a reading teacher is helping students distance themselves from texts far enough that they can think about what they're reading before they react. Every text we read influences our attitudes and behavior. Most of us know how powerful words such as "free" and "sale" affect our spending habits. Or how headlines at checkout counters compel us to fork over a few more bucks for our groceries. Later, when we've had time to reflect upon just how "free" that third box of cereal really was (buy two, get one free), we realize that we have trouble eating one box, let alone three. Or when we see that our favorite celebrity isn't really getting divorced (except in her next movie), and that the whole magazine is fluff.

Teaching students to read familiar cultural texts doesn't mean they'll change their behavior, but it might mean they'll think before they act. I'd rather students act deliberately instead of impulsively. I want them to challenge some of their assumptions and consider how those assumptions were constructed in the first place. Teaching them to read cultural texts is a start.

Cultural Consumption: Products and Values

After these initial exercises to help students realize they can read cultural texts, we begin a more in-depth exploration of cultural consumption. First, we think about products we consume and how those products are sold to us; second, we think about the consumption of values.

Advertisers don't want consumers to think about the ads they produce; they want them to consume the products they advertise. Advertisers don't want students to read their ads critically because this will expose the fallacies that exist in most advertisements. Drinking Mountain Dew will not produce the same charge as skydiving or rappelling. Wearing Nikes will not improve athletic ability. Using Grey Poupon will not elevate social status. The more closely students read product advertisements, the more clearly they understand how Madison Avenue manipulates them.

One example in Misty's paper discusses Olympic champion Jackie Joyner Kersee:

> When I first read this ad I felt like I was reading a sad story about making it in the world rather than looking for shoes to buy. It says, "There were times when you were growing up in East St. Louis, when you thought you would never fit in. That you wished that your life could be

as normal as other people's normal lives seemed to be."
Now this ad is definitely not selling you shoes. I think it's
feasting on the emotions of deprived adolescents, who,
when growing up, don't feel like they fit in.

In actuality, though, the ad is about shoes—Nikes. Misty
continues:

> I think Nikes target the high school teenagers and athletes
> who are searching for a way to fit in. We wear certain kinds of
> shoes because other people wear them . . . because of the so-
> cial status . . . I was in Biggs once and saw a nice pair of black
> suede shoes. I really liked the shoes until I saw what kind of
> brand it was. I didn't want to go through all of the trouble of
> possibly being made fun of if I had a generic shoe on.

> *Misty Frost, grade 11*

Reading the ad critically now sparks a memory about Misty
trying to "fit in" before. I don't pretend that teaching students to
"read" their own cultural consumption or the ads that influence
that consumption will change the way they consume, especially
as adolescents seeking peer approval. It may affect their habits as
adult consumers, though, once they gain more confidence in
themselves and their identity.

Misty's reading of the Nike ad focuses on the advertisement's theme—the traditional American "rags-to-riches," "pull
yourself up by the bootstraps" individualism that has long fueled
our cultural psyche. Misty phrases it this way: "They make you
feel like you can start at the bottom of the barrel and work your
way up to an Olympic gold medal."

To help students learn to "read" ads, I model a reading myself, discussing the cultural assumptions about people and events
in a sample advertisement. I tell them to consider the ad's denotation, the images that literally appear on the page, as well as the
connotation, what those images imply.

For example, one ad I use proclaims, "He Runs Like He's On
Duracell." Literally, the ad pictures Dick Clark sitting in a director's chair with the profile of a Duracell "AA" battery below. But
the ad implies a number of things about our culture:

114

1. that we value youth and appearance and wish we could stay as young as Dick Clark looks
2. that we value and trust celebrities and accept their testimonials (even though the products they endorse often have nothing to do with how those individuals achieved celebrity status)
3. that on the surface we value quality (even though Duracell isn't necessarily a higher quality battery than the Energizer—the ad claims "Nothing Lasts Longer," but no evidence is provided to validate that claim)

Students then clip ads that depict a constructed view of reality and practice "reading" them orally in small or large groups. To facilitate their readings, I suggest they think about the following questions:

1. About what kinds of things can we as readers be influenced?
2. Can we be given certain ideas and attitudes subliminally if we are not attentive? How?
3. How do advertisements document our national culture? Do they help us define who we are as a people?
4. What kind of people do we look up to and idolize?

A number of students choose to read alcohol ads, and as Mark's paper shows, analysis papers need not lack voice. He begins with a poem:

> Well, well. If it's not another ad for a beer or wine.
> The party in the bottle,
> Anywhere and anytime.
> You drink it. I drink it, too.
> As well as all those model human beings we see on the tube.
> Beautiful women in beautiful places.
> Handsome men with smiles on their faces.
> Beers brewed in the purest of places.
> A delicate wine for all kinds of happy-go-party cases.
> Another ad, commercial or what not
> Gets us thinking of Jim Beam and pop.
> Or some Bartles and James,

"Thanks for your support."
Maybe a glass of vodka for after work.
Yet another commercial for a beer or wine.
Alcohol,
The party in a bottle.
Anywhere.
Anytime.

Mark incorporates slogans and stereotypes in the satirical introduction to his paper, then shares his reading of two particular alcohol advertisements: Smirnoff Vodka and Godiva Liqueur. Here's what he says about Godiva. Though his reading of the name may not be what the advertisers intended, he makes an interesting argument.

THE REAL SIN WOULD NOT BE TASTING IT
GODIVA

Now that your mind's on the name, let's look at it. Say the name of the liqueur very slowly. God diva. Sounds kind of like it should make the drinker God-like. Or that it is a drink of the Gods . . .

To drink with, or of the gods, to indeed become a God, would that be appealing? Would you like to be God, possibly of Roman mythology, or maybe The God, the one and only supreme god of Christian beliefs?

And to those who are religious to the point that they would take offense at the suggestions that I made, remember, the Real Sin is not to taste it.

If you're still thinking about that name, then perhaps you might recall something about the entirety of the name. Come on, I know you can do it. Horse, lady, naked lady as a matter of fact. "Hmmm, where have I heard Godiva from . . ." Well, if you're referring to Lady Godiva, then you're probably right. Why do you think they have the horse carriage on the label? That's right, to symbolize Lady Godiva's historic horseback ride through the city. She was so good a horse rider that she was able to ride the horse bareback, and I'm not just talking the saddle here. This fantastic voyage was made by some long-haired, naked chick, riding with no saddle and no lipstick . . .

Religion, money, sex. Yep, it's a catchy thing, that ad is.

Mark Singh, grade 11

Mark's reading of the word *Godiva* and of one particular Godiva Liqueur ad shows his ability to deconstruct the way a product is represented and marketed. His analysis is playful but makes a point: that advertisers prey on our desires and ambitions.

Pam reflects on the stereotypical construction of "alcohol worlds" in her paper:

> The people don't look like the average person who just got off of work and came in to relax, or that fat, lazy drunk who's been there since they opened. Everyone is young, barely old enough to drink. They look like models with well-built bodies and teeth so straight and white you think they drink straight-up bleach.
>
> *Pam Allen, grade 11*

Pam makes an interesting point, even though she doesn't seem to realize it: "Everyone is young, barely old enough to drink." In fact, many critics suggest that the kind of ad Pam describes purposely targets new markets for their products: teenagers nearing the drinking age. Though Pam doesn't focus on the target audience, JaVonna and Dave do in their papers.

JaVonna argues that ads for OLD ENGLISH 800 target young black men "to bring down the African American male." The beer's label explains that the name has its origin in the New England slave trade. "Over thirteen years ships made 61 trips. This is how the bottle got the '800'—61 times 13 rounds off to 800." The thirty-one crowns on the label relate to the thirty-one crowns early slave traders charged per slave.

> People who are alcoholics often are a slave to the bottle, and maybe the advertisers think they'll be buying a slave to their product every time they produce a 40-ounce bottle of OLD ENGLISH 800.
>
> *JaVonna Buckhanan, grade 11*

117

Dave's comments echo JaVonna's when he says that although it often appears minorities are forgotten in beer ads, "in many instances they are the specific targets of ads for other, less traditional beers":

> Proof of this is abundant in the selling of malt liquor beverages. With names like Powermaster and King Cobra, these beverages cater to primarily young, inner-city, black youths, looking for an inexpensive product with a high liquor content. Curiously, there is a common thread between the commercials for the malt liquor and the regular brew. The malt liquor ads use the same formula—beer = pretty women + good times. So there is a similar exploitation of women as the mover of a product intended for men. A somewhat controversial ad has a beautiful woman touting the attractiveness of her "Colt 45 man." A clear link between the attraction of the opposite sex and the consumption of alcohol as portrayed by the advertisers.
>
> *Dave Collins, first-year college*

Each of these writers displays the ability to read ads critically and convey their reading in writing. Each writer's voice comes through in the analysis. Mark, Pam, JaVonna, and Dave show how advertisers capitalize on consumer weaknesses. They don't indicate, however, that they themselves have been manipulated by alcohol ads, that their personal lives have been affected—at least not in these papers. This isn't the case with all of my students. In her paper, "Alcohol Lies," Kali says that advertisers "prey on your dreams":

> They tell us beer doesn't do anything but make you loosen up, feel good, and have a great time. What they don't tell you is that you'll be so loose you can't walk, that the only time you'll feel good is after you vomit, and the great time you have will only scare your children. How come they never show that in the ad? I'll tell you why. Sales. That's all they care about. Sell the product at any price. But what if the price you, the consumer, have to pay is your life?
>
> My father is an alcoholic. I have many painful memories of abuse and anger caused by his drinking. Sometimes I think my

father would sell his soul for another bottle of Jack Daniel's.
My father has sold his life and Miller Company holds the title.

Basically, all I am trying to say is that we have been de-
ceived. We were told that alcohol wouldn't harm us and
now we are dying of liver complications. When will it end?
Are the American public so desperate to escape from our
problems that the only place we have to turn to is a bottle of
vodka? People, listen to me. If things are so bad you want to
escape, sleep for a day or two. That way the only person
you hurt is yourself. Please don't drink because unless
you've been in my position, you don't know how it hurts.
Damn the distilleries. Damn them all to hell.

Kali Evans, grade 11

Kali's writing is expressive and passionate. Most of my students don't relate similar stories, but teachers should make room
in their classes for students like Kali, who need to unload the
same kind of baggage. Within the context of this assignment—to
read advertisements critically—Kali found room to unpack a burden she'd been carrying around for years.

As their teacher, I don't want to pry into students' private lives.
I don't insist they write confessional pieces to share their pain. On
the other hand, if reading critically provides an outlet for working
through personal difficulties, I want students to know this forum is
available, that I am open to all the stories they wish to tell. In other
words just as students in independent reading-writing workshop
classes make reading and writing their own, I want my students to
engage personally even when working on a common assignment.

Carolyn's reading of Polo advertisements may not be as personal as Kali's response to the liquor ads, but her personal insight
reveals her engagement. Her introduction shows how her reading
is associated with past experiences:

Who would have suspected that a mere one-half inch by one-
quarter inch stitching of a horse into every article of clothing
and accessory produced by a single manufacturer would one
day merit billions of dollars? Evidently, Ralph Lauren did.

His line of clothing and accessories entitled "Polo by
Ralph Lauren" premiered in the early 1960s and continues to

prevail in today's fashion world. His choice of a title and logo is puzzling considering that he was an American entrepreneur, and the Europeans originated and dominate the sport of polo. Why didn't he choose a baseball player swinging a bat symbolizing an American pastime instead of a man (whom I envision wearing a pleated red and green plaid skirt and knee-high stockings) riding a horse with his polo stick in hand? Perhaps people think they establish a rapport with royalty by purchasing and wearing these garments. Americans continue to be enthralled by royal families . . . and connect the sport of polo to the lap of luxury.

Carolyn has a mental image of polo that influences the way she reads ads for Ralph Lauren's clothing. She associates the sport with European royalty, with whom she says Americans are "enthralled."

Carolyn's reading of the ads are also influenced by other reading she's done:

If Ralph Lauren promoted his real name on his apparel, the American public would be appalled, for it is anything but regal. Lauren is a pseudonym for Lipshitz. Can you imagine the labels of his clothing reading "Polo by Ralph Lipshitz"? When I think of the name Ralph Lipshitz, I picture a balding, middle-age man with protruding buck teeth bending over and scooping up a pile of cow manure on a desolate farm. On the other hand, the name Ralph Lauren sparks an image of a classic-looking man with well-defined features and tortoise-shell-rimmed glasses sitting in front of a fire with a good book.

Although not everyone's reading of the two names would coincide with Carolyn's, she shows how great an impact names have. My hunch is that most readers would agree that "Lipshitz" constructs a very different mental picture than "Lauren," and that Ralph Lipshitz realized that difference when he changed his name.

From the sport to the name, Carolyn gradually focuses on the conscious construction of a product image. Now she zeroes in on the logo itself:

120

Each infamous Polo pony is strategically placed and embroidered in a contrasting color depending on the article of clothing so that it is clearly visible. On all oxford-type shirts and button-downs, the pony resides on the upper left-hand side. The pony sits on the side of every Polo-by-Ralph-Lauren sock just low enough that when someone sits down and their pant legs rise up a bit, the pony is spotted. Even on men's ties, the logo is centered high enough that it shows when the buttons of a sport-coat or suit jacket are fastened. A trademark of excellence has been established by those who wear Polo by Ralph Lauren.

Carolyn explains that attaining this excellence costs consumers three times as much as a similar wardrobe purchased in a department store at the local mall. To obscure the cost of Polo merchandise, Lauren creates an atmosphere in his stores that distracts buyers from this disparity:

> The atmosphere of the Polo displays and stores contributes to the appeal of the clothes. Hardwood floors, wooden trunks, railings tipped with gold, all of the clothes on wooden hangers, and a large gold plate with "Polo by Ralph Lauren" engraved in it hung above the cash register establish feelings of warmth and prestige. A tag similar to a small greeting card is attached to each garment. The card tells of the fine quality and tradition of the product. For instance, the tag of a maroon and green plaid flannel oxford reads, "This Polo by Ralph Lauren product is an expression of quality craftsmanship and integrity of design, from the selection of the fabric to the execution of every detail." Ralph Lauren attempts a personal approach in reassuring that his quality and attention to detail precede the price. The tag lures customers to read it before searching for a price, because it is suspended from a button of the shirt while the price tag hides inside of the collar.

> *Carolyn Burke, first-year college*

Carolyn's paper shows her ability to read critically, research, and connect what she already knows with what she's learning. Her paper is unified and focused. She knows how to use specific detail to engage her reader. No, she's not writing about Huck or

Hester, but if students can produce writing this critical and convincing about other texts, shouldn't we legitimate those texts, too?

Cultural Consumption: Ideas and Philosophies

Other legitimate texts to which many of my students have responded positively include news transcripts, songs, contemporary short stories, magazine articles, and classroom dialogues. In this section I focus on the idea of war and patriotism and discuss how certain texts can both shape and reflect personal philosophies.

In a recent unit I asked my students to read the following texts: two newscasts covering a homecoming parade for Desert Storm veterans; an article from *Esquire* called "Why Men Love War," by William Broyles; Walter Dean Myers' *Fallen Angels*; the movies *Casualties of War* and *Apocalypse Now*; Tim O'Brien's story "On the Rainy River"; and songs from the 1960s including "Soldier Boy" and "Masters of War."

The news transcripts, both from broadcasts on June 10, 1991, were shared several years ago at NCTE. Viewers can write networks for transcripts or tape news broadcasts and compare different versions of the same story. The first is from NBC with Tom Brokaw:

Brokaw: It was called Operation Welcome Home: today's blizzard of confetti . . . a one-mile-long, four-hour celebration for the men and women of Operation Desert Storm. There were some protesters, but for most New Yorkers this was a long-awaited chance to cheer for something.

Stan Bernard: Lower Broadway, the financial district . . . General Norman Schwarzkopf, Defense Secretary Dick Cheney, and a New York native, General Colin Powell—led the way . . . Over four and a half million spectators. Tons of ticker tape and confetti rained on the marchers, more than half of whom served in the war against Iraq . . . it is hard not to be moved by the sight of the 24,000 marchers and the cheers.

Spectator: It was a special thing that these guys did for us, and I think they deserve something. I think we have some making up to do.

*Bernard:*The rough treatment of Vietnam veterans was fresh in many minds, and a contingent of Vietnam veterans marched in this parade.

Spectator: I think . . . we need to tell everyone we really support them.

Bernard: There . . . [was] an attempt to break through police lines to disrupt the parade. They were overwhelmed by the police and the sentiment of the crowd.

There was a display of military hardware. And a few New Yorkers wondered if this jet would make it out of town before it was stolen and sold for parts.

In this financially hard-pressed city, it was a parade that was privately paid for, and the surplus of at least a half a million dollars will go to support families of casualties of the war. But this was the celebration that so many came home alive and well.

The second transcript is from ABC and Peter Jennings:

Jennings: Is New York too crowded? Not today. Too noisy? Not today. Too dirty? Not today.

Spectator: This is really showing what New York is about.

Jennings: Whether it was a renewed sense of self-esteem or the brilliant June weather or the simple love of a big party, more than a million spectators turned out to cheer more than 24,000 marchers.

The New York Stock Exchange, normally a den of feverish commerce, paused for a moment of silence and a moment of song, led by a local hero born and bred in the Bronx.

Spectator: "God bless America, my home sweet home."

Jennings: The sentiment was not unanimous. At last night's ecumenical service, Defense Secretary Dick Cheney and Desert Storm Commander Norman Schwarzkopf were interrupted by protests. And the parade itself served as an unhappy reminder of New York's current obsession: money.

Jeff Greenfield: Victory parades go back thousands of years to the Roman Days of Bread and Circuses to feed the masses. Of course, in New York in 1991, there is no bread to pay for the circuses.

Jennings: Faced with a three-and-a-half-billion-dollar deficit, the city, for the first time in history, turned to private funds. Half a million dollars came from the Kuwaiti government, millions more came from private companies and individuals.

After the parade ends, after the ribbons and banners are put away, the shadows of Desert Storm will remain: Saddam Hussein still in power, the Kurds in danger, uncounted thousands of innocents dead. And maybe those very concerns led to the sense of urgency in today's celebration. When heroes are marching around the streets, no one has to worry about what is waiting around the next corner.

Most of my students think of the news as "truth," even if they rarely watch it. The news is a place to learn the facts about any issue or event. TV news is often the only way many students, and many Americans, find out what's happening in our society.

These two newscasts both include some of the same information:

1. Twenty-four thousand people marched.
2. The parade was held in New York's financial district.
3. Norman Schwarzkopf was involved in the celebration.
4. Because the city faces financial difficulties, the parade was privately funded.
5. A few protesters interrupted the festivities.

If, however, TV viewers obtained all their information about this parade from one of these broadcasts and no other source, their perceptions of this event would differ greatly. Each of these stories, while communicating certain facts, nonetheless constructs different realities about war, patriotism, foreign and domestic affairs. After reading both transcripts aloud in class, I asked students to share their "readings" in writing.

Misty writes that even though both newscasts address the same topic, the tone of each is different:

> Basically, they've constructed different realities. Peter Jennings constructs "the reality" of the parade to be some kind of stupid facade to cover up the problems that still remain about the war and economic debt. The voice in this transcript is sort of sarcastic. For example, in the seventh para-

124

graph, Jeff Greenfield says, "There's no bread to pay for the circus." This transcript definitely shows a pessimistic view.

The NBC news is optimistic. Tom Brokaw understands the deficit but doesn't slam it up in New York's face. He talks about how the men deserve the parade. The Vietnam experience is fresh on our mind, and we don't want to repeat the negative feelings. The patriotism appeals to the reader. If I had only read this transcript, I would never know about the shadows that still lurk in the Middle East or all the problems with New York finances.

Misty Frost, grade 11

Misty adds her own opinion, which echoes her reading of NBC's broadcast: Desert Storm veterans deserve recognition. Despite her opinion, she clearly is able to articulate how each transcript constructs a different reality. She understands how tone affects "truth"; ABC's "sarcastic" tone, slamming New York's financial difficulties in its collective face, changes her reading of the story, even though, as she admits in her response, both broadcasts cover the same topic.

Pam's analysis of the effect of tone echoes Misty's:

Jennings sounded almost as if we had lost the war, as if he was talking about some massacre instead of a parade. Brokaw was all happy-go-lucky. He was like the parade was so honorable or something.

Pam Allen, grade 11

Though students' language may not always be eloquent, they are learning to read critically. Paul's response is a good example:

In the NBC transcript they point out the bad things but cover them up quickly with the good things going on. In the ABC transcript they started out with the good things leaving you with the bad. Sort of like eating a sweet and then being fed an old moldy sandwich . . . but in the NBC one they used the reverse leaving you with a good sweet taste of a turtle-nut sundae.

Paul Napier, grade 11

Amy's reading concentrates on the use of language and supportive arguments—or lack thereof—to construct a view of the celebration parade:

> I think ABC was taking the cynical approach because they want you to see the whole picture, that basically all those people died for nothing. The use of the word "shadow" in the last paragraph is especially effective because it adds a sense of sadness. The "shadow" of that memory will always be in our minds.
>
> NBC obviously wanted us to feel good about what we accomplished by going over there (although they never say anything about what was actually accomplished). They want us to forget about the hardships and numerous problems for a while and enjoy something positive.
>
> *Amy Price, grade 12*

Each of these students demonstrates through writing the ability to read critically, to understand how realities are constructed. They are more conscious now that news programs manipulate viewers by what they include and don't include in their stories; that the connotative language newscasters use creates tone and shapes opinion; that the order in which certain facts are presented affects viewers' final impressions of an event.

Many Americans limit themselves to one source when forming their opinions about a certain topic. I want my students to examine different sources, different constructions of reality or "truth." I hope the cumulative effect of different sources will lead students to more sophisticated questions and more sophisticated understanding. An anonymous response I recently read sums up my feelings about helping students think critically:

> I fully realize that I have not succeeded in answering all of your questions . . .
>
> Indeed, I feel I have not answered any of them completely. The answers I have found only serve to raise a whole new set of questions, which only lead to more problems, some of which we weren't even aware were problems.
>
> To sum it up . . . in some ways I feel we are as confused

as ever, but I believe we are confused on a higher level, and about more important things.

The following discussion reveals some of the confusion that took place later in the semester as we shared our readings of Walter Dean Myers' *Fallen Angels* (1988), William Broyles' "Why Men Love War" (1984), and Francis Ford Coppola's *Apocalypse Now* (1979). I started the discussion with a question about Broyles' essay:

J.G.: So what do you think about men loving war?

Robert: It's true.

Misty: You'd miss war—maybe the bonds you had together—even stronger than marriage.

Justin: I don't think it's true—even in *Fallen Angels*, they're scared, they don't want to be there.

Robert: It relates to *Fallen Angels*—they're missing their squad at the end.

Julie: I don't think they're missing the war, they're just not sure how to relate to the real world.

Amy: They love war because they can be heroes—like the place where the guy jumped on the grenade to save his friends.

J.G.: What do you think, Amy, about loving war because you get a chance to be a hero?

Amy: I think it's stupid.

Matt: Men are men. Who wouldn't like to kill someone for no reason if they could get away with it? What man wouldn't do it?

Misty: I think men are primitive.

Kelly: That's how my brother's friends are.

Pam: It doesn't have to be men.

Marisa: You have to have a motive. Maybe you don't want to kill them, but you do want them to disappear.

Mark: Who played war as a child? When you play you have a particular state of mind.

Bobby: Little boys are brought up to like war. They get G.I. Joes for presents.

Amy: Girls have grown out of it, but guys haven't.

Mark: Have any girls here played laser tag?

Amy: Women can separate the game from reality.

J.G.: Let's focus on Broyles' article for a minute and the metaphors he uses for war. Do you remember any?

Bobby: War is like sex.

J.G.: What passage supports that?

Bobby reads: "Sex is the weapon of life, the shooting sperm sent like an army of guerrillas to penetrate the egg's defenses—the only victory that really matters. War thrusts you into the well of loneliness, death breathing in your ear. Sex is a grappling hook that pulls you out, ends your isolation, makes you one with life again" (p. 62).

Justin: I don't agree.

Amy: When you think of sex, you think of . . . conception.

J.G.: So war is like conception?

Amy: More than it's like sex.

J.G.: Does anyone ever think of sex as a conquest?

Matt: Yeah, you get bragging rights with your buddies.

Amy: I don't think males do it for bragging—I think they do it to feel better about themselves.

JaVonna: Girls and guys both do it.

Matt: You see young girls marrying old guys, having their babies, just so they can get their money.

J.G.: So how is war like sex?

Matt: When you go to war, you try to overpower the enemy. When you have sex, you try to overpower women.

Discussion bursts forth from all around the room—guys nodding their heads in agreement with Matt, protests from many young women in the class, one or two saying women overpower men, too. Everyone talks at once, and I don't get any of this transcribed.

J.G.: Are there other metaphors for war in this essay?

Robert: War is theater. Government gave soldiers a script—they just didn't finish the last act.

Matt: Just like in Desert Storm. It was always on TV. It was like a show.

J.G.: Any other metaphors?

Justin: War is beautiful.

I read this passage from the article: "There's something about a firefight at night, something about the mechanical elegance of an M-60 machine gun. They are everything they should be, perfect examples of their form. When you are firing out at night, the red tracers go out into the blackness as if you were drawing with a light pen. Then little dots of light start winking back, and green tracers from the AK-47s begin to weave in with the red to form brilliant patterns that seem . . . as if they had been etched on the night" (p. 62).

Justin: I don't agree—killing isn't beautiful.

Bobby: The author doesn't talk about what happens on the other side—the people who get shot and killed.

I praise Bobby for noticing what the author excludes.

J.G.: Based on what we've read or watched, can anyone fill in what the author leaves out?

Examples follow: Chef's decapitated head from Apocalypse Now; the bodies hanging in the trees; the baby who is mined in *Fallen Angels*, exploding in a soldier's face.

It's getting near the end of the period, so I ask one more question.

J.G.: Could a woman have written this?

Amy: No.

J.G.: Can women write about war?

Mark: They wouldn't have written about war. They would've written about how they're more moral and mature than men and so wouldn't fight in the first place.

Misty: Women would write about the sentimental side of war, about the friends they made and experiences they shared.

J.G.: How does Walter Dean Myers' book fit into this discussion?

Robert: He wrote about the bad part of war and the friendships, too.

J.G.: So do all men love war?

Robert: I don't think Myers loves it.

BELL

I don't think our discussion resolved anything about whether or not men love war. Some students would insist they do; other would disagree. Their shared "readings," though, show how using a variety of sources complicates individual viewpoints. Yes, Broyles says, "War is beautiful," but Bobby points out what Broyles ignores: the people who get shot and killed. Students then refer to Coppola's film and Myers' book to show specifically some of these exclusions: decapitated heads, hanging bodies, exploding babies—hardly beautiful.

Just as students realized earlier that Peter Jennings and Tom Brokaw construct different views of the Desert Storm parade, they now point out how Myers, Broyles, and Coppola construct different views of war. Broyles may love it, but Robert is convinced that Myers doesn't.

We see, too, from this discussion that males' and females' prior experience and socialization affects their reading of each of these pieces, especially "Why Men Love War." The metaphors discussed—particularly "sex is a weapon"—make this clear. Females don't think about power and sex in the same sentence; apparently some males do. Females in this class don't see sex as a game.

Male student attitudes toward both war and sex are game-like. Little boys, Bobby says, play G.I. Joe; women, Amy responds, can separate the game from reality. One of the things that interests me is how males and females relate their own gender's experience and how they read those of the other gender. Mark connects playing war as a child with playing laser tag as a teenager, implying that this state of mind approximates the attitude soldiers have. Kelly calls that state "primitive."

These gender differences toward war and sex surfaced again after we watched the movie *Casualties of War.* Shortly after Sergeant Meserve (Sean Penn) saves Private Erikson (Michael J. Fox) early in the film, he orders his entire platoon to rape a young Vietnamese girl they've kidnapped. Erikson is the only soldier who defies the order. I ask students to respond in their journals to this construction of a wartime experience. Notice how males and females read this text differently. One male student responded,

> In normal cases rape is never justifiable. But in war there is chaos, and chaos in war brings out the evil animal instincts in man. In war anything is justifiable. She was nothing but a gook anyway. Her life was worthless.

Another wrote,

> In war there are no rules and regulations. If someone was to be put on trial for rape which happened in a war, especially a sergeant, it would be ridiculous. He's fighting for us. He's on our side.

Mark's response equating war and sex may be more poetic, but his attitude is similar to that of many of my male students:

> Machine gun (we'll just call it a "gun") pumpin' back and forth. The miniature "explosions" from each "bullet" forces your arm (pelvis) back, the arm's (pelvis's) strength pushing forward. Men (semen) trudging (swimming) upstream against the current. Breathing hard from the running ("working"), the "burst" of happiness as you finally "shoot" your target. Your target "collapses." Oh yes, war is sex.
>
> *Mark Singh, grade 11*

Angie's response is representative of most of my female students:

> Men love war because they think that they can maybe prove themselves. They want to show everyone how masculine they are, that they can kill.
>
> When Sergeant Meserve raped the girl, he did it to show he was a man. Raping a girl doesn't make you a man, it makes you a monster. He used sex as a weapon.
>
> *Angie Holbrook, grade 11*

Besides examining how different genders construct war-time experiences, I ask students to consider if black and white constructions of war differ. In addition to reading Walter Dean Myers' *Fallen Angels*, which focuses on the Vietnam experiences of a predominantly African American platoon, we also read Tim O'Brien's short story "On the Rainy River," which explores the dilemma a white college graduate faces when he receives his draft notice. Both the novel and short story explore antiwar themes, but the construction of the characters' backgrounds and attitudes toward war differ.

One of the advantages of using different sources in relation to the same subject is that students can more easily read the differences—in this case the different assumptions the authors make about going to war. Amy and Krista capture those differences in their journals:

> O'Brien's family had money and social power, something Perry's hadn't had. O'Brien felt that because of this and the fact that he was in college with a bright future ahead of him, he was in no danger. He thought they would only draft the less fortunate kids. Richie had nothing going for him. He didn't have the money to go to school or the opportunities O'Brien had. For example, when Richie found out he was going to Vietnam, he was a little scared but saw it as a chance to get out of Harlem and experience life. When O'Brien got his draft notice, he saw it as a sort of dying; his life was being ruined instead of enhanced by the knowledge that he might gain from getting out into the world.
>
> *Amy Price, grade 11*

> O'Brien might've disagreed with the war, but he wasn't as radical as most of the protesters. The editorials [he wrote] didn't have as much feeling; like he said it was more intellectual than feeling. The war just didn't involve him. Until he got his draft card.
>
> Perry's situation was a little different. He had to go. It was his way out. It was a way for a future, for a life. He came from a single-parent family living in the inner city. His mom didn't have the money to send him to college and neither did he. Richie was a pretty good basketball player, but a knee injury pretty much shattered his dream of turning pro-

132

fessional. Richie could either fight in the war or let the inner-city way of life swallow him up.

Krista Whitaker, grade 11

When we assign students reading and writing, we never know exactly how they'll construct our assignment in their own minds. I expected that everyone would restrict their discussion to comparing the novel and the short story. JaVonna, a black female, surprised me, though, contrasting her reading of *Fallen Angels* with contemporary African American culture:

At the beginning of this class we discussed factors which make you see things differently. Race definitely made Walter Dean Myers tell his story of Vietnam different from any other [author we've read]. He showed the racial sides of things like when he says, "how they got to stick together"— it's funny because nowadays African Americans don't stick together. All they think about is getting over and if killing another African American is what it takes, they'll most likely do it.

JaVonna Buckhanan, grade 11

The final texts for this unit were songs from the sixties, including "Soldier Boy" and "Masters of War." Read in the context of the historical background I provided and the other sources we discussed, students were able to speculate about how listeners might react if their only source about war were one of the songs—just as they speculated earlier about a viewer's reaction to Peter Jennings' or Tom Brokaw's newscast. Look at Paulette's response to "Soldier Boy":

If this was how people really thought about war, they probably were blindfolded about a lot of things. This song sounded to me like this soldier was going on vacation and would return home soon.

Paulette Wright, grade 11

Amy's reaction is similar:

133

In "Soldier Boy" there's no objection to war and men going to it other than the fact that they'll miss them.

Her reaction to "Masters of War," on the other hand, reflects the antiestablishment climate of the middle and late sixties:

In "Masters of War" the country's leaders tell everyone to go fight for their country and "be all they can be" when they sit behind a desk and watch the war on TV.

Amy Price, grade 11

Krista captures the historical contrast of music in the early and late sixties:

In the early sixties the music was innocent much like that of the fifties. Going to the prom, wearing blue velvet dresses and getting married the week after graduation. But after a few years, when Vietnam began to heat up, so did the music. Uncle Sam was taking away the innocence of life and life was taking away the innocence of the music.

Krista Whitaker, grade 11

Unfortunately, adolescents grow out of their childhood innocence and learn of war and drugs, greed and bulimia. As teachers, we discover, just as Holden did, that we can't catch them as they fall. Students will learn, whether we like it or not, that cruelty and pain are part of their lives. We might prevent some of that pain, though, if we teach our students to read the contemporary texts that bombard them daily, texts not typically read in schools: texts about alcohol and appearance, politics and patriotism, sales and sex.

Though students lose much of their innocence as they mature, advertisers and politicians count on "innocent" consumers to purchase their products, elect them to office, support a war. Teaching students to read product and political texts more critically can help them make more informed choices. Amy summed it up at the end of the semester when she said, "If you're not critical and a little suspicious when you read or watch something, you're only going to receive the information that the media wants you to hear."

I'm not trying to breed cynical students, but readers who are "critical and a little suspicious" will understand that when they consume products and ideas, they're consuming a whole set of values and philosophies, too. Including a variety of contemporary cultural texts as part of our curriculum and teaching students to read those texts can lead students to this understanding and to more critical consumption.

CHAPTER 6

Using Writing to "Read" Films

Back-to-basic traditionalists think a healthy dose of the three Rs is just the prescription to cure what ails American society, but as my students say, "Get real!" The reality is that without attacking the big V, we'd only be healing part of the patient. Sure, readin', writin', and 'rithmetic are crucial to literacy, but in this age of VCRs, MTV, and thirty-second sound bites, visual literacy is crucial, too. As I suggested in Chapter Five, teachers should expand students' reading to include nontraditional texts, one of which is the video text. This chapter extends the discussion begun there and focuses on the way film constructs "reality" and how teachers can help students become more perceptive readers of film.

A problem often arises, though, when we use visual media in our classrooms. "It's a free day!" Jason blurts out when he sees the TV/VCR cart. Toby kicks back in his desk, locks his hands behind his head, and yawns. When the lights dim, Mandi searches her purse for M&Ms, and if the film is a black-and-white documentary, a third of the students are asleep within five minutes.

For many students viewing is a passive activity; for teachers, however, viewing should be active, critically engaging students, teaching them to read films the way they do—or should—books. To help students become more critical readers of films, teachers should first help them reflect upon how they read print.

I start by writing the letters B-I-R-D on the board, asking students to spend a minute or two jotting down the first image that comes to mind. Paulette sees a "white seagull flying over the ocean, then scooping down into the water and back out." Bobby describes a "bald eagle in a tree with no leaves." Robert sees "pigeons in a park fighting for food." Angie imagines a whole flock of birds, Misty spies a fat bluebird in a backyard tree, and JaVonna sees Tweety Bird from Looney Tunes. I ask my students what a kindergartner who knew the alphabet but couldn't read might see. "Only the letters B-I-R-D," they reply.

I follow this discussion by putting an illustration of a bird on the overhead, and now most students see the same thing as would a kindergartner who can decode the illustrated symbol even though she can't read words. While the letters B-I-R-D and the picture of the bird are both symbols, the picture is a more direct translation. Even so, students' prior knowledge influences their reading of still pictures. Paul knows the image he sees is a crane; Misty thinks the bird is a stork; Angela sees an ugly duckling.

When children are very young, they begin to associate the pictures they see on TV with the pictures they see in books. On TV the pictures move and the people and images are smaller than in real life, but gradually children come to see these images as "real." They don't question the director's intent, the filmmaker's technique, or the fact that people on the screen are only acting. As many children get older, they continue to passively accept what they see on TV or in films as a representation of reality. Anyone viewing this representation, they believe, will perceive that same reality.

When twenty people attend the 1 P.M. matinee of *Robin Hood: Prince of Thieves*, noncritical viewers assume that all twenty see the same film. Not true. Just as people read words and images differently, so, too, do they read *Robin Hood* differently. Two of the twenty watching the film have skimmed Joe DeChick's review in *The Cincinnati Enquirer*, "Tale of Yore a Bore," and are predisposed not to like it. Six have heard from friends how exciting the film is. Three adolescent girls think Kevin Costner is a hunk and like the film no matter the quality. Four are distracted by thoughts of work and have trouble concentrating on the movie. In fact, there would be twenty different readings of *Robin Hood* at that matinee showing.

As teachers, we can help students become more visually literate by making them aware of how they read films. Besides showing them how their backgrounds affect their readings, we can teach them to view films more critically. We can make them aware of how directors attempt to manipulate their emotions, of how different camera angles and shots affect their perceptions, of how music and sound effects work in conjunction with visual imagery.

To help my students become more critical readers of visual images, I show them the famous picture "My Wife and My Mother-in-Law," by cartoonist W. E. Hill. I tell them to write a sentence or two describing what they see. Krista concludes the "gal" is "wealthy" because of the "big hat" and "feathery material around her neck." Paulette doesn't see the "gal" Krista does, but an "older woman who looks like she is hurting inside." Marisa writes,

> I see a woman. She has on what looks like a fur coat, a hat with a feather on it, and a choker. She's not looking straight at me, but is turned half-way around.
>
> *Marisa Moore, grade 11*

Even if students have seen the picture before, they like re-seeing it and especially explaining to others that the young woman's chin is the old woman's nose, and the old woman's chin is the young woman's chest. Misty realizes this in the middle of her writing:

> I see a middle-aged woman with a white scarf that looks like a polar bear over black curly hair. She has a large nose and is frowning. She has a feather in her scarf. Damn! I just saw it. A young woman. She is looking at the wall we can't see.
>
> *Misty Frost, grade 11*

When I'm sure everyone can see both the young and the old woman, I put a copy of a picture from the movie *Witness* on the overhead. I explain to my students how reading a picture is similar to peeling away layers of an onion. On the surface of this particular picture, we see three people: an adult male in the foreground, an adult female and child in the background. If we look more closely, we see that the two in the background appear to be inside a wooden structure—probably a house—and are framed by a doorway. The male in the foreground is outside the house. We notice he is dressed in contemporary clothing, that he wears an expensive-looking watch, has a suit coat draped across his right arm, above which appears a gun strapped in a holster to his side. He doesn't seem to be threatening anyone with the gun; we might conclude he's a detective. The woman in the background wears a long dark skirt; she and her son's clothes are plain compared to the man's. If we are familiar with Amish culture, we recognize the woman's traditional hair covering.

Since the figures in this picture are juxtaposed, more sophisticated readers might explore symbol and theme. The figure in the foreground dominates the picture because of his larger size and the bright light that shines on him. The smaller figures stand in shadow. The picture suggests a clash of cultures, one dominating the other; in fact, that is one of the themes of *Witness*, which stars Harrison Ford and Kelly McGillis. I offer this reading to students as one of many possible readings. My Pennsylvania and Ohio background and my training as an English teacher explain, in part, how I read this picture and, later, the film.

Then I give students a picture from *The Grapes of Wrath* to read. This shot, from early in the film, shows two farmers confronting a man on a tractor who has been sent to evict these "Okies." I ask students to use writing to read this shot as I did the shot from *Witness*. Marisa begins this way:

> I see three men, two in the foreground and one in the background. One of the men in the foreground is threatening the man in the background with a rifle. The man in the background is on a tractor. I assume that there's a conflict that happened or is about to happen.
>
> *Marisa Moore, grade 11*

Marisa's reading covers the scene's surface and hints at what possibly underlies this shot: one man is threatening another in a conflict that has occurred or will occur. Amy speculates further:

> The two men seem to be protecting whatever is behind them—most likely a farm based on their attire and grassy environment. This could be a labor dispute; the man on the tractor could be a "scab."
>
> *Amy Price, grade 11*

139

Students enrich each other's reading by talking about their own readings. So we talk:

"It looks like the afternoon to me because of the shadows," Justin starts.

"I think it's summer, too, because the brush along the side looks dry," Matt adds.

Misty follows these comments by nailing down a more precise time period. "The brush made me think it's the dust bowl."

Paul shifts the focus from the setting to the action. "I think the guys on the ground are trying to defend their land."

"The guy on the tank doesn't look afraid to me," T'Keesha responds.

Angie clarifies for the class what she believes the piece of machinery to be: "It's a tractor, I think."

"It's interesting you say 'tank,' T'Keesha," I interject. "What chance does a guy with a rifle have against a guy on a tank?"

"He could shoot the driver," Bobby responds.

"Yeah, but what would the owner of the farm do then?" I ask.

Kelly answers, "Get another driver."

"So what literary conflict is at work here?" I ask, and Misty replies, "Person versus machine."

Not every reading is as close to the "truth" of this scene as the ones I've included. Julie guessed the man with the gun was an escaping slave. Tammy set the time much earlier than the thirties, back when Oklahoma was still the "frontier." But most students concluded that the scene is set on a farm, that the man on the tractor was trespassing, and that the men on the ground were protecting what they believed to be rightfully theirs. By sharing their readings with their peers, everyone can continue to speculate and understand the collaborative nature of reading.

I show my students two more pictures from *The Grapes of Wrath*. One shows the Joads pushing their loaded-down vehicle over a dusty mountain road; another focuses on Ma Joad as she tries to convince state agents that her dead mother is actually sick so they'll be admitted to the "golden" land of California.

Students write their readings of these pictures, too, starting with what strikes them first, then peeling away successive layers of meaning as they read below the surface. They use what they know about sequencing and cause and effect, and draw conclusions based on what the three pictures suggest to them. After sharing their various readings, students are on their way to becoming more visually literate.

After reading still pictures, my students and I discuss factors that influence the way people read films. My own knowledge of film was enhanced by Johnson and Bone's *Understanding the Film* (1986), which my friend Tom Romano was using in his filmmaking class when I student-taught there.

My students need to learn, as I learned myself, that filmmakers take advantage of "involuntary attention." When we're out walking the dog, a blaring horn from a passing car rivets our attention even though we may have been concentrating on tomorrow's lesson plans. In fact, people spend most of their time not paying attention. Knowing this, filmmakers use various techniques to divert our attention when we least expect it, especially in suspense movies.

"Intensity and size" is one such technique. Making something brighter, louder, or bigger (e.g., placing an object or character in the foreground) quickly focuses viewers' attention.

Directors also use "novelty or contrast" to influence our readings. In *Tootsie* a man pretends to be a woman challenging traditional attitudes toward "male" and "female" roles. In *Witness*, the filmmaker emphasizes a clash of cultures.

Filmmakers also know that viewers' past experience influences their reading. When we see a film, we bring our total life history along for the viewing. Young children would not recognize the gun strapped to the detective's side in *Witness*, but teenagers would. The more we read films, the more familiar we become with filmmakers' codes and techniques. We associate white with the good guys and black with the bad guys. We know that riding off into the sunset marks a western's conclusion.

I talk to my students about conformity, too, though I'm not sure what effect I have on them in the face of peer pressure. When students are unsure of their own reading of a film, they often claim the reading of others in class just as Stephanie from Chapter Three did when she assumed the same stance on "issues" as did her more confident peers. Despite this tendency, I urge students to trust their own perceptions and readings. "Most films don't come with teachers' guides," I joke, "so my readings aren't 'correct' or 'definitive.'" I want them to know what Eldon Miller

taught me years ago when I was enrolled in his Guided Independent Reading class: teachers don't have all the answers.

In conjunction with conformity, students need to reflect upon
their prejudices. "Ethnocentrism," I tell them, "is the tendency of
one group of people to think of the customs of others in terms of
their own—and to find those customs odd or even wrong. If you
see a film you don't understand, instead of saying, 'That was dumb
or boring,' try to open your mind and put aside your prejudices."

After discussing these factors that shape our readings, students are ready to read films. In my Vietnam and the Sixties class,
I contextualize the era as part of the "American Myth": that Americans were destined to be pioneers who would complete what
Crèvecoeur called the "great circle" in the "westward course of
empire" (Hellmann 1986). This westward course began in the Far
East and progressed through the "Near East, Egypt and Persia,
Greece, Rome . . . Spain, France, and England" (p. 5). We discuss
the Puritans' "errand into the wilderness," and famous pioneers
from fact and fiction: Lewis and Clark, Daniel Boone and Natty
Bumppo. We read Steinbeck's "Leader of the People," in which a
grandfather tells his grandson about "westering," or leading
wagon trains across the prairies and over the mountains, until finally, they reach the frontier's edge at the great Pacific.

Before we see our first film, I share excerpts from William
Lederer and Eugene Burdick's *The Ugly American* (1965), which
was originally published in 1958. The novel, set in a fictional
Southeast Asian country, portrays Americans as loud, obnoxious,
and arrogant. Instead of learning the language of the people, the
Americans hobnob at parties while the Communists slowly win
away the country's peasant soul.

Senator John F. Kennedy read *The Ugly American* as a challenge to the moral fiber of the American character, and had copies
sent to every member of Congress. Two years later, as president,
he established his "New Frontier," calling for the President's Physi-
cal-Fitness Program, the Peace Corps, and the build-up of American Special Forces. When Kennedy told Americans in his
inaugural address to "ask not what your country can do for you,
but what you can do for your country," one of the things they
could do was support our pioneer role in the New Frontier: Vietnam. There, Americans could test their moral fiber and finish the

mission the Puritans had begun. The Green Berets embodied this sense of national purpose and perpetuated the American Myth.

Within this context, we begin our film study of Vietnam with John Wayne's 1968 movie, *The Green Berets*. When Wayne first expressed an interest in making the film, presidential aide Jack Valenti told Lyndon Johnson that the "hawkish Wayne 'would be saying the things we want said'" (Hellmann, p. 90). Consequently, Wayne enjoyed full Pentagon support. I tell students to view the film critically, thinking about John Wayne as director and actor, about the familiar icons of the frontier west (the American camp is named Dodge City, for example), and about the film's implied message.

I remind students to think about visual images, music, lighting, juxtaposition of characters and scenes, and the other filmmaking codes we have studied. I insist they watch the film with pen in hand jotting down details they believe to be significant.

From the opening lines of "The Ballad of the Green Berets" ("Fighting soldiers from the sky") to Colonel Kirby (Wayne) walking with a Vietnamese orphan into the melodramatic sunset, my students take notes and respond to the film in writing. Here's part of Chris' reading:

> The American Myth is that "life is a John Wayne movie." Let's look at *The Green Berets*. It was basically like this: John Wayne: "Well howdy pilgrim/soldier. Let's go out there and kick some Injun/V.C. tail. We've got a fort/base camp to defend. So let's get the horses/choppers movin'. We've got a supply wagon/C-130 cargo plane comin' in."
>
> What we have here is Hollywood telling our teenage boys that, "You might have missed out on the old West, but here is your second chance. Quit playin' cowboys and Indians and pick up an M-16 and give it a real try."
>
> *Chris Edrington, grade 11*

Here's how Brad reads the same film:

> *The Green Berets* portrays the Americans as a group of big, bold, fearless men who show up like Superman to help someone in distress. They tell the American press that it's their duty to prevent Communism from taking over the

world, and then they march right over and start fighting. They even have time to spare to fix some little girl's foot, a scene that was used just to play with your emotions, and to make the Viet Cong look even worse.

Brad Welage, grade 11

By the time we get to *Apocalypse Now* (1979), students are viewing films more critically, reading with a heightened awareness of how filmmakers portray Americans in Vietnam. Here's the beginning of Jack's review:

The Green Berets told the story of the great American: the "Fighting soldiers from the sky" who were going to save the world from the evil forces of Communism.

But *Apocalypse Now* talks about "the end" of the great American. It is a movie intent on questioning our values and our reasons for being involved in Vietnam.

Unlike *The Green Berets*, in which the depictions of evil and good are easily distinctive, *Apocalypse Now* makes us consider the gray area. Instead of seeing barbarian Viet Cong robbing equipment from dead U.S. soldiers, we see cruel Americans open fire on innocent Vietnamese school children . . . turn[ing] our self-image upside down.

The first image we see is Captain Willard, and the camera projects his image upside down! We don't see strong, disciplined Americans demonstrating their superior skills like we see when the media interview the Green Berets; instead we see a single distressed American, lying in bed (getting soft) smoking a cigarette and drinking shots of whiskey.

Willard finally does get out of bed, and . . . he shatters the mirror in front of him.

This sets the tone of the movie: this movie was made to shatter the image we have of ourselves as Americans, to disprove the American Myth.

Jack Singh, grade 11

Chris, Brad, and Jack clearly understand how these two filmmakers construct images of America and Americans in the 1960s. Wayne's film was made during the height of the war. Its purpose:

to inspire Americans during the Vietnam War, as Olivier's Henry V inspired Britons during World War II. Seen in the context of this course and viewed from a historical distance, the responses of Chris, Brad, and Jack prove less than inspired. They, of course, have been shaped by that distance as have all Americans since the sixties; they are less trusting of government in general and politicians in particular. Their perception of the United States as "benevolent savior" had already been "shattered."

Kali recognizes that the "shattered" images of *Apocalypse Now* cast a shadow on the American character that *The Green Berets* did not. One image in particular bothered her. When Lance and Captain Willard crawl through the trenches near the Do Long Bridge, Lance snuggling the puppy he claimed after Willard murdered a boatload of Vietnamese civilians, "Lance jumps to the top of the barricade and stares off into the line of fire, his and the puppy's profile contrasting in the shallow light . . . In that instant in which Lance takes a look at the world he is a boy, but by the time the image reaches his eye he is a man." Just prior to this Lance had taken a hit of LSD and was marveling at the rainbow of light reflected in the river below the bridge as if he were back home watching Fourth of July fireworks. Then Kali continues,

> In the next few days after watching the film, this scene repeatedly popped into my head. I also kept thinking about the scene following a shoot-out the soldiers had on the river . . . where Lance is screaming over and over again, "Where's the dog? We've got to go back and get the dog!" It was like he had lost his best friend. That puppy was the only pure thing in that filthy war. It represented all that is good in life. Just like those boys fighting for their lives. They went into that war with pure hearts and they returned corrupted. No one should have to see what they did.

Kali always found ways not only to make my assignments her own, but to make intensely personal connections. Writing about films of the Vietnam War was no exception. She titled her paper "All the Children Are Insane," a line from the Doors' song "The End," which Jack alludes to in his paper. The following passage explains her title and illuminates her own understanding of Colonel Kurtz:

> Once Colonel Kurtz had it all together. But war drove him crazy. He chose to support the dark side of life. As he said, "IF is the middle word in LIFE." What does *if* mean to you? *If* could mean anything. It is the unknown. We can't depend on it. We can't depend on anything anymore. Not even ourselves.
>
> "You must make a friend of horror," Kurtz said. What was his horror? What was it that he was so afraid of? I think I know. I think it is the same thing we are all afraid of. Ourselves.
>
> Admit it. At some time or another we have all had thoughts that frighten us. I have them all the time. In fact, I had one yesterday. It was more like an afterthought. Suddenly, for no reason I can explain, I took my pencil eraser and put a burn on my left wrist. Then it hit me. I was damaging myself. Why? I was horrified because I understood it. It was to feel something other than the dull ache inside of me. That same dull ache I'm sure Colonel Kurtz felt. That feeling that everything is lost and there is nothing you can do about it. So you befriend it. You try to become comfortable with it. You make it your comrade. You make it your friend. It is the horror. IT IS YOU.
>
> *Kali Evans, grade 11*

Kali's thoughts are frightening. She and I have talked about them, more than once. Perhaps one reason her last paragraph clutches us closer is that we recognize our own shattered images in the mirror of Kali's writing. As English teachers we hope the literature we ask our students to read reflects, at least in part, their own lives. Films offer similar reflections, and as Kali shows us, sometimes the connections they make are frightening.

The last exercise to help students understand these reflections follows logically from our semester of film study. Students makes short videos of their own about some aspect of war and the sixties. I share a short video I filmed the first time I taught the class and explain the process from conception to final film. I chose an unrelated subject matter so as not to influence student videos. *A*

Barbie Mirror uses familiar icons—Barbie and Cabbage Patch dolls—to expose the emphasis our society places on appearance and materialism. The plain-faced Cabbage Patch doll is ridiculed and ostracized in the video; Barbie conspicuously consumes and exercises. While Barbie worries about what to wear to the prom, the world watches Violence wage ugly wars and Poverty destroy human souls. I used pictures from news magazines, excerpts from Marge Piercy's "Barbie Doll," a soundtrack from Michael Oldfield's *Tubular Bells*, and the two dolls to make my point.

I show students the script I wrote and tell them to script their own videos. After watching *A Barbie Mirror*, we discuss what worked and what didn't. Some of my shots need to be held longer, for instance, especially ones where I expect viewers to read excerpts from the poem. After students critique my film, I turn them loose in groups: to read and research; collect images, text, music; and script their videos, mindful of the message they wish to convey.

Jammie, Misty, and Jeremy research the 1970 killings at Kent State. Their video uses Crosby, Stills, Nash and Young's "Ohio," a taped interview with a teacher enrolled at Kent when the four students were shot, images from magazines and newspapers, and headlines written on the twentieth anniversary of the riot.

Jack, Herb, and Kevin were enrolled in this class the same semester American soldiers lost their lives in Iraq. Their film, *The Stigma*, questions American attitudes toward the soldiers of two wars: "Why," they asked, "were veterans of Desert Storm welcomed with victory parades while Vietnam veterans were spat upon?" Besides effectively conveying their theme, this group exercised the most patience in the process of shooting their video. Not satisfied with a blurry shot or improper exposure, they shot and reshot their script until they were satisfied. Their painstaking efforts paid off in a high quality video that I now share with other classes.

I know that teaching students to read films critically helps them better understand the construction of knowledge. Oliver Stone's *J.F.K.* represents a different picture of John F. Kennedy's assassination than does the report written by the Warren Commission. I want students to be aware of these different constructions, but I also want them to engage in creating the medium themselves. The best learning is in the doing. Working through the process of producing and reflecting upon their own videos

147

stretches students' appreciation of the work involved in filmmaking and, at the same time, reinforces the concept that knowledge is constructed.

For these students, writing functions as a tool to probe the depths of themselves as readers and viewers, as thinkers and citizens. Teaching is a political act, and asking students to challenge the status quo is a political statement. Although we don't have the right to impose anyone's ideology on our students, teaching them to read the ideologies that underlie the films they watch makes them better readers. Chris understands that *The Green Berets* is a John Wayne western in disguise; Brad recognizes that the same film perpetuates the "Superman" myth left over from World War II. These students aren't just reading the "plot" of the film; they're reading between the scenes.

Once during a presentation to other teachers, I discussed the use of film to raise students' critical consciousness. I showed them *The Stigma* to share the good work my students had done. Only three months had elapsed since the fighting of Desert Storm. A few members of the audience were disturbed by the students' film. It didn't reflect the same spirit of patriotism they felt as American citizens who had supported our efforts in the Middle East. The next day when the workshop continued, they wore American flag lapel pins to express their disapproval.

I was surprised at their reaction, but I can't shy away from the political nature of teaching. Had Herb, Jack, and Kevin made a more "patriotic" film, chances are they would have offended other viewers' sensibilities. If we don't teach students to think critically, we teach them to accept the roles society imposes upon them whether or not they like those roles or find them just. Using writing to read films is one way we can help students to cast their own roles and script their own lives.

CHAPTER 7

Constructing Relationships

The first year I taught introductory composition at Miami University in Oxford, Ohio, I was asked to submit a syllabus outlining and explaining the course. I had been teaching only six years then and still wasn't beyond writing a weekly lesson plan. Of course, I had unit plans in mind that would last anywhere from two to four weeks, but the most I ever committed to paper was one week at a time. After writing a semester syllabus at Miami, though, I knew I'd never revert to planning week by week. I liked seeing the semester mapped out before me, readings chosen, activities planned, rationale written. Seeing the destination and course my students and I would travel comforted me; I crave organization.

The subsequent syllabus I wrote for Women and Men, a class for high school juniors and seniors, reflects the sense of organization I learned at the university level. I explain in writing that in this course students will examine the construction of gender: how different roles evolved for men and women, how parent-child relationships affect gender, how the media portray males and females. The central focus, I tell them, is better understanding of the influence of society and culture on our thinking about gender. Just as I felt more secure knowing where my students and I were headed, I think they, too, welcome that security. The next lesson I needed to learn was not to be so bound by the syllabus that I couldn't adapt my plans.

This past semester students were to begin exploring male-female relationships in week number ten of the course. They would read Irwin Shaw's "The Girls in Their Summer Dresses," S. I. Kishor's "Appointment with Love," and Joyce Carol Oates' "Four

149

Summers." My syllabus called for reading and discussing the first two stories in class and assigning the third, a much longer story, for homework. After our discussions of Shaw's and Kishor's stories, students would write about "Four Summers," analyzing the evolution of the narrator's relationship with men and how those experiences shaped the woman she became. Upon review my plan struck me as solid: the progression from group to individual reading made pedagogical sense, the stories and activities reflected the course goals. I had made my plan and was sticking to it. Then I enrolled in Tom Romano's graduate course, "The Teaching of Writing."

Robert Frost says in "The Road Not Taken" that "way leads on to way." Despite the concrete foundation my syllabus provided, I deviated from its safely paved road and risked another route. The destination was the same, but the different stops, twists, and turns led us down a more fruitful path than the one I previously planned.

On the Road

When I read Marcia Stapleton Snively's "This Is Serious" in *Writing with Passion* (Romano 1995, pp. 57–58), I thought it a perfect introduction to this unit on female-male relationships, and though I hadn't planned on students writing dialogues of their own, that seemed a natural succession. Snively was a high school junior when she wrote this dialogue about a teenage boy trying to convince his girlfriend to have sex with him. At one point Cathy asks Gary if he loves her, to which he responds, "Why is that so important: Love doesn't have that much to do with it." Later, when all of Gary's previous hands have failed, he plays the trump card he's sure will win him the pot he's sought: "I hate to say this, but if you won't, somebody else will . . . You would if you loved me, Cathy." But Snively's Cathy, not about to be manipulated by Gary's threat, has kept back a joker of her own, which she plays in the last line of the dialogue: "Love doesn't have that much to do with it, remember?"

As soon as I read this short, clever dialogue, I knew my students would find it amusing but also recognize its truth. To begin the unit I asked Erik to read Gary's part and Kristin to read Cathy's. They read it well, Kristin especially enjoying the last line. When they finished, we talked about the tension between the boy and girl and how Cathy used Gary's words against him. I pointed out what Tom says about dialogue: that students should think of it as a "dramatic encounter" rather than "mundane chitchat," that it "reveals emotions, examines ideas, explores issues, expresses desires" (p. 57).

Women and Men is an issues-oriented class. I want students to engage in a great deal of analysis, first articulating what they believe about gender, then exploring the origin of those beliefs. Writing their own dialogues between a male and a female struck me as a different way to begin this analysis, one I was certain they'd find interesting and fun.

During the same class period that we read and discussed "This Is Serious," I asked students to pair up for the last twenty-five minutes and write dialogues between a male and female character. This first deviation from the road of my syllabus veered sharply off course. For example, instead of exploring issues and examining ideas, Sara and Joey ripped off a commercial—the one about sexual harassment in which the woman shrinks before the viewer's eyes—and changed the ending:

Joe: There's a couple of things that need to change.

Mary: Like what?

Joe: You know, dress a little sexier, show off those nice legs.

Mary: Joe, stop. You're being silly. Why would I do that?

Joe: We're talking about your job here, Mary.

Mary: No, we're talking about sexual harassment.

Joe: Shut up, you can't prove anything.

Mary: You're right, except for the recorder in my pocket.

Some students were more thoughtful. Amanda and Brigid wrote about a dilemma many teenagers face. When Wendy reveals she's pregnant, Troy reacts: "Well, do something. You can't have a baby. I got football and college." Though the rest of the dialogue isn't as developed as it could be, it isn't a commercial rip-off like Sara and Joey's. For the most part, though, I was disappointed with the results. Where was the substance and creativity they'd seen in Snively's piece? Where was the exploration of issues, the examination of ideas we'd just discussed? What these students had produced was more "mundane chitchat" than "dramatic encounter." What had gone wrong?

Several things, now that I think about it. Twenty-five minutes wasn't enough time. We'd done no brainstorming. We read only one model, which I think did work as a catalyst, but not as I intended. High school students think about sex—surprise—and "This Is Serious" struck a chord. Many of them quickly decided upon sex as the topic for their dialogues, hoping to produce something humorous as Snively had; unfortunately, they forgot the depth. After the disappointing collaborations, I thought of abandoning this "dialogue trip" but decided to follow the detour a little while longer.

That night I assigned Irwin Shaw's "The Girls in Their Summer Dresses," which generated the best discussion we'd had to that point in the course. If you don't know the story, a husband and wife of five years spend the day in Manhattan, their sole goal to enjoy each other's company. But the wife can't help noticing the way her husband ogles other women. She lets it be known that his ogling hasn't gone unnoticed, and they spend the rest of the story discussing his "habit" and what it means to their relationship.

Most of my male students defended the man's "natural" tendency to look. They praised him for being open: he doesn't attempt to conceal his gazes and he's honest with his wife about it. He can't help it, he admits, but his glances mean nothing. Most of my female students labeled his habit offensive and claimed his glances did indeed mean something: that he didn't love her as much as he claimed. They said that if he did, he would at least be discreet (all the while admitting it's natural for both men and women to look).

"My problem," Heather says, "is how he looked at other women," pointing to Frances' line, "You look at them as though you want them" (p. 224).

"But he hasn't done anything about it," Erik quickly responds. "He says he hasn't touched another woman in five years."

"Yeah, but just the fact that he says, 'In a way that's true,' would be enough for me to show him the door," Heather replies.

"He's been faithful. What does she want?" Mike asks.

"How long will that last, though?" Sarah wonders. "When Frances says, 'Someday . . . you're going to make a move,' he says, 'Maybe.' What do you think about that?"

"I think he's just trying to get her off his back," Mike answers, and discussion continues.

These students made it clear to me they could analyze

Shaw's story and support their opinions, not just with personal experience—although that shaped their readings—but with textual references as well. I was interested in their different interpretations of the same line: Sarah sees cheating; Mike, paranoia. This discussion convinced me that my students didn't need to write analysis papers at this point; we'd done that earlier in the semester. I knew they could do it; they were doing it now. Dialogue carries Shaw's story. Perhaps I could give them another crack at writing dialogues of their own.

The next day we read Hemingway's "Hills like White Elephants." I originally planned on using this story later in the semester, but because it is almost entirely dialogue, I decided to include it as part of this unit. Amanda read the role of the woman, and Tom read the part of the man. The story is set outside a railway station in Spain at a crossroad in this couple's relationship. When Amanda and Tom finished reading the three-and-a-half-page story, confusion spread across my students' faces, as it had across mine the first time I read it. "What is this about?" they wondered.

"Think about the lines 'simple operation' and 'letting a little air in,'" I told them. Holly tentatively ventured, "Abortion?" and discussion took off.

It was time to write. I asked students to brainstorm general topics important in female-male relationships. They generated these and more: obsession, trust, deception, cheating, money, dating, abuse, sex, jealousy, possessiveness. From there I asked that they generate four to five specific stories they could tell related to some of the topics on the larger list. Once they had a smaller, more personal list, I told them to describe the two they'd most enjoy writing about, explaining briefly how each would unfold. I collected those, starred the one I thought most promising, and wrote each student a brief note. Then they drafted the story that most interested them—whether it was the one I liked best or not.

Most students wrote exceptional stories, dialogue driving their plots. The best ones were either personal narratives or fiction based on fact. Some of the purely fictitious pieces became too fantastic, as had some of their earlier dialogues. (Yes, jealousy and deception can lead to bloodshed, but since they hadn't in my students' lives, those stories didn't ring true.) While students drafted, over a period of several days, I presented short minilessons based on the reading I was doing in Tom's graduate class. Ralph Fletcher's book, *What a Writer Needs*, offered some of the best ideas. Chapter Seven, "Beginnings," suggests different kinds of leads from "dramatic" to "leisurely" (1993, pp. 82–84). I shared some of these with students and am certain they paid off. Not one story began, "It all started when . . ."

Angie followed Fletcher's suggestion about "starting at the end":

> "Look, I'm wearing the shirt you got me for Christmas," Brian said as I stood in front of him with my oversized book bag on one shoulder and a pile of books gathered at my chest. I just stood there and smiled. These were the first words spoken between us in close to a week. I began walking past him on my way out of the biology room as we brushed shoulders gently. I didn't want to touch him. I knew if I would ever touch him again, memories of him, or should I say us, would start rolling back, and sure enough, the next bell during English class, I began thinking about our past.

Angie engages me immediately, letting me hear Brian and see her—encumbered by books and backpack and memories. Her story promises to explain the week of silence broken by Brian's words. Angie adds tension when her narrator fails to respond to Brian's attempt at reconciliation. The story itself was Angie's response. It proved painful to write. Tears welled up in her eyes when we talked about her draft. I even hinted that perhaps not enough distance existed between her relationship and the story, but Angie was determined to write. Though painful for her, this piece was one of the best I received, because though she fictionalized the names, the story was her own.

We discussed endings in class, too. Once again, Fletcher's book proved helpful. At the beginning of Chapter Eight, he quotes Eudora Welty: "I think the end is implicit in the beginning" (p. 91). The memories triggered in Angie's lead result in this conclusion:

> I wish I could end on a happy note, like I talked him into going to a rehab center or something, but it is all really sad. Sad that Brian is a stupid teenage boy wasting his life away

to drugs, and sad for me that I was stupid enough to stay with him for four months.

Angie Richter, grade 11

Angie doesn't glamorize what happened, as a number of students did in their endings. Her boyfriend's drug use drove a wedge between them that only deepened with time. Writing the story allowed Angie the objectivity to analyze what had happened; fictionalizing it provided her a dose of the therapy she needed.

Holly, too, profited from our minilessons over leads and conclusions in her story, "Cheaters Never Win":

Lead
"John, what if Michael finds out? He'll kill us! You have to leave now or else you are going to mess things up for us. Please, John!"
Conclusion
"Michael, I . . ."
    "Save your breath for the judge."

Holly Clay, grade 12

Holly's story develops too quickly. Her characters, Kara and Michael, need to talk more about the dissolution of their marriage. Despite the paper's shortcomings, Holly's lead and conclusion are satisfying. She's developing as a writer.

Another minilesson that worked revolved around a piece of advice novelist Richard Price gave Fletcher when he was enrolled in one of Price's writing courses: "The bigger the issue, the smaller you write . . . You don't write about the horrors of war. No. You write about a kid's burnt socks lying on the road" (p. 49). I wasn't sure Price's advice penetrated any of my students' consciousness, but as I reread Larrisa's writing, I'm convinced it did.

Larrisa's story begins in the hot month of August:

A kitchen. Plenty of windows that light streams through. Blue walls and white counters. Cows. Cow towels, cookie jars, and pot holders. A girl who just turned sixteen the previous winter. Yet reluctant to get her license. Her mother scrubbing the vegetables for dinner.

Though the story is about an evolving relationship, the girl's reluctance resurfaces at the end.

> It is February. It is cold. And Laura still has no license.
>
> *Larrisa Breeze, grade 11*

I didn't pay the license much attention the first time I read Larrisa's story; I got caught up in the relationship. As I read it now, though, I see that the license is no small thing, but symbolic of the girl's relationship, which, like the weather, has grown cold. Larrisa wrote "smaller" to reflect larger issues, just as Price had advised, a sophisticated move on her part.

Kristin uses a house to represent a relationship, and though there isn't one particular recurring detail as there was in Larrisa's piece, Kristin extends the metaphor through the story. Her characters talk about their dreams:

> "Do you remember how we would try to decide which rooms would be for our children? Or how we would decorate them? I remember we sat in the wallpaper store . . ."
>
> "Forever," she said interrupting. "We could never decide if we wanted the border with the clown print or the one with different animals."

Later, the main character Sandra says,

> "I used to think about this house as our life. It had been here forever. It was sturdy. Never falling apart. Sometimes it would need a new coat of paint, or the back porch steps fixed, but it would always be standing, stable."
>
> "I'm sorry," Tim said.
>
> "There's no reason to be sorry. We just have our own worlds. Our own separate houses."
>
> "I know what you mean. I guess our house needed too many repairs."

Besides using the house as a metaphor for the relationship, Kristin repeats an important word in her lead and her conclusion: "forever." They sat in the wallpaper store "forever" dreaming about their future; the house had been there "forever." Their relationship, ironically, wouldn't last as long.

In her semester portfolio Kristin writes,

> I won't lie. I've never really been good at writing dialogue. I didn't really have a choice in the matter, though . . . As I started writing this piece, the words just began flowing onto the paper. At first glance, you'll probably wonder, "How is this about a high school student?" True, it is about a married couple, but the problems they deal with apply to the relationship that I am currently in. For example, in the story it shows how the couple slowly drifts apart and becomes less trusting of each other. This also began happening in my own relationship, so I transposed my own personal experiences into the relationship of the story.
>
> *Kristin Leder, grade 11*

Kristin zeroes in on the factor that I believe made these stories work and the original dialogues fail: personal experiences grounded these pieces in reality. Instead of fantasies or commercials, the students' own lives spurred their writing, even if they wrote fiction.

Kevin is a prime example. He has never been a particularly strong student; in fact, he's failed my class before. He doesn't fit into any social group in school. In his journal he writes that he hates it here. Sometimes students ridicule him, question his sexuality. He's a senior who just wants out.

After sharing a passage from Fletcher's book about "The Art of Specificity," which shows the extent of a drug problem at a local high school without ever mentioning the word "drugs" (p. 49), Kevin caught on and transferred the lesson to his story, which was based on one of his relationships:

> Kara notices Steve clinching his fist and the thumping of his foot on the floor. Steve sees her rolling her eyes and turning the wheel real fast on sharp turns. "I swear if you turn another corner like that, I'm making you get out and I'll drive," said Steve.
>
> *Kevin Jones, grade 12*

Kevin shows the tension between the couple without ever mentioning anger or frustration. The rest of his story developed that tension and rang so much truer than the earlier dialogue he'd written at the beginning of this unit. Most of my students wrote stories more realistic than their earlier collaborations. I think their stories were successful for these reasons:

1. They related to the models I shared.
2. The group brainstorming sparked possible topics.
3. The independent brainstorming personalized those topics.
4. The brief descriptions they wrote, to which I responded, offered immediate feedback.
5. The minilessons provided helpful writing strategies.
6. They were immersed in their topic through texts and talk.

When my students turned in their "final" drafts, I wrote comments in the margins, usually questions, and then some sort of summary response. Most papers earned A's and B's. Because I'm concerned about editing, I also put a check mark at the end of the first ten lines where I noticed mistakes, if they'd made that many errors in the paper. If students made more than ten mistakes, I didn't want to demoralize them or so divert their attention away from content that they became more concerned with fixing mistakes than with telling their stories. I want them to realize both are important. Before I passed papers back, I asked Kristin if I could share one of her college papers with the rest of the class.

Kristin is a student who just entered my class second semester after a "totally frustrating" experience with English at a local community college. At the end of her sophomore year, she opted to take a college English course her junior year instead of one of the courses offered at Lockland. (This is the same Kristin who used the "house" metaphor to describe a relationship.) Kristin was happy to share her paper. In fact, she gave me two, and pointed out a comment on one about her paper saying "next to nothing." The college instructor had bled red ink all over Kristin's paper noting mistakes, stylistic preferences, and editorial comments such as the one Kristin showed me.

I wanted students to realize that not everyone responds to student writing the way my colleague Linda Tatman and I do. I told them I thought this instructor's responses were inexcusable and shared what Kristin had said after getting her first paper back: "I'm disgusted and never want to write again." As an English teacher, I realize my responsibility to help students learn standard written English. I constantly struggle with how best to do that. At the same time, if my responses convince students they should never write again, how will I ever have the opportunity to teach them the conventions of written English? Students must want to write again.

I shared another story with this class. A few years ago Bob failed my class first semester. At that time we had a course scheduled second semester for first-semester failures. Bob was my only student in that makeup class. One on one, Bob was fine. He was cynical and lazy but bright as well, and as my only student, he decided to do his work. Bob never gave me a break—the luxury of an extra free period. He was there every day.

On one occasion I asked him to write a persuasive letter about any topic directed to the audience of his choosing. He wrote about open lunch and addressed his letter to the high school principal. Bob poured himself into his draft, working harder than he had all semester. I think he truly believed he could persuade the principal to reinstate open lunch, which had been discontinued several years before.

Bob was so excited when he finished his first draft, he couldn't contain himself. His writing was competent, but his draft contained some careless errors. "Can I go see Mr. Heller now?" he asked. I decided not to squelch his enthusiasm.

"Sure," I replied.

Bob ran from the room and found the principal walking down the hall. He showed his letter to Mr. Heller, who immediately reached for the pen propped behind his right ear and began marking the mistakes that glared at him. When Bob returned to the room, he was cursing. "I can't stand that man. I never want to see him again."

I told students this story—not naming the principal, who had left several years before—so they'd know some readers never get past mistakes no matter how worthy the content.

On that note, I passed back their papers, and told students to read my comments and attempt to correct the errors in the lines I'd checked. I walked around the room helping anyone who invited me. Out of this work, spontaneous minilessons were born.

"Mr. Gaughan, what's wrong with this?" Bobby asked me.

Bobby's first line read, "Jake quit." A good lead, I thought. What did he quit—a job, a sport, school? I wanted to read on. Why had I checked this line? His second line read, "Why? We haven't messed around in a long time." Bobby's mistake was a common one, particularly since many students were unfamiliar with writing dialogue; many had used direct address in their papers but didn't know how to punctuate it. I told Bobby where he needed a comma and used this example to help other students see how much difference one comma can make.

Another lesson comes from Kevin's paper. He had written, "Kara notices Steve clinching his fist and the thumping of his foot on the floor." Although I hadn't checked this line, I had suggested Kevin consider "tightening." Becky realized that cutting *the* and *of* "sounded better." Parallel constructions do sound better even when we can't name them.

I continue learning from students as I attempt to teach writing. I never know how they'll react to my comments. Like most writing teachers, I often doubt that students even read them. No doubt about Sarah, though. Her story is about a teenage girl attending her first fraternity party, a bit wary, but eager nonetheless. When a young frat man says, "I expect sex, especially when I'm drunk," I wasn't surprised that Sarah's character responds, "Well, sorry, your luck just ran out."

At the end of the story, as the girl is about to leave, the boy apologizes and the girl agrees to stay: "Jay smiled. Angel grinned. The front door closed." I wrote, "Excellent writing! I'm not sure I believe the end, though." This was one of the best papers I'd ever seen Sarah write even if I didn't find her conclusion convincing. When I collected her paper after Sarah had corrected mistakes, I noticed she'd written a new ending:

Jay smiled. Angel walked out. The front door closed.

Sarah Noelcke, grade 11

Should I be happy? She obviously read my comments, but is this new ending hers or mine? Sarah's conclusion suggests that teachers can shape student writing, with either positive or negative effects. We shape students, too, not just their writing. If I'm honest, I have to admit that my response to Sarah's conclusion communicates more than my reaction to her writing; my values are embedded in my comments. Perhaps talking to Sarah about Angel and the values she wanted to communicate through her character would have been a better tack to take.

To help students think about how relationships shape young men and women, I asked them to write reflective memos when we finished this unit. Mike, I discovered, took our discussion about "The Girls in Their Summer Dresses" out of the classroom and into his own relationship. Like most of the male students, he thought it permissible to look but not touch:

> I asked my girlfriend about it. Boy did I get an earful. I really don't think that it is all that bad if you look as long as you don't break your neck to try to look, but that's not what Tara said. She said that it was rude to be out with one person, then stare at someone else. After listening to this I had to sit there for a minute to think about what it would feel like to be out with a girl and have her stare at another guy. I wouldn't want it to happen. So maybe the woman [in the story] did have something to worry about.
>
> *Mike Foster, grade 12*

During our discussion of Shaw's story, Mike had commented that the man in the story was only trying to get his wife "off his back," that she had nothing to worry about. Putting himself in his girlfriend's shoes made him rethink the story.

From Angie's letter, I learned that her father had been a "druggie," shedding more light on the story she'd written:

> Writing the story helped me come to terms with our break-up . . . Before I was making excuses for him, now I feel like he hurt me for no reason, so I shouldn't feel sorry for him, but do worry about him . . .
>
> *Angie Richter, grade 11*

Writing about her relationship proved therapeutic for Angie. Commenting upon that writing placed her story in a larger context for me, and probably for her, too. Juxtaposing her relationship with her father and her boyfriend in her memo explains why her boyfriend's drug use upset her as much as it did. Angie's father left her when she was six.

Finally, commenting upon "This Is Serious," the dialogue that prompted our detour, Katie writes, "[the conversation] is all too familiar . . . I've always been able to relate to guys better when we are just friends . . . but when it comes to boyfriends and sex, I get totally confused" (Katie Bass, grade 11).

Brigid writes that "This Is Serious" explains the pressures placed on females in relationships:

> She asked if he loved her; he replied, "What does love have to do with it? Everybody's doing it." Exactly what a woman doesn't want to hear . . . Towards the end of the dialogue, the male uses that catchy phrase, "If you loved me you would." All she has to say is "What's love got to do with it?" Strong woman.
>
> *Brigid Erwin, grade 11*

In the syllabus for this course, I tell students I want them to articulate what they believe about gender and to explore the origin of those beliefs. Though we detoured from our original route, students still expressed their feelings about gender and traced their origins. Angie's relationship with her father shapes her relationship with her boyfriend: she didn't want to be hurt again. Mike's relationship with his girlfriend informs his reading of Shaw's story: initially he thought it acceptable to look at other women in the presence of his girlfriend, but when he imagines her looking at other guys, he reconsiders.

Writing this chapter helped me reflect on the impact of immersion. Being immersed in reading *Writing with Passion* and *What a Writer Needs*, teaching Women and Men, writing new assignments sparked by reading, commenting on students' papers, and reflecting on all of this now helps break down the walls between taking classes, teaching, and living. I realize how my interaction with students and colleagues shapes my teaching and learning.

In the same way students were immersed in reading and writing about relationships. But they weren't just reading and writing *about* relationships; they were constructing those relation-

162

ships through their reading and writing. Mike and Heather read the relationship between the couple in Shaw's story differently because of their gender; Angie wrote the "truth" of her relationship as she made sense of her own and her boyfriend's actions, especially in light of her relationship with her father. Immersion is the key. Just as I had been immersed in reading, writing, and teaching, so had my students been immersed in thinking about relationships.

If we want to break down walls between living and learning in our students' lives, we need to immerse them in topics that concern them both in and out of school. Angie and Mike broke down walls; the rest of our students can, too.

CHAPTER 8

Reflecting on Gender: Analyzing Discourse, Composing Portfolios

"Water boils at 212 degrees Fahrenheit, right?" I ask students in my Women and Men class.

"Right," they agree; 212 degrees is the boiling point of water. What they forget, though, or maybe never knew, is that altitude affects boiling point: at sea level water boils at 212 degrees, but not at ten thousand feet above sea level.

After that example from science, they try on this one from math: "The sum of the angles of an equilateral triangle equals 180 degrees." Most students remember this theorem, so they agree it's true. In this example, though, students limit their thinking to the Euclidean model of plane geometry. When I hold up a large beach ball I've hidden behind my desk and show them the equilateral triangle taped on its surface, one point at the pole, two on the equator, it isn't hard to convince them that these three right angles total 270 degrees.

I "test" students with questions similar to this early in the semester, then ask them to freewrite. "Why," I say, "would an English teacher ask you to take such a test in a course called Women and Men?"

Michael writes,

So we can become more open-minded. We are conditioned by society to think certain ways, and one of those ways is that men are dominant. By this test we are expanding our thinking, opening up our minds to new ideas, different ways of thinking. To start us on the right track, Mr. Gaughan has

shown us how we think now. I think that getting rid of feelings [of sexism] is one of the main goals of this course.

Michael Keller, grade 11

Sara adds, "We have set ideas and are unwilling to look beyond the obvious . . . You wanted us to not be so quick to believe."
One of my jobs as an English teacher is challenging students' assumptions. I try to set a reflective tone from the start. Reflection doesn't always come naturally to students. They need
practice. Using journals, memos, and portfolios affords them opportunities for that practice. I was happy to see Michael and Sara
challenging their own assumptions and making connections in
these early reflections.

Discourse Analysis

I've always encouraged my students to talk in class—especially in
large- and small-group discussions—but I'd never asked them to
reflect on the way they talk. Talking before peers in class is a
learned behavior. I've observed my own daughter Amy interact-
ing with friends in our neighborhood and in class at school; she's
two different people. In school she's guarded, carefully weighing
her words, less willing to speak. At home she chatters with no
trace of self-consciousness.

The same holds true for my high school students, but it
seems I have to relearn this lesson every year when a new group
of ninth-graders enters my classroom. We sit in a circle and I in-
vite them to talk. They avert their eyes, giggle, pick up pens and
doodle—anything to avoid making fools of themselves in front of
me and their peers. Of course, every group has one or two self-
assured young people who plunge into the icy waters of silence
encircled by their desks, but even these students are unaccustomed to participating in the kind of dialogue I have in mind.
One key component is listening—listening so they can respond
intelligently to classmates, make assertions, support them, challenge others, push themselves and their peers to learn more
about a particular topic.

Whatever these students do when they graduate, learning to
talk will benefit them—whether it be in a college classroom, on

the job, at a community meeting, or coaching their daughter's soccer team.

Usually by the second semester of their ninth-grade year, students are much more comfortable dipping into class conversations. Since there are only two high-school English teachers at Lockland Senior High, chances are good they'll take another class or two from me when they're juniors or seniors. By then most of them look forward to class discussions.

Still, I wondered if students were aware of *how* they talk to one another, especially in the presence of the opposite sex. I decided to find out. Students in my Women and Men class agreed to an experiment. For one period that week, only females could speak; the following day, only males. Those of us not speaking would observe, take notes, and reflect upon what we learned. I insisted upon unanimous agreement for this experiment and got it.

Students had read a packet of poems about mother-daughter relationships before these classes met. Their charge was to discuss the poems and their observations. I transcribed the discussions and include short excerpts from each:

Females

Misty F.: We're supposed to run the show ourselves.

Amy: It's about time!

Paulette: I want to start with the introduction, where it says "the birth of a daughter has been seen as a kind of failure or disappointment in our patriarchal society" (Lifshin 1978, p. ix).

JaVonna: Yeah, I agree.

Several others nod their agreement or verbally agree.

Paulette: I'd like to talk about "Fish Story" (Olds, p. 17).

She reads the poem.

Misty F.: I think it's about a mother bearing her child.

Paulette: I think it's sick the way she's looking at her own daughter naked in the tub.

Amy: I think it's sad. She feels she's losing her attachment to her daughter, a "shrimp in her sea" (Olds, p. 17).

Missy: This poem reminds me of "Abuse" (Steinbergh, p. 27).

Everyone turns to the poem and Missy reads.

JaVonna: The mother's frustrated.

Misty F.: A lot of mothers get frustrated with having to deal over and over again with a crying child.

Paulette: That's no reason to abuse it.

Misty F.: I'm not excusing what she does.

Amy: Your privacy is taken away when you have a kid. I don't think society understands what it's like to be a mother.

Misty F.: I don't know how I'll react when I have a child.

Misty G.: Aren't you scared you'll yell at your kid, maybe even hit 'em?

Misty F.: Yeah, and they'll call 421-KIDS.

Paulette: Then they shouldn't have a baby.

Amy: But nobody knows what's gonna happen. Nobody would ever have a baby if they worried about everything that could happen.

JaVonna: I'm the oldest in my family, and I think parents try stuff out on the oldest and then try not to make the same mistakes on the younger kids.

Amy: Yeah, like a trial run.

Paulette refers her peers to an article in the packet about mothers and daughters.

Paulette: What do you think of the mother admitting to her daughter, "I'm jealous of you"?

Misty F.: I think fathers are more jealous of their sons than mothers are of their daughters.

Paulette: I think it's more between mothers and daughters.

Amy: I think mothers try to live vicariously through their daughters.

Paulette: Yeah, like mothers try to make their daughter's hair look just like theirs and they dress them up the same way they dress.

Someone makes a leap from a daughter's hair to bald men, and a raucous discussion follows about marrying soon because all men are going to go bald, buying stock in Rogaine and making a bundle; someone suggests that men have hair on their posterior to make up for the lack of it on their heads, then Paulette reminds everyone they've gotten off track, and someone suggests reading "First Menstruation" (Bass, p. 58).
     Crissy reads the poem.

Misty G.: It's sad that she's afraid to talk to her mom about it.
Kristina: When you grow up you stop tellin' your mom some stuff.
Amy: I'm just the opposite. I tell my mom more now.
Misty G.: The older woman in the poem takes the place of the mom.
BELL

     In the next discussion the following day, my student teacher, Mr. B., participated with the male students.

Males

Matt: I think it's true that men see the birth of a daughter as a failure. They want to have a boy they can call "Junior."
Mr. B.: I have a friend named Eric who named his daughter Erica.
Matt: I think it's more than a name. They want to teach their boy sports like football and baseball. They don't want to watch a girl playin' some stupid sport like tennis.
Mark: I don't think it's the first name that matters. Men want a boy so they can carry on the family name.
Mr. B.: What poems did you like?
Justin: I didn't like any of 'em. I thought they were all stupid. Who wants to read a bunch of poems written by women about women? How can we talk about something like "First Menstruation"?
Matt: Maybe it's like boys getting pubic hairs.
Mr. B.: How about reading "First Menstruation," Justin?

Justin reads.

Mr. B.: Do you think males communicate differently with their fathers than females do with their mothers?

Matt: I think when we get pubic hairs, we start thinkin' we're a man.

Mr. B.: Starting to menstruate is a definitive sign of a girl becoming a woman. Is there a similar sign for guys or is it more a series of things?

Matt: With women, their first bra is a sign they're a woman.

Several males nod, but no one comments.

Justin: Look at "Mother, the Same Witch Haunts Us" (Steinbergh, p. 26). It's a woman doin' the same thing to her daughter that her mother did to her.

Mark: What does "sign with blood" mean?

Mr. B.: Do you think that's a reference to menstruation?

Matt: Yeah, that could be it. She has to live the same experience to understand her mother. Women get all sensitive about abuse [referring to earlier lines in the poem]. Guys think they're supposed to take getting hit like it's no big deal. We don't even call it abuse. Women want to have someone to talk to. I think that's why men have worse tempers.

Paul: I like beatin' up on my dad.

BELL

When I finished transcribing these excerpts, I made copies for each member of class. I also included the transcript from Chapter Five, the female-male discussion about war. Students had not seen this transcript before, and I wanted them to read all three before they reflected. (See Figure 8–1.)

I had never done this in any class before, so I was unsure what students would write, what they would see in their own and each other's words. I was prepared for a flop but was pleasantly surprised. Krista entitled her paper "The Conversation Game":

In the first discussion with both sexes about how men supposedly love war, the men and women were basically at each other's throats . . . Everything that was said sparked another

Women and Men: Discourse Analysis

Read the following three discussions, one of which occurred earlier this year in Contemporary Culture. That discussion was open to everyone in class. The second is from Women and Men and was open to females only. The third took place the following day and was open to males only.

As you read, think about the language used by males and females. What assumptions underlie the language? Do you agree with the assumptions that are made? Does the language reveal anything about the speaker?

What differences do you detect from one discussion to another? Do males and females interact differently when speaking in same-sex groups as compared to mixed-sex groups? If so, how?

What conclusions can you draw from these three discussions about males and females, about the way they use language, about the way they interact? Do you think these discussions are typical? In other words, if you observed three other student populations divided the way these were, would the discussions be similar? Would the second and third discussions have been different had there only been females in the room for the second and males in the room for the third?

While you're reading the transcripts, highlight words and phrases that you think will help you answer some of these questions. Note the speakers of these particular lines—who preceded them and who followed?

Write a paper analyzing these three pieces of discourse. Think about how to best organize your thoughts and how to support your conclusions. Be sure to quote specific words and phrases in your paper as part of your support. Try to make this the most thorough analysis you've done all year.

Figure 8–1

argument . . . It was almost like they couldn't wait until the person was finished speaking just so they could pick a fight with them.

In the girls' discussion the talk was more free and flowing. There weren't very many breaks between topic changes and those who talked, did so openly. We talked about everything that could relate to the discussion (except for the hair incident) and still needed more time than we had.

I think our talk went more smoothly because women have always been "allowed" to talk openly. It is expected of us. Throughout time, women have very easily shared their problems with each other. Women are more sensitive and more communicative than men. Because of this our discussion was more unified and we got a lot more ground covered.

In the guys' discussion, I noticed the talk was very stiff and almost forced. There were longer and more periods of silence. It seems like no one really had anything to say . . . No one was very open and everyone seemed cool and aloof. I think the result of their discussion was because of the way they were raised . . . Most guys don't talk much, except about sports and women.

Krista Whitaker, grade 11

Krista notes clear differences among the three discussions. She makes points about flow and tone and awkward moments of silence that the transcripts don't reveal. She theorizes, too, about why the conversations played out as they did: women have been "allowed" to talk openly, at least with each other; they're expected to discuss their problems and respond sensitively to others' needs. Men, on the other hand, have not been socialized to talk about much besides women and sports—and when they talk about women, they don't talk about relationships. So when asked to discuss the assigned poetry, they were essentially on foreign ground.

Perhaps it was unfair to make males respond to mother-daughter poems. Maybe I could have found father-son poems for them. Actually, I hoped the males would use the poems as a catalyst for discussing parent-child relationships.

I thought, too, of how often teachers expect females to empathize with males, assuming females can and will make connec-

tions to their own lives. For years girls read books with male pro-
tagonists with whom teachers expect them to identify. Is it unrea-
sonable to expect male students to make the same leap?

I don't think so, but as evidenced by some of my male students' comments, it is. Angie notes this difference in attitudes in
her reflection:

> Males left the impression that they were superior . . . Matt
> saying, "They [men] don't want to watch a girl playin' some
> stupid sport like tennis." Also, Justin's comment, "Who
> wants to read a bunch of poems written by women about
> women?" Like the poems were not worth their time and
> women are not good enough for them.
>
> When it was females only they said they were scared
> and insecure about the future. They were scared about how
> to treat their kids or what they would end up like. They re-
> ally looked to the future searching for hope and change.
>
> *Angie Holbrook, grade 11*

Tom claims to be "stuck in the middle" of the males and females in this class—his good buddies sit to his right, his girlfriend
to his left. He resents how some of the female students lump all
men together: "So here comes Matt speaking before he thinks," to
which Misty responds that "men are primitive. . . not Matt, but
men." Misty is Tom's girlfriend.

Tom explains that because he feels "stuck" he usually remains silent in class, but writing this reflection provides him a
much-needed forum. He uses his paper to take shots of his own,
shots he feels justified taking:

> I don't like this discussion because females talk about men as
> a whole, not as individuals. I don't like or love war. Like Amy
> said, "Women can separate the game from reality." So can I.
>
> Women are always being discriminated against, but in
> these discussions we're the ones that are primitive, can't
> separate games from reality, nonsentimental, going to go
> bald and have to get hair off our butts to make up for the
> lack of hair on our heads. It just makes me wonder.
>
> *Tom Link, grade 11*

As these conversations transpired, I recorded my observations. Tom rarely spoke, but I could tell he was seething underneath. I'm glad I asked him to reflect on our class discussions; I'm glad Tom's writing makes him wonder.

Justin agrees with Tom in his reflection, claiming some of the female comments were "sexist": particularly he notes at the beginning of the female discussion when Misty says, "We're supposed to run the show ourselves," to which Amy responds, "It's about time":

> They make it sound like the men run everything. If that's the way women feel, I guess that's the way it is.

Interestingly enough, though, Justin does notice a difference in tone between the male-female conversation, which he says was "more of an argument," and the female-only conversation, which was "more of a talk in everyday life":

> They conversed about things they knew about. It wasn't anything new to them, so there wasn't any disagreement.
>
> *Justin Morris, grade 11*

Misty learns something about herself as she analyzes the three discussions. For her the way males and females are socialized clearly makes a difference in the way they talk to each other:

> When reading the discussions, I realized for the first time that women and men talk differently when they're together or separate. I never really believed it. I always thought that I would say what I wanted regardless of gender surroundings. However, through comparing the discussions, I found when women and men are secluded, they tend to be more open. Their opinions are much more "explicit" when there's no one to refute their opinion.

Even though females do refute each other several times in their discussion, Misty doesn't characterize or perceive those comments as threatening. She acknowledges that some disagreement occurred in the same-sex discussions, but she glosses over its significance:

In the [female] group there wasn't much disagreement. We were civil. [We] basically agreed and when we didn't there wasn't a big spat about it.

Misty Frost, grade 11

In *Sounds from the Heart: Learning to Listen to Girls*, Maureen Barbieri admits her own "low tolerance for conflict" (1995, p. 91). At the time Barbieri was teaching seventh grade at an all-girls school near Cleveland, Ohio. When a *New York Times* piece reported that Forrest Carter, author of *The Education of Little Tree* (1976), was a former member of the Ku Klux Klan, Barbieri was as disillusioned as her female students. Instead of promoting "honest discourse," typically one of her primary goals, Barbieri was upset with herself, feeling she taught students not to face disillusionment but to run away from it (p. 98).

I understand her predicament. Little Tree's story is so humane. Why "ruin" students' reading with this piece from the *New York Times*? In the end, Barbieri and her students did discuss Carter and what was being written about him.

Many of Barbieri's female students—and mine—are the "nice girls" Carol Gilligan writes about, "always calm, controlled, and quiet" (Barbieri 1995, p. 61). They want to speak openly but without the discomfort of argument. When we free girls to speak together, removing the pressure many of them feel in coed classrooms, they may be more inclined to express their real feelings. Reflecting upon the female-only conversation, Marie writes, "It was like we knew the guys were there, but we blocked them out. Because of this we could get more personal."

Like Barbieri, I want to promote honest, open discourse in my classroom. I want to create a nonthreatening environment in which students will express what they truly think. I need to be sensitive to males and females and continue to encourage productive dialogue. Maybe showing students how they talk to one another will not only make them more critical, but boost their confidence as well. In the end, all of us must learn to talk together.

Portfolios

Besides reflecting on the way males and females talk to one another in my Women and Men course, I ask students to explore gender roles, stereotyping, sexist language, and male-female relationships. At the end of the semester, they compose course portfolios that allow them the room and distance they need to make sense of the work they've done. I know, though, that students will write more in-depth reflections at the end of the semester if I give them practice reflecting during the semester. So each week I assign two to three reflective journal entries in class—to respond to a discussion, to analyze a fairy tale, to react to an ad—and two entries out of class—to record any related observations about gender they perceive outside the classroom. I want to continue to tear down the walls between the world and school, living and learning. Keeping a journal can help.

Here's an out-of-class entry Tracey wrote:

> It was really weird that I got a job [as a telemarketer] just when we were studying Women and Men in English. During my interview with one of my soon-to-be bosses, he made a remark like "You have that innocent-sounding voice that men can't refuse." I found that very offensive. I mean what does it matter the type of voice I have just so long as I have one at all. Then it made me wonder, if my voice wasn't so "innocent" as he called it, if I would still have gotten the job.
>
> *Tracey Gibson Hoskins, grade 11*

Tammy commented in her journal that a male teacher asked his class, "Do any of you girls have a tissue?," which made her and Jenny roll their eyes, because, she said, she's more aware of stereotypes since she's been taking this class. Students wrote about "Men at Work" signs (even though women made up part of the crew); division of labor (including the minor input men contribute in childbirth); the reality of the glass ceiling in the Cincinnati business community. I'm convinced that giving students practice reflecting upon their work and their world throughout the semester produces more sophisticated portfolio reflections at semester's end.

Dennie Palmer Wolf says in "Portfolio Assessment: Sampling Student Work" that portfolios hold great promise for self-assessment because human beings can be personally demanding and thoughtful when it comes to shaping work that matters to them. She goes on to say that the problem with much school-based assessment is that it actually prevents students from becoming thoughtful respondents to and judges of their own work. The emphasis on objective knowledge, the one-time nature of most exams, and the fact that assessment usually comes from without instead of being a personal responsibility offer students lessons that impair their capacity to thoughtfully judge their own work (Wolf, pp. 35–39).

Portfolios provide students with opportunities to evaluate themselves, to make sense of their own learning. They decide what is important instead of relying on me to test them. Taking charge of evaluation reinforces their learning. They have to articulate not only what they learned but why that learning is significant, how each artifact they include in their portfolios relates to a larger pattern of meaning. In Women and Men, students divide their portfolio into two parts. In Part One they include artifacts that address course content; in Part Two they include samples of memorable writing. The final component of their portfolio is a "Dear Class" letter explaining the significance of each artifact. (See Figure 8–2.)

In Part One of her portfolio, Krista includes questions from the "test" I mentioned at the start of this chapter; a freewriting about gender and authority; notes she took about sexist language; a mother-daughter poem she wrote after reading Mary Brosmer's

---

Women and Men: Portfolio Project

Compose a portfolio of the work you've done this semester that reflects your learning about the following:

1. women and men
2. your writing

Part One

Choose items that clearly show what you've learned: reading that made an impact upon you; notes you've taken; papers you've written; responses to your reading, listening,

---

Figure 8–2

and viewing; newspaper articles you've read; freewritings about discussions you've had with friends or relatives, etc.

Think about your class work first: the quantum logic test, *Fried Green Tomatoes*, the gender discrimination video, *Out of Control*, sexist language, fairy tales, peer evaluation, gender stereotypes, mother-daughter poems, *Of Mice and Men*, same-sex discussions, discourse analysis, sexual harassment, silencing, *Kindred*, *The Color Purple*, violence, "How Far She Went," "The Rape of Mr. Smith," etc.

As you review your work, look for threads that connect what you've done this semester. Put items in your portfolio that reflect those connections.

Part Two

As you review the writing you've done this semester, try to be an objective critic of your own work. Has your writing improved? If so, how? If not, why not? Include pieces in your portfolio that reflect how you have grown or remained static as a writer. Try to show your ability to tackle a range of topics and compose a range of different types of papers. Try also to show depth in your writing by including all the drafts of one piece or by showing your ability to consider closely the complexities of a particular topic.

Letter

Write a two-part letter that explains your learning about (1) women and men, and (2) you as a writer. In the letter explain each item in your portfolio and what it shows about your learning. The letter should be clear, well organized, and truly reflective of your learning. Show how you've grown as a writer by making the letter an interesting and informative piece of writing itself. Your letter should be approximately three to four typewritten pages, double-spaced, equally balanced between Parts One and Two.

Figure 8–2 Continued

"Mama"; a journal response to a class discussion about rape; and a short piece on sexual harassment.

In her letter Krista writes, "I included the test because it shows how much I've learned and how I've grown this semester . . . If you don't know injustice is there, you don't know how and when to look for it."

Krista's second item is a freewriting:

> We were to write about a professor of a college history class. I was the only person [in my class] to make the professor a woman. The reason I did that was because often I look at those in authority and picture them as female. I think that directly relates to the way I was brought up. My parents taught me that women are not less than men, that we are equal [Krista's four siblings are all female]. I was taught that nothing could hold me back just because I was a girl. Not many people are fortunate enough to be raised in a home like I was.
>
> *Krista Whitaker, grade 11*

In this section of her portfolio, Krista includes one artifact from each of the main units we studied: some reading, some writing, notes, and a test. Her letter helps me understand what Krista values. Her mother-daughter poem reinforces what she says above about her family and how fortunate she feels. Krista attributes her teaching Sunday school to the model her mother provided. She understands that all the students in her class are constructed differently by their backgrounds, that maybe they didn't picture a female professor because of the way they've been raised.

Part Two of Kim's portfolio includes an intensely personal piece about a time she fought off a male companion in the front seat of his car. For Kim, the writing was therapeutic.

> My last piece was "Laughing in the Park." This piece was difficult for me to write, but it means a lot to me personally. It helped me to try and deal with the situation and to eventually maybe even let it drift to the back of my mind. This was also my favorite piece. I wrote it even though it caused

some pain to go back and remember what had happened. Yet writing this piece seemed to help somehow.

Kim Frederick, grade 11

When she wrote it earlier in the semester, Kim wasn't willing to share this piece with anyone but me. Still, it was pivotal for her. What we were learning in class about sexual harassment and violence toward women was made immediate for me when Kim summoned the courage to write this memory. It clearly represented Kim's learning; she had to include it in her portfolio.

Colleen includes a one-page story we read called "The Rape of Mr. Smith" (Ruth 1990, pp. 283–284). In her letter she writes,

> By simply comparing rape to a holdup, the author could convince almost anyone of the ridiculousness of implying that a victim "asks" for it when she is raped by not struggling, having a previous history of sexual activity, walking in a certain place at a certain time, or wearing a certain outfit. The sheer cleverness of the writing suggests to me the power of writing to change thinking and force people to look at things in a different way. More than teaching me about culture or myself as a writer, this piece showed me something about writing.

Colleen Joyce, first-year college

Krista, Kim, and Colleen use reflective writing as a tool to evaluate their own emerging literacy. Of the dozens of pieces they could have included, they chose a poem, a narrative, a short story. Sunstein and Potts write,

> Portfolios are a cultural "site": As we mine our personal histories, we can better understand our definitions of literacy. Like an anthropologist in the field, a portfolio keeper begins to see themes in her artifacts as she collects them. Over several revisions and responses from others, those themes begin to shape her understanding of how her own history shapes her literacy. (1993, p. 9)

179

The portfolios aren't for me but for students. In *Horace's School* Ted Sizer writes that portfolios are primarily educational rather than assessment tools. "They are designed to help students rather than to help those who must do such legitimate sorting; they are, at their best, good tools for 'diagnosis.' However, their function is not to measure as much as to guide, and that bias may make measurement more complicated than it would otherwise" (1992, pp. 160–161). Students' portfolios teach them what is important about their learning.

At the same time, I do learn things from their portfolios that I would never have learned without them. For example, Colleen wrote a piece about her relationship with her grandmother, which I read during the semester. That would have been the end of that, but in her portfolio letter I discover more:

> I sent a copy of "Grandma's Final Gift" to my mom and dad. I did not think much of it until my mom called me to tell me how much she loved it. She made copies for all my sisters and all her brothers. That brings me to my fourth artifact, a letter from my Uncle Tom telling me how much he enjoyed it. I could not believe how much everyone in the family liked this paper, and would be lying to say I was not flattered. I realize that they are all biased; they all know and love me and my grandma. Nonetheless, my confidence in my writing was bolstered considerably. I also enjoyed the feeling of knowing I was able to make my family happy with my writing.
>
> *Colleen Joyce, first-year college*

Besides discovering that student writing travels beyond the walls of my classroom, I learn what reading and writing projects worked. If a number of students include positive responses to particular units, I know to continue using that same material. If their responses are negative, I consider adapting it or trying different projects altogether.

Using portfolio evaluation also encourages students to reconsider papers they have written and how they might be improved. I ask that they include all the drafts that went into producing one work of writing. Kenyata writes,

I looked through all of my drafts very carefully. I also had Fonika read the writing over just in case I had overlooked something. Then I revised my paper, taking sentences out that I thought got a little off the subject or that I really just didn't need. I also made a couple of new sentences containing things I thought the reader should know.

Kenyata Guin Packer, grade 9

I found that most students voluntarily collaborated as Kenyata and Fonika did to improve individual papers and help them compose the best portfolio they could. They started to realize the importance of audience and to value the aid of an objective critic. In the process they learned to become more critical of their own work.

I also ask students to focus on two mechanical mistakes that recurred through the semester. Students aren't fond of editing, and I don't think portfolios make them fonder, but composing them can help students focus on conventions.

Leah writes in her letter:

As I was looking over my papers, I found two mechanical mistakes that appeared frequently. They were putting the two words "a" and "lot" together as one word. And using the word "they're" when "their" needs to be used. To eliminate "a lot" of these mistakes, I revised my paper orally to make sure everything sounded okay.

Leah Brown, grade 10

Kelly echoed this strategy:

I've learned that if I read my writing out loud to other people, then I catch more mistakes than just looking and reading it myself. I noticed I have a problem using homonyms. I still get "effect" and "affect" mixed up all the time. I've learned that if I use "affect" as a verb, then I've used it right.

Kelly Parker, grade 10

Portfolios often slap students in the face, waking them up to reflect on their own writing processes, shaking them out of comfortable assumptions. Portfolio reflections help them think about how they think. If the sacred ground of science and mathematics can be challenged, then so can attitudes, beliefs, and behaviors. The test questions at the beginning of this chapter show students that the rules of the game shape the truth, that human consciousness limits what we can know for sure. What's true in plane geometry may not be true in solid geometry. The sun revolved around the earth for years until Copernicus showed up.

Standardized tests and objective criteria can similarly limit what we can know for sure about our students, and they can distort our own attitudes about students' abilities to read and write. Asking students to reflect upon their observations, experiences, and conversations in writing can expand those limits. Composing course portfolios in which students reconsider their work can help teachers learn more about their students, but more importantly, it can help students learn more about themselves.

CHAPTER 9

Taking Charge of Learning

When Max Morenberg, co-director of the Ohio Writing Project, told me I was expected to deliver a fifty-minute presentation to my Project peers, my nervous stomach began churning. It was the summer of 1983, and I'd taught only one year. Now my teacher and colleagues expected me to teach them. What did I know? I had experienced some success with a basic revision activity my first year teaching (actually it was a more of an editing exercise); perhaps I could walk teachers through that and show them the one student example I'd saved that year.

When Max and I discussed my presentation, he suggested I read Nancy Sommers' "Revision Strategies of Student Writers and Experienced Adult Writers" (1984, pp. 328–337). I did—after which I completely revised my presentation.

Ever since, I've been convinced of the importance of sharing my work with other teachers. Just as I constantly revise my teaching, so, too, do I revise my presentations. I've never presented the same topic the same way twice. Something always changes: the audience, the purpose, and me as a teacher-presenter. Each presentation I construct is influenced by these variables.

When I present, I learn more about my teaching, my colleagues, my profession. Each presentation I give is interactive, and each interaction teaches me something new. Working with other teachers, considering their questions, listening to their responses, pushes my thinking, improves my teaching. When presentations go well, my confidence climbs, and I get professionally charged. If presentations can do this for me, why not for my students?

So we talk about presenting and its similarity to writing. Oral presentations, I tell students, must be written first, either word for word as a State of the Union address would be, or outlined as a teacher's lesson plans would be. The process is similar in both cases:

1. Inventing
2. Planning
3. Rehearsing/drafting
4. Revising (in light of rehearsal)
5. Polishing
6. Publishing (in class)

The rhetorical situation is similar, too:

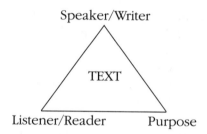

The speakers will be the students presenting; the listeners, their peers and me. The purposes vary depending upon each particular project. The text the students create will not be a paper but a presentation.

After studying two units in Women and Men, one on silencing, the other on violence, students finish the year with an independent project. They must find a creative means, other than writing a paper, to exhibit what they've learned. They can further explore one of the subjects we discussed in class, research a particular aspect of the topic that interests them, conduct interviews, or read additional materials.

Bryan read about victims of date rape and its impact upon them. His motivation for this project emanated from an incident a close friend of his suffered. I knew Bryan to be sensitive to others' feelings—he hated conflict in class—so I wasn't surprised he wanted to aid his good friend. I was also aware of Bryan's musical ability. I didn't know, though, that he could compose.

For Bryan's final presentation, he wrote the music and lyrics for "Torn Up Inside":

She came up to me in tears.
I wanted to reach out.
But it seemed as if she couldn't tell me
how she felt.
So I kept on talking,
hoping she would tell me why.
I knew something was wrong.
You could see it in her eyes.
I noticed the bruises
that she had on her face.
And when I tried to touch her,
she pushed me away.
She just shook there
like someone in the cold night.
What can I do for her
tonight?

Refrain
Torn up inside,
wishing that someone would be a friend.
But no one could understand
how she felt.
So all that she did
was hold it in.
Hoping that no one
would find out.

She began to talk to me
about that night.
She told me that
she wanted to die.
I didn't know what to say
to her.
Should I talk
or not say a word?

She told me that she tried
to push him away.
That's when I knew
what happened on that date.
I told her that she always
had a friend,
but I knew inside her torture
would not end.

Refrain

Bryan Harrison, grade 12

Bryan synthesizes the last two units of this class into his song. His friend was silenced—"all she did was hold it in"—as was he: "Should I talk or not say a word?" Bryan experienced the distance date rape creates—And when I tried to touch her, she pushed me away"—and the confusion that follows: "What can I do for her tonight?" Bryan asked us to respond in writing to the lyrics of his song and to share our own responses. He explained his composing process and discussed his research, which included reading several essays and interviewing a rape crisis counselor, all of which culminated in the music and lyrics of "Torn Up Inside."

Bryan appeared at my classroom door with a portable electric piano, which he placed on several desktops at the front of the room. When he began to play, my easily distracted fourth-period students quickly focused on the words and music. Bryan's voice evoked the emotional pain and personal torment expressed in his lyrics; his piano accompaniment established the mood. When he played his last note, students applauded spontaneously. All of us knew we'd witnessed a bright moment.

I wished I'd videotaped Bryan's performance. I wanted other audiences to witness the possibilities. The next day I approached Bryan about repeating his song. He wasn't able to get the piano for fourth period but did later in the day. Members of seventh bell hadn't been studying women and men but could still appreciate Bryan's composition. Not surprisingly, their response matched fourth period's . . . and I got it on tape.

Students create all sorts of ways to publicize their projects. Nioka designed a trifold pamphlet for victims of abuse complete with phone number for a women's crisis center in Cincinnati. Vicky created a montage of photographs and magazine cutouts depicting differences between lust and love. Nicole and Janette wrote and performed a play about a wrestler using steroids and purging himself to "make weight." Jackie and Charity put Calvin Cathy from Rosa Guy's *The Friends* (1974) on trial for abuse. Tara, reserved and far from popular, played several parts in the "radio" ad she wrote with such lack of inhibition, I couldn't believe she was the same person. Her peers were so impressed they vocalized their approval and applauded her performance.

In *Horace's School* Ted Sizer writes,

> Going to school is practicing to use one's mind well. One does not exercise one's mind in a vacuum; one rarely learns to "think" well with nothing but tricky brainteasers or questions embedded in a context that is neither realistic nor memorable. One needs to stimulate its exercise with engaging ideas in an equally engaging setting." (1992, pp. 25–26)

Creating that engaging setting is a constant struggle teachers face with each new year and each new class. Maintaining that setting for an entire year or even a semester is nearly impossible. It's difficult to be engaged ourselves five or six periods a day, 180 days a year. Students find it just as difficult.

Still, if we consider the many talents our students bring to our English classrooms, and are willing to let students take charge of their learning, we may find ourselves and our students engaged more often. Consider Mark and Mike.

Each fall when spirit week precedes the annual homecoming festivities, we count on the two of them to "dress out": one day as a couple of "dorks" from *Revenge of the Nerds;* the next as color-coordinated superheroes. Both like to draw; both like to dress; both like attention.

It comes as no surprise, then, that when given the opportunity to draw and dress for class, Mark and Mike swallow the bait. After studying how advertisers manipulate consumers in Contemporary Culture (see Mark's analysis of Lady Godiva Liqueur in Chapter Five), students were given a number of options for their final presentation.

Mark and Mike chose to sell a difficult product (ask former President Bush) to a target audience not inclined to clamor for it the way they would Barbie dolls or Power Rangers. Broccoli. How to sell that, I wondered?

Their prewriting included an illustrated story board depicting six scenes:

1. A long-haired Dr. Frankenstein–like creature (resembling Mark) transforms the last subject, a pigtailed child, into a member of his "mutant army."
2. A bald mutant emerges from a transformation machine.
3. A caped crusader proclaiming himself "Broccoli Man" surges unexpectedly onto the scene.
4. The doctor commands his patient, "Get him!"
5. Broccoli Man transforms the mutant back to her former self.
6. The doctor succumbs to Broccoli Man, who instructs kids, "Make broccoli part of your day!"

On presentation day Mark and Mike dress before class begins and wait in the hall for their performance. Mark enters class first dressed in a white lab coat, long unkempt hair jutting out from his head. His subject—a peer who volunteered—follows behind. Laughing demonically he begins his experiment, its ultimate goal the demise of Broccoli Man. Mike bursts into the room, dressed in pea-green tights, long green cape flowing behind, his head covered with a Halloween "mask" right out of the movie that bears the same name.

Would such an ad get younger viewers' attention? Is the genre one with which they're familiar—evil antagonist seduces young innocents, who can be saved by the only superhero powerful enough to battle the forces of darkness? Of course. Is it responsible advertising? Probably not. Mark and Mike's ad reinforces the violence kids witness in Saturday morning cartoons. Will it sell broccoli? Better than any ad I can imagine. Have Mark and Mike learned anything about the world of advertising? I think so.

I believe what Tom Romano says in *Clearing the Way* about "good faith participation": students "must write and interact with that writing . . . share the work of their peers, talk about their writing processes and choices . . . [and] practice . . . the craft they are learning" (1987, p. 127). In other words, students must immerse themselves in classroom projects, making assignments their own, maximizing their potential as learners. Some critics might call this "broccoli" project fluff. I doubt Mark and Mike would. Neither would I. When more traditional academic projects cross their paths, Mark and Mike can take charge.

Teachers need to create space in their classes for students to capitalize on talents and other intelligences that don't traditionally reside under the umbrella of English/Language Arts. I need constant reminders myself. When we do give students room to present their talents, talents we aren't aware they possess, we're often pleasantly surprised. As an evaluator I have to keep in mind that student presentations are more about process than assessment. I have trouble quantifying the learning of Mark and Mike's skit or Bryan's song, but if Sizer is right, students learn to think well when they're engaged.

Providing students with more opportunities to take charge of their learning continues to drive my pedagogy. That doesn't mean I neglect them or fail to intervene in their learning process. Most students are willing to take charge, but they need support. They don't want to be thrown into the pool without a "learning preserver" floating nearby. Before students begin presentations, I tell them they should consider the following as part of their preparation:

1. The point
2. The means by which they will make that point clear (role-playing, panel discussion, talk show, dramatization, debate, mock interview with author/character)
3. Strategies to engage their audience (asking us to write, to listen, to think, to discuss, to view)
4. An interesting lead
5. A memorable conclusion
6. A balanced presentation (members should share equally in preparation and presentation)

When we had nearly finished *The Education of Little Tree* (1976) in my American Dream class, Vicky, Robert, and Angie led a fifty-minute discussion over pages 161–216. (See Figure 9–1.)
They chose to outline their presentation in four segments

Education and the American Dream:
The Education of Little Tree

As you read this novel, write down page numbers of Little Tree's significant educational experiences; then jot a quick note to yourself about each experience (e.g., on p. 10 Little Tree learns about people using flags to justify taking more than their share). After every third note, choose one of the educational experiences and write a one-page response. Write about the educational experience itself, when you learned something similar and from whom, and any other connections you can make that relate to Little Tree's experience and your own. These entries will be important for class discussion.

You and a partner will sign up to lead discussion once during the reading of the novel. You can use your written responses and your classmates' as one way to spark discussion; you should also consider other related educational issues that you've experienced or observed. Each group is responsible for bringing in one or two related readings from outside of class. (Start reading *Time, Newsweek, The Cincinnati Enquirer* and other publications for articles about education.) You should copy the articles for each member of the class and tie in the outside reading to the book.

Think about how you can focus the discussion and keep the class interested and involved. You might have us write, read, or role-play. Think about what you want us to get out of your presentation, then design activities that will help us realize your expectations. Keep thinking about how education relates to the American Dream. You will have the entire class period to make your points.

Please type a one-page agenda of the activities you have planned (list your purpose, significant page numbers from the book and brief notes, outside articles that you consulted, planned activities and the order in which they will occur).

Take charge of your learning and have fun with this!

Figure 9–1

and divide up the speaking responsibilities among the three of them. Vicky opened by sharing the poem "A Philosophy" by Grantland Rice and having her peers discuss the poem's relationship to the novel.

Angie and Robert chose passages they believed most significant from this section of the book and solicited student response. Then Vicky played a recording of Kenny Loggins' "Conviction of the Heart" and asked her peers why they thought her group included this song as part of their presentation.

Their final activity asked students to imagine themselves as Little Tree and respond in their journals to one of the following prompts:

1. You and your grandpa are walking through town after making a run to the Crossroads store to sell your whiskey. While walking down the street, you become interested in your surroundings. You aren't paying attention and end up running into a white woman. She proceeds to yell and scream accusing that you were trying to grab at her body and that you and your grandpa tried to attack her.
2. After a few years you find yourself going to a school. It is a school for minorities. You notice that there are not only Native Americans there, but Mexican and African Americans as well. These are two of groups of people you have never seen before.

In this novel the orphaned Little Tree learns more from his Native American grandparents about surviving in the natural and human world than any white institution could possibly teach him. He learns a life philosophy his grandpa names "The Way."

Robert, Angie, and Vicky explore Little Tree's learning in their presentation by asking their peers to compare their reading of the novel with two new readings. They engage the class immediately by having them read and respond and end by asking them to imagine and write. They help their peers empathize with Little Tree and, in the process, achieve new understanding.

In each of my classes I ask students to accept more responsibility for their learning by teaching their peers. Group presentations can last anywhere from ten minutes to an entire period. This spring one group of ninth-graders conducted firsthand research on interracial dating. They videotaped interviews with their peers, the principal, and Carlsie's father; they wrote a script set in a restaurant with two couples, one white, one black and white; they read articles and chapters from a book they found in the library; they wrote questions and scenarios to which they had their classmates respond. They dimmed the classroom lights, set up desks with linen tablecloths, lit candles, played soft jazz, and acted out their script, raising the primary problems interracial couples confront: acceptance from friends and family, peer pressure to date within their own race, the psychological pressures to conform. So engaged was the audience, the group asked if they could continue their presentation the following day. We all agreed.

As students witness their peers' presentations and as they practice presenting themselves, the quality of their own presentations improve. So pleased have I been with most of this student work, I decided upon a radical idea for my Contemporary Culture class. Instead of giving students a syllabus the first day of class outlining week by week the subjects and activities we would explore, I gave them a list of possibilities and asked them to check those they'd be most interested in studying:

_____ Family	_____ Journalism	_____ Race
_____ Education	_____ Violence	_____ TV/Film
_____ Sexuality	_____ Health Care	_____ Music
_____ Propaganda	_____ Patriotism	_____ Advertising

After selecting the six most popular topics, students chose the unit they wanted to teach with three or four of their peers. We spent the first week or so planning and conducting preliminary research. I shared folders of materials I'd collected over the years related to each topic; we visited the public library to find more. (See Figure 9–2.)

Keeping in mind the importance of the "learning preserver," I modeled the first unit and made my teaching explicit to students. Besides engaging students in the topic, I wanted them to

Contemporary Culture and Mass Media: Group Project Unit Plans

Plan a unit on the topic your group chose to study in Contemporary Culture. Your plan must be typed and include the following:

1. Resources—list the title of each article, song, movie, book, poem, story, etc.

2. Activities—list each activity you will use during your unit: brainstorming, freewriting, role-playing, reading, discussing, writing, viewing, etc.

3. Evaluation—list each way you will check your classmates' understanding—debates, papers, quizzes, etc. There must be at least one paper for each unit that may be any of the following types: persuasive, narrative, explanatory, drama, short story.

4. Rationale—a one- to two-page typed rationale should explain your purpose, strategies, and reasons for teaching as you've decided.

A preliminary plan is due before you begin the unit; a final plan is due when the unit is complete. The final plan should include additions and changes—new resources, activities, and forms of evaluation. Explain what you changed and why. This final plan should be submitted in a pocket folder and include all the handouts used during your unit.

Considerations:

1. What are the most important issues you will address during your unit? (For example, with music you might want to examine censorship, the objectification of women, or how particular cultures are reflected in different types of music.)

2. How will you engage the class each day? (That is, what will you have them do to sustain their interest and, at the same time, give them the opportunity to learn something about English, contemporary culture, and mass media?)

3. Who will be in charge of each activity? Who will make copies (before class)? Who will lead discussion? Who will type handouts? Who will assemble the preliminary and final plans?

Figure 9–2

understand why I was doing what I was doing. I'd never taught a unit on AIDS before, but had just read Alice Hoffman's *At Risk* (1988) that summer and thought it might be a novel students would read. The story revolves around an eleven-year-old girl who contracts HIV through a blood transfusion. (I had budgeted money the spring before for a class set of paperbacks but hadn't committed to a title.) The topic of AIDS is one I believed would engage students.

I typed a list of resources and gave students a copy:

At Risk, Alice Hoffman

"A Day with a Global Killer," *The Philadelphia Inquirer*

"The Dilemma of a Good Samaritan," Michael Perry, *Newsweek*

And the Band Played On, HBO (1993)

On the first day of the unit, we brainstormed myths about AIDS, which included these:

1. AIDS is a gay disease.
2. AIDS is God's punishment for homosexuality and promiscuity.
3. AIDS can be contracted from toilet seats.

The next day we did what a colleague of mine at Miami University, Karen Powers-Stubs, calls "round-robin journal responding." Students write for several minutes in their own journals, make eye contact with a peer who finishes when they do, trade journals, and respond to their peer's comments. This continues through three or four rounds, students carrying on a dialogue with several peers in writing. In this case students explored the myths they'd generated and how they believed the myths were constructed.

We read Hoffman's novel and noted how different characters perpetuated some of the myths we explored. *At Risk* is particularly effective at showing the emotional and psychological effects of all those "exposed" to a person with AIDS.

When we weren't reading or discussing *At Risk*, we examined other perspectives (magazine and newspaper articles, a film) and, for our final activity, role-played in class. For this role-playing a student in the school district is diagnosed HIV positive and the board of education must decide how to deal with that student and her family. Students assume the following roles: board of education members, the infected student and her family, administrators, the student's peers, and concerned citizens from the community.

In small groups students spent fifteen minutes brainstorming what they believed each group would say. Then we held the meeting. Students wholeheartedly acted their parts, with such vigor in some cases that I'm convinced they weren't acting. The intensity of the board meeting rose as prejudices freely flowed. Students learned about the complexities and difficulties such a dilemma presents.

When the unit was complete, students were to detail their learning in writing. Here's part of what Dana wrote:

> I have to admit, I used to immediately associate the AIDS virus with homosexuality. The book *At Risk* gave me a different perspective . . . I learned about its effect on innocent children. The role-playing activity involving the Board of Education and a family's fight to keep their child in school was an enriching activity. Playing the role of the child with AIDS gave me a chance to "try on another person's shoes." Believe it or not I really felt offended . . .
>
> *Dana Baynard, grade 12*

On the final day of this unit, I explained to students my rationale and purpose: to explode some of the myths they generated on day one. We reviewed the variety of activities in which we participated: brainstorming, round-robin responding, reading, viewing, role-playing, and writing. Students exhibited their learning through journal entries, discussion, and reflective writing. Now it was their turn to plan their own units and lead us through a two-week lesson plan.

Dana, Shannon, Jeni, and Brandon planned a unit on racism. In their preliminary rationale they admitted that, as students, they encounter racism even if it isn't as overt as it was in the 1950s. They said they hoped people would engage in an open exploration of their topic, conceding that they might not change their peers' minds but at least they would make them confront other views:

> In order to do this we plan on brainstorming myths that are common with racism. We think and hope this will really get the class thinking about racism and how bad it really is . . . We will be watching *Mississippi Burning*. This movie is jam-packed with horrible forms of racism. We will read a story called "Exchange Value" (Johnson 1987) and write our thoughts out in a journal. There will be a pop quiz on this story just to see who is doing their reading and who is not. And we will write a paper on one of the following:
>
> 1. our views of racism
> 2. a time when we faced racism
> 3. an opinion paper on the Jerry Springer show
> 4. whether any of the myths we discussed are true

This group created a number of other activities including reading the poem "Blacks" from J. Bennett's novel *Skinhead* (1991), exploring racism in rap music, and reading W. P. Kinsella's "Black Wampum" (1978).

In another unit on journalism, part of Vicky and Brian's presentation included video clips from a local news broadcast. They told us to notice how the pictures and interviews worked in tandem to construct each story. The first, about an incident of vandalism, pictured the letters "KKK" spray-painted on the side of a church, even though the anchor never mentions the Klan in his report. Whether they bear responsibility for the vandalism is never stated, but it is certainly implied.

Vicky and Brian pointed out the broadcaster's tone of voice and choice of language. They asked us to comment on what we noticed and how the stories were constructed.

They gave us pictures that accompanied a different newspaper article and asked us to construct the story that might fit those particular pictures. When the group I was in named a hospitalized child "Little Joey," Vicky and Brian pointed out how our use of connotative language constructed a clear bias.

Turning teaching responsibilities over to students helps me

see what they understand about their topic, what they deem important, and how well they can articulate their learning to peers. Some critics might assail me for neglecting to teach students; I should be planning the units, choosing the reading, leading discussion, deciding how to evaluate the students' learning. I admit I'm a bit uneasy about relinquishing so much control. My role in this class shifts to modeling and facilitating, knowing when to intervene and when to stand clear.

When the semester ended, I asked students to evaluate what we had done. Their responses helped assuage my anxiety. Janie wrote, "It helps us to learn [the topic] more when we do the research and then teach about it." Keri claimed, "This class gave me the opportunity to be heard."

Brian liked bearing more responsibility and noticed the shift in "power":

> I think that putting the power and responsibility in our hands will help us be leaders in the future. . . Letting us choose the topics also helped keep our interest. Sometimes the topics teachers choose bore students so they don't want to learn. Also working in groups helps us to work with others well. This will help me in the future, since being in the navy I will be working with groups to complete jobs.
>
> *Brian Re, grade 12*

Annie had trouble believing I would really turn teaching over to students: "At first I thought that even though we chose the topics, that the teacher would choose what we studied about it and how we went about it, but it wasn't like that."

Denise had done short presentations in other classes but never been given the opportunity to plan an entire unit: "The two-week time span was good, because we had a chance to go into depth with our topic, rather than just brushing the surface. I would suggest this activity for other classes."

Amy enjoyed the freedom this opportunity afforded her but learned something about the burden of teaching, too:

> This class was a new experience that I really enjoyed! In every other class, you have to talk about and learn about

what the TEACHER decides. But, this semester, we chose what we learned and in turn learned more. I know that knowing I helped choose the topics alone made me more interested in what was going on in class . . . I realized just how hard it is to teach. I used to think it was really simple, but now I realize just how complex it is! I think that one of the biggest problems with school is how extremely boring it is! People are always sleeping—and sometimes I'm one of those people. I get so tired of the same thing every day! But, in this class, it's been different. We've talked about things that affect us! Things that will help us when we leave here. Math and science—those things we'll probably forget before long. But, things we've learned about AIDS and violence— these things we'll remember! We will be faced with these issues when we grow up—and that's what matters—isn't that what we're here for?

Amy Davis, grade 12

The positive comments about the semester were unanimous. Though some students griped about bearing more responsibility than some of their peers or about getting into arguments within their group, they all agreed I should extend the same opportunity to students the following year. My own feelings are mixed. I am heartened that students' final evaluations were so positive. I discovered resources I can use in future classes. Most discussions were lively and engaging.

Sometimes, though, poor planning led to poor classes. Overreliance on one group member affected classes when that person was absent. Sometimes groups neglected what I thought were important aspects of their topics. Some of the exercises designed to evaluate student learning were not thought out as well as I had hoped.

I compensated for some of these flaws since I participated in all the class discussions. If Terry's group only mentioned two positions on welfare reform, I could add a third or fourth. If a key group member was missing, I could assist the other members of that group. In the future I may want to balance teacher and student control. Despite some of the shortcomings, though, this experiment inspired students, shifted responsibility, and provided them with a chance to take charge of their learning.

Student presentations in this class did exhibit their understanding of contemporary issues in ways that single papers would not have. Students were engaged and called the class valuable to their futures—not an accolade to be lightly dismissed. As Amy said, when students take charge of their learning, they learn more, and ultimately, that's why we teach.

CHAPTER 10

Constructing a Curriculum

When my colleague Linda Tatman and I approached our principal several years ago about offering semester courses in place of English Nine, Ten, Eleven, and Twelve—Regular and College Prep— we weren't met with the enthusiasm we hoped for. Maybe next year, we thought.

Two weeks later our principal approached us: "Tell me more about these semester courses." At the same time the state of Ohio was pressing school districts to document how teachers intervened with students who weren't mastering course content. Apparently, the principal thought, semester English courses would allow more flexibility in scheduling intervention periods for students who needed it. We were told to proceed with our plan. So with a little luck and a lot of pluck, English Nine, Ten, Eleven, and Twelve died at Lockland High School and semester courses were born.

Linda and I designed a number of courses organized by theme or genre:

War and the Holocaust

The American Dream

Contemporary Culture and Mass Media

Vietnam and the Sixties

Reading-Writing Workshop

Women and Men

Contemporary Fiction

Advanced Writing

Poetry and Plays

Fantasy and Reality

Goodness and Evil

Innocence and Experience

We wrote descriptions for each course and waited to see which ones students would sign up for the following school year. We planned to write a syllabus for each popular class that summer and order new books.

Part of our motivation was to write courses both we and our students would find more interesting than the traditional ones already in place. But something else drove these new courses, too. Both of us had experienced last-period nightmares, if you know what I mean: night dreams, usually triggered by ninth-grade boys who'd terrorized middle-school teachers and been low-tracked for years (see Chapter One). As part of this reconstruction process, we hoped to end the nightmares.

Students could be grouped heterogeneously in these courses, we told the principal and counselor—some courses for ninth- and tenth-graders, some for eleventh- and twelfth-. We reasoned that breaking up tracks would help students with low self-esteem—they'd be working closely with students who had a more positive self-image. Students in the upper tracks would learn to work with peers of varying degrees of ability and with different interests. Our classes would be a microcosm of society.

Of course, things don't always work the way you plan them. We believed offering students so many choices would increase the odds they'd take an English class they really wanted and enjoy it more; after all, they signed up for it. That often wasn't the case, though. Because the school is small, students who needed the fourth-period chemistry class (the only one offered that year) couldn't take Women and Men, which was offered the same period. And sometimes a tenth-grader or two would slip into a course specifically designed for older students.

When I first wrote the course description for War and the

201

Holocaust, I imagined a sophisticated exploration of that era with eleventh- and twelfth-graders. Scheduling difficulties arose, though, and the course became a follow-up to Reading-Writing Workshop, a course new ninth-graders take. Fortunately, numerous young-adult titles address World War II and the Holocaust, so I've adapted the course for a younger audience.

Despite some of the difficulties, returning to the days of English Nine, Ten, Eleven, and Twelve never crosses our minds. Semester courses make so much more sense to us and our students.

We like heterogeneous grouping, too. Problem students don't always rise toward the top as we hoped; in fact, sometimes better students sink toward the bottom. But, for the most part, students are learning more and our classrooms are more productive places.

In the course of researching and writing these new courses, I've learned about American history; our role in Vietnam; the plight of Jews during the Holocaust; the way American society constructs gender roles. I always read with "teacher's eyes" now—whether it be a "My Turn" article in *Newsweek*, which might fit into the immigrant unit in my American Dream class, or a poem about voice I discover while reading an issue of *Rethinking Schools*. I review the "Young Adult Literature" column in *English Journal* and browse the children's section of local bookstores. I talk to friends and colleagues who share similar interests. In pursuit of interesting resources for young people, I've read dozens of poems and plays, essays and articles, stories and novels, many of which my students have been willing to read. I've attempted to create a classroom environment in which students share explorations similar to my own. I never stop learning.

Partly, I suspect, because I've never taught the same course the same way. Each year I rewrite the curriculum. I don't know how I could do otherwise. I repeat activities that work, adapt lessons that almost work, eliminate projects that bomb. I'm lucky I have the freedom to change. Since I've liberated myself from the shackles of textbooks, I've joined my students to create curriculum. Now teaching is always fresh for me, as I hope learning will be for them.

Just as students explore the construction of knowledge in each of my classes and construct their own knowledge with peers, teachers should undertake similar explorations. Why let an anthology cloud our vision with the shadow of tradition? Why let a rigid course of study impede student progress? Just as students need to take charge of their learning, teachers need to take charge of their curriculum.

We need to rethink what we do. We can start by composing a teacher portfolio to help us reflect upon our teaching the same way we ask students to reflect upon their learning. In the same way the National Writing Project proposes that teachers of writing should write, I propose that teachers whose students keep portfolios should keep portfolios themselves.

The first teacher portfolio I composed was not specifically for the purpose of reflection, though. As a tenured teacher on a three-year evaluation cycle, I was to evaluate my own teaching the years my principal didn't evaluate me. A number of options were suggested, including surveying students, videotaping our teaching, inviting a colleague to observe us, or using some other means. I opted for "other means" and composed my first teaching portfolio.

Even when administrators do evaluate teachers, they typically catch just a slice of the total teaching pie. That slice might be thirty minutes second period on three different occasions because that's the period the principal is free to observe. Or maybe they see two different periods, but for only thirty minutes each time. Even if they're particularly conscientious principals, they never get more than a taste of our teaching.

I thought a portfolio would help my principal get the overall flavor of what I do in the classroom. After reviewing numerous artifacts, I decided to represent my teaching with four different names: (1) Teacher, (2) Teacher As Writer, (3) Teacher As Learner, and (4) Teacher As Presenter. Below is the table of contents from that first portfolio:

Teacher

1. Contemporary Culture Syllabus
2. Your Education: An Exhibition
3. Group Exhibitions
4. Student Samples (Chad Welage, Fonika Thomas, Vicky Edrington)

Teacher As Writer

5. Introductory Portfolio
6. Reflections upon Adolescence
7. Using Language to Learn

Teacher As Learner

8. "Chastising the Idiots"/ "I Do with the Crew"/ "Face the Music"
9. Reading List
10. Videotape

Teacher As Presenter

11. Portfolio Reflections: Expanding the Possibilities
12. Portfolio Evaluation
13. Presentation to Board

Besides actually including each of these items labeled for easy reference, I wrote a reflective letter explaining the significance of each item:

Dear _____:

Since portfolios show me the range and depth of my students' work, I thought a teaching portfolio could show you the range and depth of my work. Just as students reflect on the work they've done for their portfolios, I've reflected on my work and include some of it here for my self-evaluation. I've categorized items under four headings: (1) Teacher, (2) Teacher As Writer, (3) Teacher As Learner, and (4) Teacher As Presenter. Below are my reflections upon each of these items.

Teacher

1. This is the first year I've taught Contemporary Culture and Mass Media. I got the idea for this class at last year's National Council of Teachers of English annual convention. Two teachers from an Eastern prep school team-teach a class on popular culture. The "mass media" part comes from another session I attended about the importance of teaching students to become more critical about the media, especially since they're bombarded by it daily. I want this class to en-

gage students in a critical examination of contemporary issues such as race, class, and patriotism. At the beginning of most units, students brainstorm related cultural myths and spend their time exploring and challenging these myths. Within this context they reflect upon conservative, moderate, and liberal views and learn how to position themselves in relation to controversial subjects.

2. One topic I ask students to examine in Contemporary Culture is their own education. They read articles and stories that reflect different educational philosophies; interview teachers, parents, peers, and administrators; collect representative samples of work they do in each of their classes. Then they reflect upon the kind of teaching and learning they find most useful. This is the unit Vicky Edrington has agreed to discuss in the "Let's Talk Schools" segment of the next board meeting.

3. I've endeavored this year to make students more responsible for their education. In each of my classes students have to lead discussion over assigned readings; in addition to this my American Dream students have to choose their own related readings and design a fifty-minute lesson for one class. These have been some of the best classes we've had all year. Many students have proven how responsible and creative they can be when it comes to engaging their peers. The handout on "group exhibitions" explains the process students go through when planning their own lessons.

4. The next three pieces were written by students. Chad Welage explains in his "Dear Class" letter the items he included in his first-semester portfolio. The fifth paragraph is particularly interesting because Chad reveals how another student opened his eyes and showed him a perspective on patriotism he hadn't considered. I'm always encouraged when students learn from each other. The next piece, by Fonika Thomas, should give you an idea of how I respond to students. While I didn't write a lot on this draft, you can see that I try to praise what's working and question what isn't. Fonika and the rest of her class entered these pieces in a local essay contest. You've seen the third piece before, but I include it anyway because I'm proud when students achieve this kind of success outside of school [Vicky's piece was

published at a local writing program]. I also respect the work Vicky did on this: it went through a number of substantive revisions before it reached final draft stage.

Teacher As Writer

5. One of the tenets of the National Writing Project is that teachers of writing must write themselves. This section shows some of the writing I've done this year. I include the "Introductory Portfolio" letter to show that I write with my students when I get the chance. It also shows that I model what I want them to do. I asked students to assemble a portfolio at the beginning of the year to emphasize that the "stuff" of their lives is important to their learning and worth reflecting upon.

6. "Reflections on Adolescence" was written for the *Lantern* [the school district's newsletter]. I like to quote students in articles, (1) to publicize their good work, and (2) to show readers that students engage in important work and can be thoughtful about that work.

7. E. M. Forster said, "How do I know what I think until I see what I say." In other words, writing is a tool for learning. I believe in the importance of that tool and try to get students to believe it, too. We do lots of short writings to help make clear what often is vague until we see our thoughts on paper. I include "Using Language to Learn" to show that I practice what I preach. This is the first of a sixteen-page exploratory piece I wrote about sexist, racist, and political language. [I later revised it for Chapter Four of this book.]

Teacher As Learner

8. If teachers aren't learning with their students, then they're probably not as engaged as they need to be in their teaching. Fortunately, I still have a lot to learn. The three student pieces by Andrea, Jack, and Vicky were written last year. We had just read several articles about censoring music and discussed how the authors use emotional, logical, and ethical arguments to persuade their readers. I like the students' writing because each positions him- or herself differently, and they employ what they have just learned about persuasive techniques. They show me perspectives I hadn't

considered and that they can write convincing arguments. Now I use these three pieces as models for other students.

9. Just as teachers of writing should write, teachers of reading should read. I include this reading list to show what I've been reading lately. Three of my students missed a film and test about the internment of Japanese Americans during World War II, so I told them they could read *Farewell to Manzanar* (Houston 1973) and take a test on it instead. But first I had to read it myself. I read the novel, took notes, and wrote a test for the three of them; as it turned out, though, none of them did the reading. Oh well, at least I enjoyed it. I read Harry Crews' *Body* (1990) for the fun of it—it's a novel about the obsessiveness of bodybuilders. I'm reading Ira Shor's *Freire for the Classroom* (1987) to improve my teaching.

10. I'm including the videotape to let you know a little more about the Ohio Writing Project. I cued up the segment where I reflect upon what I've learned about teaching writing. There is also a brief explanation by Andrea Davis about a form of peer response we used in her class this year.

Teacher As Presenter

11. Besides teaching, writing, and learning, I think teachers should share their work with other teachers. This fall Linda and I presented at NCTE in Louisville with a colleague from Miami. I'm including the proposal I wrote for our workshop. We had the maximum of sixty people in attendance and heard a number of positive comments from them when the workshop ended.

12. I devised the Portfolio Evaluation form for our Lockland assessment of junior writing. I feel good about this project because we're finally talking across grade lines, something we should have done a long time ago. I respect Kathleen Krause and Karen Carlin and hope our association will affect the teaching of language arts in Lockland and benefit students in the long run.

13. The last item is an outline for a presentation I hope to use with the board of education. I want to give them a sense of the kind of work high school students engage in

and how essential it is that students become responsible for their own learning. I'm challenging my students to accept this responsibility, an invitation many of them are reluctant to accept. I've renegotiated their "contract." Instead of pretending I'm a fount of knowledge and students are empty receptacles waiting to be filled, I'm asking them to construct knowledge collaboratively by reading, writing, and thinking critically. I'm convinced this is the best course for our students here at Lockland, and I know they are capable of meeting these expectations. Maybe more people should renegotiate teacher-student, parent-student contracts and watch students show what they can really do.

Please accept this portfolio as my self-evaluation. Thank you for your attention.

Sincerely,
John Gaughan

If my principal were willing to read this letter, watch a two-minute videotape, and skim through thirteen items, he'd have a much better sense of my teaching and professional involvement than his few observations would ever provide. I'm not sure he read it all, but in the end that didn't matter. Though I originally composed the portfolio for him, I discovered in the process that it was really for me. I constructed meaning from my teaching life that year, from my interactions with students, from my presentations with colleagues. This portfolio is an accurate reflection of what I've done well.

Of course, what I've done well isn't the whole story, or the whole pie, to use my metaphor. I offer no slice of teaching that leaves a bad taste in my mouth, and I'd be lying to say I hadn't baked those slices, too. In my most recent portfolio, I provide a slice of failure.

JaVonna, a junior, was a young mother trying to balance child care and school. She'd been more successful as a sophomore, but was finding it more and more difficult to reach school on time or even to show up at all.

I knew JaVonna's journal entry and my response to her should be an integral part of this next portfolio because the reading and writing was so fresh in my mind. JaVonna took advantage of the postsecondary options program her junior year, taking two classes at a community college and two classes at Lockland. She may have thought she could better juggle her schedule since she was enrolled in fewer classes than a full-time junior. Of the classes she did take, one was college English and one was high school English.

Apparently, JaVonna didn't feel as prepared for her college course as she thought she should have been, so throughout the year she used her journal to vent her frustrations.

Neither Mrs. Tatman nor I had ever taught JaVonna to write a five-paragraph essay, she complained, or how to compose an outline. I had to agree that I hadn't done either of those things, and I guessed my colleague hadn't either. It was JaVonna's other complaint that irked me: that I didn't teach students to write argument papers. I began writing furiously in the margins of JaVonna's journal reminding her of the extensive unit on argument first semester then I realized she probably wouldn't be able to read a thing I'd written. My handwriting is small and practically illegible, especially when I write fast. So I decided it was worth typing a response and attaching it to JaVonna's journal:

JaVonna:

All year you've been complaining about your education at Lockland, and though I responded in your journal, I'm not sure you'll be able to read what I wrote, so I'm typing a more complete response.

You say, "None of my classes have actually prepared me for college," and that we have "set a trap" by not teaching you to write persuasive essays, outline papers, or answer test questions.

First of all, I think your journal entry itself is testimony to the fact that you've learned to write persuasively—enough in this case to convince me to respond in writing. On the other hand, I disagree with much of what you say.

"Arguing" in class discussions does prepare you to write persuasively—though oral and written discourse are different, in both cases the writer/speaker must consider audience and purpose when constructing the argument. Besides that, you have to have something to argue about—content comes first, then form.

209

Last semester in Contemporary Culture we spent over a month working on argument papers. We analyzed three student arguments and talked about what worked and what didn't. Though I don't think outlines serve much purpose (when I was in school my peers and I usually completed them after we wrote our papers because they were required), the analysis we did of argument papers did serve as a tool for organizing our persuasive pieces.

As far as preparing you for college, you've got to accept some of the responsibility. To become a better reader, read (you can't decide in college what you'll read and what you won't as you've done in my class). To become a better writer, write. You've had numerous opportunities to do both in your English classes at Lockland.

I've taught at Miami University as you know. My courses there are very similar to this course—the assignments, often identical. In the past several years numerous Lockland graduates have returned to inform me of their success in first-year college English. Many of them get A's—Vicky Edrington is one example from first semester; Amy Davis, one from this semester.

I can't believe, as a junior, you're writing off your chances for a scholarship. If you work hard and raise your grades, you'll have as good a chance as anyone.

I wrote this quickly, but I thought you deserved a response. I appreciate your honesty and willingness to take risks.

Sincerely,
J. G.

Essentially, my letter is a rationalization, an attempt to justify my teaching to a student. It made me feel better, at least initially, but it wasn't writing that worked. I don't think I convinced JaVonna of anything. Maybe I do need to think more closely about helping students structure their papers. Maybe I should better prepare them to answer essay questions or respond to writing prompts. JaVonna's journal entries angered me, frustrated me, but in the process made me think.

If I want to accurately reflect on my teaching from that year,

I have to include some reference to my dialogue with JaVonna, and I have to admit the transaction was a failure on my part. I hope that in future portfolios I'll risk exposing my failures as well as my successes.

I hope, too, I can convince others how useful teacher portfolios can be. This year, in fact, in conjunction with the Ohio Writing Project and EECAP (Early English Composition Assessment Program), the members of three English departments have agreed to a teacher-portfolio project. We will meet throughout the year, sometimes in one group, other times by department, and work on constructing individual portfolios. The immediate goal will be self-evaluation, but other secondary goals are already obvious.

As we share our portfolios, we'll be sharing our teaching: literature that works with students, successful teaching strategies, course syllabi, theoretical positions. Besides sparking each other's interest, we'll be unveiling what we find problematic: how to balance the classics and contemporary literature, where process and content intersect, the importance of a social context in an individual's education.

After teachers evaluate themselves through portfolios, I'd like to see them extend the discussion to their department and the English curriculum itself. Can individual teachers use artifacts from their own portfolios to represent the pedagogy and philosophy of an entire department? What strengths and weaknesses exist in their program? How can teachers improve the curriculum to engage more students and prepare them for further education, the world of work, and the society they're about to enter as citizens with the right to vote? How can they enrich their own teaching lives? What professional projects should they undertake as an English department?

The final product of our work, the ideal product, is a better world: students who enjoy a healthy breakfast and coming to school each morning; students whose parents care about their well-being, who attend open houses and parent-teacher conferences; students and parents and teachers and administrators with open minds willing to examine different points of view.

Of course, that final "product" remains a dream. For now we'll have to settle for "process": looking closely at our own teaching, our own department, a curriculum we can surely improve. We may never compose a product we can't revise, but that's what makes our chosen profession so dynamic.

Taking charge of what we teach—the curriculum; of how we teach it—our pedagogy; and of how our teaching is evaluated—teacher portfolios, for example—can help new teachers name themselves confident professionals and experienced teachers (some on the verge of burning out) resurrect their professional identities. Composing our own teaching portfolios shifts evaluative powers from outside to inside our departments. Armed with a defense of why we do what we do and a vision for a curriculum that makes more sense, we can march into teachers' meetings and administrators' offices with proposals for change, freeing ourselves and our students to confront the problems of the twenty-first century.

Epilogue

Mrs. Keller still teaches at Clarksdale High. She often delivers stirring lectures that rivet students' attention. I like to be stirred by good lectures myself. I remember the first time I watched Ian McKellen acting Shakespeare. On a small square stage, McKellen brought the "Tomorrow" soliloquy in *Macbeth* to life. What a facility for teaching through acting. I wish I could do the same. McKellen's delivery was powerful. The audience was awed. Besides a stunning interpretation of Shakespeare's words, which transported us, with him, back to Elizabethan England, he explicated the soliloquy line by line.

As awed as I am, as much as I learn, I realize his teaching is traditional. McKellen doesn't solicit feedback from his audience. He doesn't engage them in a dialogue about Macbeth's tragic state. He shares his own interpretation, which is extremely convincing. The few times I shared McKellen's Shakespeare with students, I tested them later by asking them to write short interpretations of their own. The most attentive students gave me what I expected: the authority's interpretation. I think a place exists in our curriculum for this kind of teaching. Learning from others can benefit students.

Think back to the rhetorical triangle from Chapter Nine:

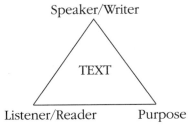

Speaker/Writer

TEXT

Listener/Reader   Purpose

When students write in Mrs. Keller's class, the audience is the teacher; the purpose, to verify that students understood her lecture; the writer, a vessel, empty before, filled now with "teacher knowledge." The text students create is shaped by this relationship. If they take good notes and/or have good memories, they write "good" papers. I think students are answering essay questions or writing this kind of paper in many contemporary classrooms, not just in English classes. Although such writing helps teachers gauge student understanding, little room exists for students to construct their own meaning or share their own interpretations.

At the same time I think an occasional lecture can be worthwhile, can motivate students, pique their interests, challenge them to learn more. I think this happened in my Vietnam class when I shared what I'd learned about the "great circle" in the "Westward course of empire." Sometimes the best way to teach particular skills is for teachers to tell students what they themselves have already learned: the rules of soccer, the most efficient way to move text on a computer, Darwin's theory of evolution.

Mr. Rosewald, though, of Westchester High, knows not to stop there. After showing students how to move text during revision, he models revising himself. Then, after explaining why he made the choices he did, he gets students involved in their own revisions. Mr. Rosewald's concern is helping individuals interact with their own work.

The student in his class has freer rein than does the one in Mrs. Keller's. The audience is not just the teacher but each student's peers, and sometimes people outside the classroom. The purpose will change with each piece of writing. Last year in my Reading-Writing Workshop, Katie asked if she could read a journal entry she'd written the previous weekend. She'd hadn't read much of her writing to that point in the semester or written anything particularly memorable. Since she was a ninth-grader whom I hadn't taught, I knew little of her ability. She began reading:

> There she is lying beneath the dirt. So cold, so alone. She needs her sissy, to hold her, to love her, to feed her, to be there for her. But I can't. I can't do anything with her. Except dream about her.

214

In some of my dreams she was a doctor. In others she was a model. But in my favorite one she was alive . . .

When it snows I like to think that every perfect snowflake is her little soft hand coming down and touching me. Then when her hands are on me, she whispers in my ear that everything will be all right . . .

Katie Brusman, grade 9

Katie hadn't read far when all of us realized we were sharing a poignant moment. When Katie's peers stopped tapping their pencils or scratching out notes, and the only sound was Katie's voice breathing life into her memory of her sister Jessica, everyone in that classroom realized the power of writing.

Katie wrote this piece about her sister because she needed to write it. Initially it was for her, but it became for us. Teachers can't plan moments like the one those students experienced. We can set up safe environments where students take risks; we can encourage students to write honestly; we can nudge them to share their work. Mr. Rosewald has received a number of pieces like "The Dream of Jessica." Students in expressivist classrooms like his have the opportunity to express themselves often, and often that expression is powerful.

It's quite possible that in a social-constructivist classroom like Ms. Bennington's at PS 891, Katie wouldn't have had the opportunity to write the memory of her sister—if the rhetoric that governs Ms. Bennington's practice were strictly social-epistemic or constructivist. That would be a shame. Students need to write personal pieces solely because they "need" to, regardless of the theory that underlies a particular teacher's pedagogy; their peers need to be part of such powerful moments.

Students in Ms. Bennington's class, however, may learn things they might not in Mr. Rosewald's. All writers are socially constructed; so are the readers who make up their audience. Teachers in constructivist classes help students understand that construction. While the purpose for a particular piece of writing may be the same for a student in either classroom—say to convince Ms. Jennings, the high school principal, to implement an open-lunch policy—the individual in Ms. Bennington's class might have an understanding or critical awareness about her audience and school politics that a student in Mr. Rosewald's might not—perhaps, in this case, to avoid sexist language or to address the concerns of members of the school board.

As a teacher, I'm more aware of my own position in the classroom, in the educational process. I realize the political nature of teaching. I know the curriculum I've designed challenges traditional notions of what should be taught in high school English classrooms. I know some teachers, administrators, and parents would consider some of the topics my students explore taboo. Understanding the new teaching identity I've constructed for myself informs my pedagogy, makes me reconsider what I teach. In Chapter Four, for example, I discuss the use of W. P. Kinsella's "Mr. Whitey." That story works well to help students think about the assumptions embedded in racist language, but I realize now that I might want to couple it with one by a Native American author. This year I'll probably use "Mr. Whitey" and "Amusements" by Sherman Alexie. My teaching "text" is different because I'm a different teacher.

Students need to be more critically aware, too—of themselves, the people around them, the cultural institutions of which they are a part. This book is about helping them achieve that awareness. At the same time, I don't want students' critical analyses to be so detached or devoid of passion that the writers feel no connection to their subject. In Chapter Five Kali Evans wrote, "Damn the distilleries. Damn them all to hell." What started as a social critique of alcohol advertisements quickly led to a painful account of Kali's own related experience. In Chapter Six when reviewing *Apocalypse Now,* Kali again moved from critical to personal response. She connected with Colonel Kurtz and the "dull ache" both of them experienced.

I'm proud of the work Kali did in my class. I'm glad she found room to locate the personal in the social, to put her own life into a larger context, to better understand society and herself. I'm proud of Katie's "Dream of Jessica," too. I don't want my social agenda to supersede individual students' needs. Katie and Kali took charge of their learning. Teachers can, too. Traditionalists, expressivists, and constructivists can learn from each other if they're willing to look over the walls that divide us and listen. Those walls are lower than we think.

APPENDIX

Selected Annotations for Reading and Viewing That Work with My Students

All of these works are cited in the References.

Films

And the Band Played On (1993)
This HBO video relates the story of AIDS in detective-like fashion. Scientists from the Centers for Disease Control accumulate evidence of the then "new" disease and try to trace it to its origin. The film exposes the political sides of AIDS, showing how the necessary funding wasn't allocated because it was considered a "gay" disease. (140 min.)

Apocalypse Now (1979)
Francis Ford Coppola's film shatters the myth of Americans as savior when American soldiers fighting in Vietnam discover the horror in themselves. One of Martin Sheen's most intense roles. (153 min.)

Casualties of War (1990)
Private Erikson, played by Michael J. Fox, disobeys his sergeant, played by Sean Penn, when he's ordered to kidnap and rape a young Vietnamese girl. The film works well in conjunction with discussions of the My Lai Massacre. (120 min.)

El Norte (1983)
An excellent film to use when students study immigration. Two Guatemalan peasants leave their village when their father is

murdered and their mother is kidnapped to seek refuge in "the North." Their preconceptions of the United States, however, don't match the reality they find. (141 min.)

Ethnic Notions (1967)
This documentary shows how African Americans have been portrayed in the media from the antebellum South to the present, and how those portrayals have shaped identity and attitudes. (56 min.)

The Green Berets (1968)
A John Wayne western in disguise (see Chris' comments in Chapter Six). I show this film before *Apocalypse Now* because it perpetuates the myth of Americans as world saviors. (135 min.)

Hairpiece: A Film for Nappy-Headed People (1985)
This animated film shows the effects of media on appearance and our culture's conception of beauty as African American women gaze into the media mirror. You can rent this film from Women Make Movies, 462 Broadway, Suite 500, New York, NY 10013. (10 min.)

Matewan (1987)
John Sayles' film about the West Virginia coal fields and the struggles between "The Company" and "The Union." I sometimes use the film in my American Dream class after the immigration unit, because, in an attempt to break the union, the company "imports" black miners and Italian immigrants, who are just trying to survive. (132 min.)

Novels/Plays

At Risk, by Alice Hoffman
The effects of AIDS on an American family, school, and community when eleven-year-old Amanda Farrell contracts HIV through a blood transfusion.

The Children's Story, by James Clavell
Clavell's story begin at 8:58 and ends at 9:23. In that short time a new teacher brainwashes a classroom full of elementary chil-

dren and convinces them to swear their allegiance to a new government. I read this aloud to students to get them to think about what the phrase "I pledge allegiance" really means.

The Education of Little Tree, by Forrest Carter
Even though it's likely the author was a former member of the Klan, this novel is a sensitive and humorous account of a Native American child being raised by his grandparents. Little Tree learns "The Way" of his people, and receives a much more humane education at home than he does at school.

Fallen Angels, by Walter Dean Myers
Richie Perry doesn't have the money to go to college so he goes to Vietnam, where he learns the horrors of war. This novel works well in conjunction with Tim O'Brien's *The Things They Carried* because Myers' main characters are African Americans with backgrounds quite different from those of O'Brien's characters. Though the book is long, and "thick" books scare many of my students, most of them thoroughly enjoy reading this novel.

Fences, by August Wilson
Troy Maxson never realized his major league dreams because of racial barriers; he doesn't want his son to suffer the same disappointment. Struggling to meet his own and his family's needs, Troy builds fences that divide him from his wife and son.

Fried Green Tomatoes at the Whistle Stop Cafe, by Fannie Flagg
I play the book-on-tape version, read by the author, of the scene in the novel when a teenage boy literally runs into Evelyn Couch at the grocery store. The language he uses is harsh, but my juniors and seniors have always reacted maturely and understood the damaging effects of words on a person's self-esteem.

The Friends, by Rosa Guy
Phyllisia Cathy, an immigrant from the West Indies, experiences discrimination from her Harlem classmates until Edith Jackson saves her. Easy enough except that Edith makes Phyllisia uncomfortable because of Edith's ragged appearance. Their relationship

develops, but not without tension, until Phyllisia finally learns what it means to be a friend.

The House on Mango Street, by Sandra Cisneros
This novel about growing up Hispanic in Chicago has sparked some of the best writing my students have done because they can relate to Esperanza and her life on Mango Street. Each short chapter reminds them of their neighborhood, childhood, or people they know, and convinces them to tell their own stories.

Kindred, by Octavia Butler
Dana, an African American woman married to a white man in 1976, finds herself transported to the antebellum South, where she must save one of her ancestors, a white slave owner, in order to exist in the present. Once readers accept the back-to-the-future premise, this novel is excellent for examining the parallels between sexism and racism, the past and present. One of my students' favorite novels.

Ragged Dick, by Horatio Alger
A true rags-to-riches story of a poor orphan who works hard and answers the door when opportunity knocks. I use this in my "Work and the American Dream" unit because it perpetuates the myth that any individual willing to work can attain his or her dreams.

Running Loose, by Chris Crutcher
Louie Banks must decide how to react when his football coach orders his team to purposely injure a black player on an opposing team. That, and its depiction of the complications of a new relationship make this one of my students' favorite books.

Stories/Poems

"Appointment with Love," by S. I. Kishor
After corresponding through letters and falling in love, a man and woman decide to meet in person, neither knowing what the other looks like. The woman in the story devises a test that the man

must pass before he can meet her. A good story to discuss the nature of love, trust, and the importance of appearance.

"Black Wampum," by W. P. Kinsella
When Billy Jawbone accidentally kills his employer's baby boy, he offers them his own baby girl. This story is good for discussing clashes between cultures and between genders.

"Ellis Island," by Joseph Bruchac
Because Bruchac is part Slovakian and part Native American, his attitude toward immigration is mixed. In his poem he imagines his grandparents on Ellis Island but also the people they displaced, both his ancestors.

"The Girls in Their Summer Dresses," by Irwin Shaw
This short story, which is mostly dialogue, involves a couple discussing the man's "annoying" habit of looking at other women. Students love to discuss what this habit says about the couple's relationship and how they view looking at others in the presence of their boy- or girlfriend.

"Mr. Whitey," by W. P. Kinsella
Whitey Bremner hires Silas Ermineskin and Judy Powderface to tend to his home and property after the death of his wife. Whitey begins to respect his new employees until his "friends" goad him, and the prejudice he'd buried resurfaces in his behavior. A good story to show how culture can shape "individuality."

"On the Rainy River," by Tim O'Brien
Whether to go to Canada or Vietnam, that is the question. Tim O'Brien's short story in *The Things They Carried* challenges readers' notions of patriotism and cowardice.

"Rayford's Song," by Lawson Inada
Rayford Butler asks his teacher if he can sing a song of his own in elementary music class, and though his peers admire the beauty of Rayford's song, they are reluctant to sing themselves because

of their teacher's reaction. This poem can be used to discuss voice, the canon, teaching, and multiculturalism.

Tangled Vines: A Collection of Mother and Daughter Poems, edited by Lyn Lifshin
The accessible poems in this collection revolve around themes of childbirth, inheritance, envy, dependence, rejection, separation, and letting go. Poets include Sylvia Plath, Audre Lorde, Anne Sexton, Sharon Olds, Nikki Giovanni, and Marge Piercy.

"the teacher," by Tom Romano
I like students to discuss the metaphor in this poem of the teacher as scoutmaster—leading, guiding, urging students on, sometimes even hoping they catch poison ivy.

"Telephone Man," by Chris Crutcher
This short story shows how prejudice is a learned behavior and suggests it can be "unlearned." The main character uses the derogatory language his father does when speaking of any race other than the Caucasian, until the end of the story when a subtle change in his own language offers promise that people can change.

Essays/Memoirs

"Confessions of a Working Stiff," by Patrick Fenton
Fenton makes his living "humping" cargo for an airline; he "doesn't get paid to think." I use this essay after students read Horatio Alger's *Ragged Dick* to get them to consider another side of work and the American Dream.

"Mike LeFevre," by Studs Terkel
LeFevre, a Chicago steelworker, was interviewed by Terkel for *Working*, his collection of oral histories. I use it in my American Dream class to discuss how work can sometimes be dehumanizing.

"Mommy, What Does 'Nigger' Mean?," by Gloria Naylor
In this personal essay Naylor explains how a term used pejoratively by whites has different meanings when African Americans

use it to address one another. The meaning of a word is not inherent but socially constructed.

"Racism in the English Language," by Robert B. Moore
This essay about racial bias in the English language generates controversy every time I use it, but it's worth it to get students thinking about how language reflects and shapes thought.

"Shame," by Dick Gregory
Much of what students learn in school is not what teachers intend to teach them. A young Dick Gregory recounts in this memoir the pain and humiliation he learned because his family was poor.

"Tell Your Children," by the Grand Council Fire of American Indians
After students have read traditional interpretations of American history, this essay shows how historians' language can shape their opinions of historical events. "They call all white victories, battles, and all Indian victories, massacres" is one example.

"The Ten Biggest Myths About the Black Family," by Lerone Bennett Jr.
Bennett argues that media images of the black family are distorted and revolve around ten major myths. African American families are more stable than the media suggests, and black men, in particular, are more responsible. A provocative essay to spark class discussion.

"Why Men Love War," by William Broyles
Broyles' essay rationalizes his wartime experiences, suggesting that he and many of his fellow soldiers loved fighting in Vietnam. War "offers a sanction to play boys' games," he says, a controversial enough statement to get most students talking. (See Chapter Eight.)

References

Alexie, S. 1994. *The Lone Ranger and Tonto Fistfight in Heaven.* New York: HarperCollins.

Alger, H. 1985. *Ragged Dick and Struggling Upward.* New York: Viking.

And the Band Played On. 1993. Director: R. Spottiswoode. HBO Video. 140 min.

Apocalypse Now. 1979. Director: F. Coppola. Omni Zoetrope. 153 min.

"The Ballad of the Green Berets." 1995. Sgt. Barry Sadler and Robin Moore. On *Billboard Top Pop Hits 1966.* Rhino Records, 71936.

Bambara, T. C. 1992. "The Lesson." In *Gorilla My Love.* New York: Vintage.

Barber, B. 1993. "America Skips School." *Harper's Magazine* 287 (1722): 39–46.

Barbieri, M. 1995. *Sounds from the Heart: Learning to Listen to Girls.* Portsmouth, NH: Heinemann.

Bass, E. 1978. "First Menstruation." In *Tangled Vines: A Collection of Mother and Daughter Poems,* ed. L. Lifshin, 58. Boston: Beacon Press.

Bennett, J. 1991. *Skinhead.* New York: F. Watts.

Bennett, L. 1986. "The 10 Biggest Myths About the Black Family." *Ebony* 41 (10): 123–132.

Berlin, J. 1988. "Rhetoric and Ideology in the Writing Class." *College English* 50 (5) : 477–494.

Brokaw, T. June 10, 1991. *The NBC Nightly News.* New York: NBC.

Broyles, W. 1984. "Why Men Love War." *Esquire* 102 (5): 55–65.

Bruchac, J. 1989. "Ellis Island." In *Rereading America: Cultural Contexts for Critical Thinking and Writing,* ed. G. Columbo, R. Cullen, and B. Lisle, 218–219. New York: St. Martin's.

Butler, O. 1979. *Kindred.* Boston, MA: Beacon Press.

Calandra, A. 1991. "Angels on a Pin." In *Outlooks and Insights: A Reader for College Writers,* eds. P. Eschholz and A. Rosa, 311–313. New York: St. Martin's.

Carter, F. 1976. *The Education of Little Tree.* Albuquerque: University of New Mexico Press.

Casualties of War. 1990. Director: B. De Palma. Westgate Video. 120 min.

Christensen, L. 1993. "Celebrating the Student's Voice." *Rethinking Schools* 8 (1):9.

Cisneros, S. 1989. *The House on Mango Street.* New York: Vintage.

Clavell, J. 1981. *The Children's Story.* New York: Dell.

Crews, H. 1990. *Body.* New York: Poseidon.

Crutcher, C. 1983. *Running Loose.* New York: Dell.

———. 1991. "Telephone Man." In *Athletic Shorts.* New York: Greenwillow.

Dickens, C. 1961. *Hard Times.* New York: Signet.

———. 1981. *David Copperfield.* New York: Oxford University Press.

Dylan, B. 1963. "Masters of War." On *The Freewheelin' Bob Dylan,* New York: Columbia.

Edwards, J. 1982. "Sinners in the Hands of an Angry God." In *United States in Literature,* ed. J. Miller, C. Dwyer, R. Hayden, R. Hogan, and K. Wood, 128–129. Glenview, IL: Scott, Foresman.

El Norte. 1983. Director: G. Nava. Cinecom International Films. 141 min.

Ethnic Notions. 1967. Director: M. Riggs. Videorecording. California Newsreel. 56 min.

Fenton, P. 1991. "Confessions of a Working Stiff." In *Outlooks and Insights: A Reader for College Writers,* ed. P. Eschholz and A. Rosa, 251–257. New York: St. Martin's.

Flagg, Fannie. 1987. *Fried Green Tomatoes at the Whistle Stop Cafe.* New York: McGraw-Hill.

Fletcher, R. 1993. *What a Writer Needs.* Portsmouth, NH: Heinemann.

Freire, P. 1970. *Pedagogy of the Oppressed.* New York: Continuum.

Frost, R. 1985. "The Road Not Taken." In *The Norton Anthology of American Literature: Volume 2*, ed. B. Gottesman et al., 1020. New York: W. W. Norton.

Grand Council Fire of American Indians. 1982. "Tell Your Children." In *United States in Literature*, ed. J. Miller, C. Dwyer, R. Hayden, R. Hogan, and K. Wood, 476–477. Glenview, IL: Scott, Foresman.

Grapes of Wrath, The. 1939. Director: J. Ford. Twentieth Century Fox. 129 min.

Green Berets, The. 1968. Director: John Wayne. Warner Brothers. 135 min.

Gregory, D. 1990. "Shame." In *Emerging Voices: A Cross-Cultural Reader*, ed. J. Madden-Simpson and S. Blake, 285–288. Ft. Worth, TX: Holt, Rinehart, Winston.

Guy, R. 1974. *The Friends.* New York: Bantam.

Hairpiece: A Film for Nappy-Headed People. 1985. Director: A. Chenzira. 10 min.

Hellmann, J. 1986. *American Myth and the Legacy of Vietnam.* New York: Columbia University Press.

Hemingway, E. 1986a. *The Sun Also Rises.* New York: Collier.

———. 1986b. "Hills Like White Elephants." In *Classic Short Fiction*, ed. C. Bohner, 461–464. Englewood Cliffs, NJ: Prentice Hall.

Henley, N., M. Hamilton, and B. Thorne. 1990. "Womanspeak and Manspeak: Sex Differences and Sexism in Communication, Verbal and Nonverbal." In *Issues in Feminism: An Introduction to Women's Studies*, ed. S. Ruth, 394–406. Mountain View, CA: Mayfield.

Hirsch, E. D. 1987. *Cultural Literacy: What Every American Needs to Know.* Boston: Houghton Mifflin.

Hoffman, A. 1988. *At Risk.* New York: Berkley Books.

Houston, J. W., and J. D. Houston. 1973. *Farewell to Manzanar.* New York: Bantam.

Hughes, L. 1991. "Theme for English B." In *Outlooks and Insights: A Reader for College Writers*, eds. P. Eschholz and A. Rosa, 328–330. New York: St. Martin's.

Inada, L. 1993. "Rayford's Song" In *Rethinking Schools* 8 (1): 9.

Jennings, P. June 10, 1991. *ABC News.* New York: ABC.

Johnson, C. 1987. *The Sorcerer's Apprentice: Tales and Conjurations.* New York: Penguin.

References

Johnson, R., and J. Bone. 1986. *Understanding the Film: An Introduction to Film Appreciation.* 3d ed. Lincolnwood, IL: National Textbook Company.

Kim, A. Oct. 25, 1990. "Burdens on Asian-Americans." *The Cincinnati Enquirer.* A-10.

Kinsella, W. P. 1978a. "Black Wampum." In *Scars.* Canada: Oberon.

———. 1978b. "Mr. Whitey." In *Scars.* Canada: Oberon.

Kishor, S. I. 1968. "Appointment with Love." In *Teaching Literature to Adolescents: Short Stories*, ed. S. Dunning, 30–32. Glenview, IL: Scott, Foresman.

Knoblauch, C. H., and L. Brannon. 1993. *Critical Teaching and the Idea of Literacy.* Portsmouth, NH: Boynton/Cook.

Lawrence, J., and R. Lee. 1981. *Inherit the Wind.* New York: Bantam.

Lederer, W., and E. Burdick. 1965. *The Ugly American.* New York: W. W. Norton.

Lifshin, L. 1978. *Tangled Vines: A Collection of Mother and Daughter Poems.* Boston, MA: Beacon Press.

London, J. 1986. "To Build a Fire." In *Classic Short Fiction*, ed. C. Bohner, 687–697. Englewood Cliffs, NJ: Prentice Hall.

Macrorie, K. 1984. *Writing to be Read*, 3d ed. Portsmouth, NH: Boynton/Cook.

Matewan. 1987. Director: J. Sayles. Warner Brothers. 132 min.

Moore, R. 1993. "Racism in the English Language." In *Experiencing Race, Class, and Gender in the United States*, ed. V. Cyrus, 152–159. Mountain View, CA: Mayfield.

Murray, D. 1990. *Write to Learn.* Fort Worth: Holt, Rinehart and Winston.

Murray, P., and L. Murray. 1965. *Dictionary of Art and Artists.* New York: Frederick A. Praeger.

Myers, W. D. 1988. *Fallen Angels.* New York: Scholastic.

Naylor, G. 1990. "Mommy, What Does 'Nigger' Mean?" In *Emerging Voices: A Cross-Cultural Reader*, ed. J. Madden-Simpson and S. Blake, 197–201. Ft. Worth, TX: Holt, Rinehart, Winston.

The New York Times. 1991. "The Ronald Reagan Basic 1984 Campaign Speech." In *Outlooks and Insights: A Reader for College Writers*, ed. P. Eschholz and A. Rosa, 508–512. New York: St. Martin's.

Oates, J. C. 1985. "Four Summers." In *Literature: Options for Reading and Writing*, ed. D. Daiker, M. Fuller Hayes, and J. Wallace, 85–100. New York: Harper & Row.

O'Brien, T. 1990. "On the Rainy River." In *The Things They Carried*. Boston: Houghton Mifflin.

Oldfield, M. 1973. *Tubular Bells*. New York: Virgin Records.

Olds, S. 1978. "Fish Story." In *Tangled Vines: A Collection of Mother and Daughter Poems*, ed. L. Lifshin, 17. Boston: Beacon Press.

Orwell, G. 1972. *Animal Farm*. New York: Signet.

———. 1991. "Politics and the English Language." In *Outlooks and Insights: A Reader for College Writers*, ed. P. Eschholz and A. Rosa, 483–495. New York: St. Martin's.

Piercy, M. 1973. "Barbie Doll." In *To Be of Use*. Garden City, NY: Doubleday.

"Rape of Mr. Smith, The." 1990. In *Issues in Feminism: An Introduction to Women's Studies*, ed. S. Ruth, 283–284. Mountain View, CA: Mayfield.

Roland, V. Nov. 10, 1992. "The Bias in Mideast News." *The Cincinnati Enquirer*. A-7.

Romano, T. 1985. "the teacher." In *Literature: Options for Reading and Writing*, ed. D. Daiker, M. Fuller Hayes, and J. Wallace, 714–716. New York: Harper and Row.

———. 1987. *Clearing the Way: Working with Teenage Writers*. Portsmouth, NH: Heinemann.

———. 1995. *Writing with Passion: Life Stories, Multiple Genres*. Portsmouth, NH: Heinemann.

Salinger, J. D. 1978. *The Catcher in the Rye*. Boston: Bantam.

Scudder, S. 1991. "Learning to See." In *Outlooks and Insights: A Reader for College Writers*, eds. P. Eschholz and A. Rosa, 323–327. New York: St. Martin's.

Shaw, I. 1985. "The Girls in Their Summer Dresses." In *Literature: Options for Reading and Writing*, ed. D. Daiker, M. Fuller Hayes, and J. Wallace, 221–229. New York: Harper and Row.

Shor, Ira (ed.). 1987. *Freire for the Classroom: A Sourcebook for Liberatory Teaching*. Portsmouth, NH: Heinemann.

Sizer, T. 1992. *Horace's School: Redesigning the American High School*. Boston: Houghton Mifflin.

Sommers, N. 1984. "Revision Strategies of Student Writers and Experienced Adult Writers." In *Rhetoric and Composition: A Source-*

book for Teachers and Writers, ed. R. Graves, 328–337. Portsmouth, NH: Boynton/Cook.

Stanley, J. P. 1977. "Paradigmatic Woman: The Prostitute." In *Papers in Language Variation*, ed. D. Shores and C. P. Hines, 303–321. University, AL: University of Alabama Press.

Steinbeck, J. 1976. *The Grapes of Wrath*. New York: Penguin.

———. 1982. "The Leader of the People." In *United States in Literature*, ed. J. Miller et al., 9–18. Glenview, IL: Scott, Foresman.

Steinbergh, J. 1983a. "Abuse." In *Motherwriter*. Green Harbor, MA: Wampeter Press.

———. 1983b. "Mother, the Same Witch Haunts Us." In *Motherwriter*. Green Harbor, MA: Wampeter Press.

Sunstein, B., and J. Potts. 1993. "Teachers' Portfolios: A Cultural Site for Literacy." In *The Council Chronicle*, Urbana, IL: National Council of Teachers of English.

Terkel, S. 1989. "Mike LeFevre." In *Rereading America: Cultural Contexts for Critical Thinking and Writing*, ed. G. Columbo, R. Cullen, and B. Lisle, 520–528. New York: St. Martin's.

Twain, M. 1984. *Adventures of Huckleberry Finn*. New York: Signet.

Vonnegut, K. 1973. *Breakfast of Champions*. New York: Dell.

Walker, A. 1982. *The Color Purple*. New York: Washington Square Press.

Weathers, W. 1990. "Grammars of Style: New Options in Composition." In *Rhetoric and Composition: A Sourcebook for Teachers and Writers*, 3d ed., ed. R. Graves, 133–147. Portsmouth, NH: Boynton/Cook.

Wilson, A. 1986. *Fences*. New York: New American Library.

Witness. 1985. In *Understanding the Film: An Introduction to Film Appreciation*, 49. Lincolnwood, IL: National Textbook Company.

Wolf, D. P. "Portfolio Assessment: Sampling Student Work." In *Educational Leadership* 46 (7):35–39.

Yagelski, R. 1994. "Literature and Literacy: Rethinking English as a School Subject." In *English Journal* 83 (3):30–36.